Knowledge Design and Determination

ABOUT THE AUTHOR

PANNEER SELVAM is born in Salem - Valappady of Tamil Nadu. He started his career as school teacher in New Delhi in the year 1991. He joins as lecturer in DIET, perundurai of Erode in 2000. Bharathiyar University were gave the Philosophy in Doctorates in Language and Education. He is the seventh diploma holder from National University of Educational Planning and Administration (NUEPA), New Delhi in 2002. In 2005, the Tamil Nadu government was given the 'Excellence Award' for his unrivalled teaching activities and some organization also. He has published more than hundreds of Research Papers and books in the field of Education. At present he is working in the department of Education, Bharathidasan University, Tamil Nadu.

ABOUT THE BOOK

Education is a comprehensive term. As we have seen, educations are bound up with human race. Its boundaries are rich and varied as life itself. Its meaning is as wide as life itself, just as it is difficult to squeeze life in a few words, in the same way; it is difficult to give meaning to or definition to the term 'Education'. This increasingly negative orientation to work is probably due to the fact that man no longer finds meaning or a sense of himself in the community or as Freud (1962) suggested, but which does not seem to exist today; his work at least gives him a secure place in a portion of reality, in the human community. Man is basically a mind, body unit and these two aspects vitally influence one another. For efficient functioning of the individual he should posse's sound health of body and mind.

❐

Knowledge Design and Determination

Dr. S.K. Panneer Selvam
Assistant Professor, Department of Education
Bharathidasan University, T.N.,India

AMIGA PRESS INC.

AMIGA PRESS INC.
H.O:- 28-A, Indra Park, St.No-9
Near-Chander Nagar, Krishna Nagar
Delhi: - 110051 (India)
Tel: - 011-22504028, +91-98736-57000
Email: - amigapress@gmail.com
info@amigapress.co.in
amigaeditorial@gmail.com
amigapub@gmail.com

Website: - www.amigapress.co.in

This edition is published by Amiga Press Inc.

ISBN: 978-93-84533-68-7

First Published 2020

Printed and bound in India by Replika Press Pvt. Ltd.

Contents

❐

1

The Problem and its Perspective

All individuals living in what has been called "an age of turbulence an age of anxiety and stress", where man's ability to cope with his environment is being taxed in new and unprecedented ways? Other generations have faced threat, peril and anxiety, but there is something different about the stress that confronts us today. Current emotional pressures are more sub title, more intangible and more pervasive. Man is now faced with a world of increased complexity in which his defensive capacities are strained; there is no way to escape and often no way to fight back.

MENTAL HEALTH

According to Hadfield Mental Health is the full and harmonious functioning of the whole personality. Nikelly (1966) suggested that the person accepts himself with his strong points and his shortcomings. Mental health involves a continuous adaptation to changing circumstances where a living being strives to achieve a balance between internal demands and the requirements of a changing environment. Fulfilment of basic human needs is the basis for good mental health. An individual tries to establish a balance between his needs and his capacity for realizing the needs. As long as this balance is satisfactorily maintained, the person remains adjusted and his mental health is retained. But when this balance is lost, he drifts towards maladjustments.

STRESS AND MENTAL HEALTH

The modern world which is said to be a world of achievement is also a world of stress. One finds stress everywhere, whether it is within the family, organization or any other social or economic activity right from the time of birth till the last breath drawn, an individual is in variably exposed to various stressful situations. This is not surprising that interest in this issue has been rising up with the advancement of the present century which has been called "an area of growing complexities and pressure".

The basic opinion of stress is that, it is fundamentally a psychological phenomenon with immediate and direct physiological manifestation as well as an experience of discomfort. The enormous number of publication related to the concept of stress has made it difficult to pin point the concept in any precise manner. More than ever before work is not seen as the root of infinite satisfaction and fulfilment, but rather a source of stress, discontentment and humiliation. Studs Terkel (1972) sum this up most succinctly – "Work is, by its very nature about violence to the spirit as well as to the body.

This increasingly negative orientation to work is probably due to the fact that man no longer finds meaning or a sense of himself in the community or as Freud (1962) suggested, but which does not seem to exist today; his work at least gives him a secure place in a portion of reality, in the human community. But the reason for this change of attitude is aptly highlighted by Terkel (1972), "the planned obsolescence of people that is a piece with the planned obsolescence of the things they make, or sell. It is perhaps this fear of no longer being needed in a world of needless things that most clearly spells out the unnatural the surrealist of much that is called work today".

It is because of the dramatic changes that have taken place in society over the last decade or two that work and life stress have become more immediate focal points of interest. This interest has reflected itself in an ever increasing research orientation into occupation stress, the impact of life events, stress and disease.

Based on Pestonjee's approach (1987), "it is natural and healthy to maintain optimal level of stress" and "success, achievements, higher productivity and effectiveness call for stress" When stressors are left unchecked and unmanaged, they can create problems in performance and affect the physical and mental health of the organism. The negative effect of stress arises when an individual fails to maintain a balance between himself and his social environment. Hence keeping up mental health is one of the major problems of the world today.

For a better understanding of mental health it is necessary to give humans, an advice of how to solve the problems of living. Hence mental health services have proliferated. People have become more involved than ever in the problems of human welfare and there are groups that seek to improve the quality of living through social, economic and medical programs promoted under the banner of mental health and mental hygiene.

MEANING OF MENTAL HEALTH

Mental Health means the balanced and integrated development of personality. It is a science that deals with human welfare pervading all fields of human relationships. A person is said to have good mental health when he succeeds in maintaining harmonious relationship between himself and his environment.

THE CONCEPT OF MENTAL HEALTH

Mental health refers to the functioning of a well- integrated personality. The concept of mental health is closely related to the concept of adjustment. All humans know that while an individual has satisfactory personality adjustment he is also likely to have good mental health. Thus the normal, well adjusted, well integrated and mature person is bound to have positive mental health.

FACTORS ASSOCIATED TO MENTAL HEALTH

Mental Health is a Fiction

It is difficult to see a person who is mentally healthy in all the aspects. Truly speaking perfect mental health is a fiction and not reality. Hence, it is always better to talk of optimum mental health in place of perfect mental health

Mental Health and Physical Health

The saying that "a sound mind lives in a sound body" is quite true. For achieving an optimal level of mental health one has to first acquire adequate physical health.

Mental Health and Efficiency

It is not essential for the successful and efficient men to be mentally healthy as well. One way is quite efficient and successful at his work or profession but he could be most unhappy full of anxiety etc.

Mental Health and Social Ability

While a mentally healthy person is sociable, it is not necessary for a sociable or socially adaptable person to be healthy minded. One may be sociable but extremely anxious to please everybody. Similarly he may be amenable because of an inherent feeling of insecurity or inferiority.

Mental Health Differs and Ethical Standards

Mental health differs from ethical standards morality, There exists, many individuals who are very moral but suffer from serious abnormalities like phobias or sex preservations.

IMPORTANCE OF MENTAL HEALTH

Man is basically a mind, body unit and these two aspects vitally influence one another. For efficient functioning of the individual he should posse's sound health of body and mind. The terrific advances in the field of preventive and medicine coupled with continued attempts in all countries to improve the standard of living of people have to a large extent enabled us to eradicate most of the disease of the body and helped to provide for longevity of human life with sufficient physical health.

A sound body has now become an easy possibility within the research of everyone. Handicaps and discards do efforts mental duality and outlook. But in contemporary society mental health has become a major problem affecting almost every person. Individuals who do not possess mental health pick up habits of smoking and using drugs and liquor.

Not only have mental health hazards significantly increased in number and complexity but these have also affected the physical efficiency of individual causing a variety of psychosomatic disorders. So mental health is now recognized as an important aspect of an individual total development and mental hygiene is accepted as an integral part of the school and college programme.

DEFINITIONS OF MENTAL HEALTH

Hadfield (1972) defined, "Mental health as the full and harmonious functioning of the whole personality. A mentally healthy person lives a fuller, happier, harmonious and effective life"

Jahado (1963) defined, "Mentally healthy person as one who actively masters his environment, demonstrates a considerable unity in consistency of personality and is able to perceive self and the world realistically"

Norma et. Al., (1991) defined, "Mental health as the various strains of environment we meet in life and mental hygiene as the means we take to assure the adjustment"

Mental health is the adjustment of an individual to themselves and the world at large with maximum of effectiveness, satisfaction, cheerfulness and socially considerable behaviour and the ability of facing and accepting the realities of life.

Crow and Crow (1962) "Mental Health is a science that deals with human welfare and prevails all fields of human relationship".

Hadfield (1972) "Mental Health is the full and harmonious functioning of the whole personality"

FACTORS RESPONSIBLE FOR POOR MENTAL HEALTH

Factors responsible for poor mental health, mental health illness and disorders into three main categories

HEREDITARY FACTORS

Sometimes the roots of mental health ailments and diseases are found in the effective genes inherited from the parents more over the inherited potentialities in terms of intellectual abilities, Psychological structure and appearance etc., put limits on one's mental health and the deficiency and appropriates of any sort in these potentialities.

PSYCHOLOGICAL FACTORS

Psychological constitution appearance and physical health of an individual affect his Mental Health. A sound body is set to possess a sound mind and is capable of making adjustment in life on the other hand poor health, physical defects ailments and disease bring deterioration to one's strength and stamina for performing one's duties. It arouses inferiority feelings and mental complexes that create serious adjustment problems. In this way improper physical psychological conditions furnish the soil for the growth of poor and ill mental health.

ENVIRONMENTAL OR SOCIAL FACTORS

It has now been established on account of various researches in the field of mental hygiene that external forces like family, school, college and society are more responsible for bringing mental illness that the hereditary or constitutional faces. Social and emotional maladjustment has been found to be the root cause of all mental illness and disorder. Student's behaviour is worst in the class and society

PROMOTION OF MENTAL HEALTH

All people face many of the same stressful situations in life, but learn to adjust with them in different ways. Emotional reactions vary from person to person depending on how an individual perceives the situation. However in coping with stressful circumstances, engaging in stress reducing behaviours, putting the situation into perspective and dealing with it immediately are much healthier. A recent document made by WHO (1994) identified a set of ten skills for the promotion of mental health. They are decision making, problem solving, creative thinking, critical thinking, effective communication; inter personal relationship skill, self awareness, empathy and coping with emotions.

The complex age in which we live with its urban orientation, job stress and other social problems appears to be conducive to mental illness. The following are some of the major factors affecting mental health.

i. In the present materialistic society individual needs and wants have multiplied resulting in dissatisfaction, alienation and frustration.
ii. The conflict provoking and frustrating situations are further accentuated by general atmosphere of insecurity hanging over the society.
iii. The competitive motive results in aspirations far beyond one's abilities which have resulted in excessive tension, anxiety, fear and guilt feeling.
iv. The hold of family and religion over men has become loose resulting in a life without meaning and values.
v. Social prejudices and stereo type have precipitated social conflicts which in turn have tended to disrupt the individual mental balance.

PROBLEM SOLVING ABILITY

Meaning of Problem Solving Ability

The 20th century educators have devoted much of their attention in trying to define and teach problem solving skills. In the early 1990s, problem solving was view as a mechanical systematic and often abstract (de-contextualized) set of skills, such as those used to solve riddles or mathematical equations as these problems often have correct answer (convergent).

Man's ability to form concept, to think, or to use language in adaptive, thus this ability helps him to solve problems. With it he is better equipped to cope with the demands of his environment and to achieve goals which he desires. In fact, this is the simplest definition of a problem solving situation – the individual has a goal and does not know how to teach or achieve the goal. He has a goal and he does not know what to do. However, in most of the learning situations the task could be achieved only through blind, trial and error behaviour with the experimenter reinforcing an arbitrary response. As a rule the individual did not have all the information available, so it was impossible for him to purser the problem as whole. The study of such situations can tell us only something about how individuals solve irrational, blind problem.

On the other hand, when all the essential information is available to the individual and some general principles can solve the problem, the problem behaviour tell us great deal about the nature of thinking and in some cases about the role of language and cognitive development.

DEFINITIONS OF PROBLEM SOLVING ABILITY

Some of the definitions of Problem Solving Ability are as follows:

- According to WOODWORTH & MARQUIS (1948),"Problem – solving behaviour occurs in novel or difficult situations in which a solution is not obtainable by the habitual methods of applying concepts and principle derived from past and principles derived from past experience in very familiar situation".
- According to SKINNER (1968), "Problem solving is a process of overcoming difficulties that appear to interfere with the attainment of a goal. It is a procedure of making adjustment in spite of interferences".

PROBLEM SOLVING APPROACHES

There are many approaches to problem solving depending on the nature of the problem and the problem. The most traditional, rational approach is typically used and involves, e.g., clarifying description of the problem, analyzing causes, alternative, assessing each alternative, choosing one implementing it and evaluating whether the problem was solved or not.

Another more state of the art approach is appreciative inquiry. That approach assert that "Problem", then it appreciative inquire include identification in the past, wishing and thinking about what we want in the future and building from our strengths to works towards our vision.

TYPES OF PROBLEMS SOLVING ABILITY

The activities of problem-solving and decision making are closely intertwined so the reader will often find mention of the two topics together.

Generally the problems under study may be: (1) Theoretical, (2) Practical, (3) Numerical and (4) Symbolic type. Every type of problem should possess the following characteristic: challenging within the capacity of the students should have many solutions, can be solved in limited time, Economic in all respects, should be real or related to the life and should be very clear.

UNDERSTANDING THE PROBLEMS:

Four Aspects of Problem Solving are:

This involves the construction of an internal representation of the problem and it requires three things:

a. COHERENCE

A coherent representation is a pattern that is connected so that all of the parts make sense.

- e.g. Solving Analogies

b. CORRESPONDENCE

There must be a close correspondence between the internal representation and the material to be understood. All of the necessary data must be included in the representation, and it must be accurate.

RELATIONSHIP TO BACKGROUND KNOWLEDGE

This is drawn from experience, using related sources of knowledge. There are some vital prerequisites to this stage: (I) every one must have the vocabulary and skills needed to solve the problem. (II) Everyone needs the appropriate tools to do the job.

PROBLEM SOLVING STEPS

There are two basic steps taken in problem solving.

1. Attending to relevant information while disregarding the irrelevant
2. Deciding how to represent the problem.

1. Attention

Attention is one of the most important aspects in problem solving. There should be a keen attention while listening or going through the problem. Divert in attention may cause a huge failure in problem solving.

2. Representation

After identifying the relevant facts, one must device what to do with them. In many cases, like word problems, one must uncover the underlying, abstract puzzle, buried in all the details.

Abstract problems use up more of our valuable working memory's cognitive space. So finding a concrete way of representing the problems helps.

Methods used include

Symbols, lists, matrices, hierarchical tree diagrams, graphs and visual images etc.

FACTORS IN PROBLEM SOLVING

In the total programme of problem solving the following factors operate.

1. Mental Set
2. Conditions of works
3. Age and Intelligence
4. Personality and Emotional factors
5. Manual work and Manipulation

CREATIVITY

Creativity as the unique characteristic of the human mind may be defined as the capacity of an individual to create or produce an entirely new or novel idea or object by the rearrangement or reshaping of what is already known. It is both innate as well as acquired and a process as well as a product. It is also characterized by qualities like universality, adventurousness and open-mindedness, a craving for change and novelty, ego involvement and divergent thinking. It does not necessarily have positive correlation with school mental health and problem solving ability.

EDUCATIONAL IMPLICATIONS OF PROBLEM SOLVING

Problem solving is an important technique in the educative process. It develops in the learner the ability to criticize, discuss and assume a constructive yet open – minded attitude to felt difficulties. The child develops the mental attitude which he carries all through the life.

Reasoning is the basis of the problem solving. In problem solving more concentration of attention is required. This should be developed of the children. Reasoning is purely mental process whereas problem solving also involves manual work also. A teacher has to pay an effective and constructive role in these aspects of education, that is, problem solving.

OPERATIONAL DEFINITION

Mental Health

By this, the investigator means the scores obtained from the Mental Health inventory constructed and standardised by M.Illayaraja Dr.M.Suresh kumar(2009) administered of the higher secondary school students.

Problem Solving Ability

By this, the investigator means the Problem Solving Ability is the scores obtained from the Problem Solving Ability tools are constructed and standardised by S.Mani.(2012) administered of the higher secondary school students.

Statement of the Problem

The researcher had framed the following statement, "A Study on Mental Health and Problem Solving Ability of higher secondary school students"

OBJECTIVES OF THE STUDY

1. To find out the level of mental health of higher secondary school students.
2. To find out the level of problem solving ability of the higher secondary school students.
3. To find out the significant difference in mental health of the higher secondary school students with respect to Gender.
4. To find out the significant difference in mental health of the higher secondary school students with respect to Medium of learning.
5. To find out the significant difference in mental health of the higher secondary school students with respect to Type of Management.
6. To find out the significant difference in mental health of the higher secondary school students with respect to Type of family.
7. To find out the significant difference in mental health of the higher secondary school students with respect to Birth order.
8. To find out the significant difference in mental health of the higher secondary school students with respect to Father's Educational Qualification.
9. To find out the significant difference in mental health of the higher secondary school students with respect to Father's Occupation.
10. To find out the significant difference in mental health of the higher secondary school students with respect to Mother's Educational Qualification.
11. To find out the significant difference in mental health of the higher secondary school students with respect to Mother's Occupation.
12. To find out the significant difference in mental health of the higher secondary school students with respect to Family monthly income.
13. To find out the significant difference in mental health of the higher secondary school students with respect to Type of house.
14. To find out the significant difference in mental health of the higher secondary school students with respect to Parent's approach on Advice.
15. To find out the significant difference in mental health of the higher secondary school students with respect to Wake up time.
16. To find out the significant difference in problem solving ability of the higher secondary school students with respect to Gender.
17. To find out the significant difference in problem solving ability of the higher secondary school students with respect to Medium of learning.
18. To find out the significant difference in problem solving ability of the higher secondary school students with respect to Type of Management.

19. To find out the significant difference in problem solving ability of the higher secondary school students with respect to Type of family.
20. To find out the significant difference in problem solving ability of the higher secondary school students with respect to Birth Order.
21. To find out the significant difference in problem solving ability of the higher secondary school students with respect to Father's Educational Qualification
22. To find out the significant difference in problem solving ability of the higher secondary school students with respect to Father's Occupation
23. To find out the significant difference in problem solving ability of the higher secondary school students with respect to Mother's Educational Qualification
24. To find out the significant difference in problem solving ability of the higher secondary school students with respect to Mother's Occupation.
25. To find out the significant difference in problem solving ability of the higher secondary school students with respect to Family Monthly Income.
26. To find out the significant difference in problem solving ability of the higher secondary school students with respect to Type of House.
27. To find out the significant difference in problem solving ability of the higher secondary school students with respect to Parent's Approach on advice.
28. To find out the significant difference in problem solving ability of the higher secondary school students with respect to Wake up time.
29. To find out the significant relation between Mental Health and Problem Solving Ability of the higher secondary school students.

NEED OF THE STUDY

These are several studies conducted on various psychological factors of students like attitude, interest, adjustment, self actualization and effectiveness. The role of students in higher secondary students is developing the personality themselves. Whether the students can be viewed as a model, director, supervisor, guide, co-worker or leader the student has a crucial role in moulding the behaviour of student. For that the student must be free from personal and psychological problems like stress, dissatisfaction, emotional disturbance and the like which is the essential thing in maintaining mental health constantly. Then only students can effectively fulfil the needs of the students as well as the society and nation. The present study sheds light on the knowledge of relationship between psychological variables like, Mental Health and Problem Solving Ability of the higher secondary school students.

DELIMITATION OF THE STUDY

This investigation has the following delimitation

1. The sample is limited to 300 students
2. The sample is taken only from Chennai, in Tamil Nadu
3. The sample is limited to higher secondary school students only
4. The sample is taken only from Government School, Government Aided School and two Matriculation Schools.

CONCLUSION

It also includes the objectives, and delimitation of the study. The overall theoretical information about mental health and problem solving ability helped in the researcher to get idea about back ground knowledge. In the following chapter relevant studies have been collected for further research work.

❐

2

Review of Related Literature

The Review of related studies is an important part of the scientific methods of research. It provides the means of getting to the frontier in the researcher's particulars knowledge. The identification of a problem of research, design and determination of the size and scope of the problems, all depends to a great extents and the care and intensity with which a researcher examine the literature related to the proposed research.

For any worthwhile study in any field of knowledge, the research worker needs an adequate familiarity with the work, which has already been done in the area of their choice. In the review of related literature, the researcher attempts and to determine what others have learned about similar research problems and to gather information relevant to the research problem at hand. The review of literature serves multiple purposes and is essential to a well designed research study.

The study of related literature saves a researcher from working on a worked topic. It further develops the insight of the investigator and enables him to develop the right type of tool. The Investigator traced out different types of research work like dissertations', thesis , journals and varieties of relevant books on education, physiology, philosophy etc., as the topic is very specific only a few number of studies have been obtained and are given below.

According to Best (1963), " A familiarity with the literature in any problem area helps the students to discover what is already known attempted, methods promising and disappointing, and problems that remains to be solved"

STUDIES RELATED TO MENTAL HEALTH

Indian Studies on Mental Health

Lucro John, A. (1990) reported that the goals of the school mental health consultation programme, is to help the consult tee to access them. The consultant helps the consult tee to identify issue or problem, and to develop problem solving skills. Effective communication skills should be a top criterion when providing consultation services. The most important trait in a consultant is the ability to establish confidence among students.

Mehra and Mishra (1991) investigated the potential moderate effect of mental health in intrinsic job satisfaction and occupational stress relationship moderate regression analysis confirm that mental health has a moderating effect on the intrinsic job satisfaction and occupational stress relationship

Mohan. T. S (1992) investigated occupational stress, coping stress, coping style, mental health states and social support in a group of executive from public and private sectors. The study was conducted on 240 executive. The major findings are private sector executive in general, experienced greater jobs stress, mental health problems and perceived greater organized support than the public sector executives. They also focused more problems than public sector executives.

Mc. Elhaney-Sandra (1993) examined the current states of US children mental health and its impact on children's ability to learn. It notes the incidence of mental disorders in children risk factors and serious emotional disturbances. It describes several model of collaboration among models, community agencies professional and parents. These models work to both treatments and prevention of mental health problems.

Kalpan Diane(1996) reported that after research by using the data from 4,141 students a theoretically informed model is proposed which specifies the efforts of failing to finish high school on the latent construct " psychological functions" in young adulthood. Result suggest that dropping out has a significantly negative effect on psychological functioning.

Doll – Beth et al (2003) reported that the National Goals 2000 emphasizes the importance of public school children's socio emotional and physical health. 20% of America's public school children suffer significant mental health problems. Aggressive or withdrawn pre scholars may later experience may later experience academic difficulties, troubles with friendship, and authority, and perhaps even fall into delinquency. School psychologists, in particular should partnership to participate in the planning and implementation of these programmes which bring together schools and communities.

Ruffolo (2004) study examined the risk and protective factors for effective mental health prevention and intervention programs. Delinquents diverted and high risk adolescents girls (N = 154) were involved. A majority of the girls reported moderate to severe depression, but only about one third had received mental health specially services. Girls in the community based in experienced more negative life events, reported more sexual abuse, more often but special education status, were more likely to come from families who received welfare, had more disruptions in living situations, exhibited more delinquents behaviour and used more negative coping behaviour than did girls in the other programmes

Kamau and Catherine (2006) studied the level of burn out, locus of control and mental health of higher secondary students in a sample 309 students of both sexes participated in the study. The male students were emotionally over extended exhausted internally controlled, anxious towards students and personally accomplished but less capable of establishing constructive relationship accomplished but less capable of establishing constructive relationship however they were more capable of coping with stress than female students

FOREIGN STUDIES ON MENTAL HEALTH

Campbell and Celestea (1988) made an investigated under the name manual for training teachers' in the dialoguing component of interpersonal cognitive problem solving. The interpersonal cognitive problem solving (ICPS) program is an education and preventive mental health program designed to teach children the cognitive and preventive mental health program designed to teach children the cognitive skill necessary to solve conflicts that frequently occur between themselves and peers or adults. The acquisition of these skills has been shown to improve overall behavioural adjustment.

Gregory Paul (1993) conducted a qualitative study of higher secondary school student's responses to the reduction in force (RIF) process, which is used by school districts to terminate students. The study describes the feelings, emotions, behaviours, mental health and reactions of students as they proceeded through RIF's Stage. Data were collected from in depth interviews with the participants and public document provided by the school district. This study concluded that the mental health of students deteriorated. The overall effect of reduction in – force (RIF) on teachers was negative effects that toughed almost every aspect of their lives.

Tanner and Jones (1997) investigated the impact of two types of cognitive style variables and three mental health problems (aggressive behaviours, elevated activity level and social with drawl) on second grade students preference for the consultation made used by a peer consultant. The models investigated were an expert or behavioural approach, a collaborative approach and mental health approach. Students responses with behavioural approach favoured for the aggressive and elevated activity level scenario and mental health approaches favoured for the social with drawl scenario.

Chamberlin, Susan (1998) conducted a study to explore the strategies of getting good mental health. The sample consisted of adults who work with adolescents (N=32). Quantitative data was collected through audio tape, semi structured interviews. Analysis of data revealed a five step process for getting good mental health. The steps were Recognizing Warning Signals, Stopping oneself and stepping back, calming oneself, thinking it through, and Deciding behaviour.

Stephanie Berzin (2008) utilized data collected from school social workers (n=1639) in the National School Social Work Survey 2008. Using a subset of questions at how school social workers partner with teacher, this study reported on the most common collaboration. Latest class analysis examined underlying sub types of school social work practitioners to assess collaborative practice models. Bivariate analyses examined including teacher professional development, improving school culture and community enhancement

Anthony F Jorm co et al, (2010) reveals mental disorders often have their front onset during adolescence. For this reason high school teacher are in a good position to provide initial assistance to students who are developing mental health problems. To improve the skills of teacher in this area, a mental health first aid training course was modified to be suitable for high school teacher and evaluated in a cluster randomized trial.

Natasi, Bonnick et al. (2011) reported that large scale natural scale natural disasters pose serious risks to mental health and simultaneously wreak have on the very system called upon to ameliorate those risks. School based mental health services have been identified as a potential mechanism through which gaps in service delivery system can be addressed in post-disorder environments. They believe that a public health framework provides a useful guide for school psychologist who may be called upon to develop school-based of care following a disaster. In this article they discuss considerations and challenges in the application of this model in the context of their experience developing school-based mental health services in New Orleans, Louisiana, USA, following hurricane Katrina.

Egger, Helen l.et al(2011), study on infant mental health fields has turned its focus to the presentation, course, and treatment of clinically significant mental health disorder, the need for reliable and valid criteria for identifying and assessing mental health symptoms and disorders in early childhood has become urgent. In this article they offer a critical perspective on classification of mental health disorders in young children.

They place the issue of early childhood diagnosis within the context of classification of psychological at other ages and describe, in some detail, diagnostic classification of mental health disorders in young children. They place the issue of early childhood diagnosis within the context of classification of psychopathology at other ages and describe, in some detail diagnostic classification that have been developed specifically for young children, including the diagnostic classification of mental health and developmental disorder of infancy and childhood a diagnostic classification for mental health symptoms and disorders in infants, toddlers, and preschoolers. They briefly outline the role of diagnostic classification in clinical assessment and treatment planning. Last, they review the limitation of current approach to the diagnostic classification of mental health disorders in young children.

Currin, James B.et Al. (2011) study explored the impact of age, historical change and gender on perceptions of mental health and mental health services. Using multi - dimensional measures to assess such perception among older adults and younger adults they expected that older adults would have less positive mental health perceptions than would younger adults, that more recently born charts of older persons would evidence more positive perceptions, and that woman, especially those more recently assessed, would also evidence more positive perceptions. To an extent, they found positive historical shifts in mental perceptions, though data also indicated that such views may have stabilized over the last decade for older persons, and interacted with age and gender in this respect. Age difference favouring younger were, in part, replicated across historical time and woman held more positive mental health perceptions than did men. Over historical time, older persons' mental health perceptions are, for the most part, increasingly positive, significant in light of the increasing proportion of older persons and changes in the mental health system itself.

STUDIES ON PROBLEM SOLVING ABILITY

Mark . J. (1996) studied on "the relationship between mental imagery and problem solving ability". A study of 44 separate accounts, reporting mental imagery associated with discovery was examined. The study analyze report of mental imagery according to the following three factors (I) Possible causes for the reported perception of mental imagery and (ii) At what a stage of the problem-solving process, imagery and reported involved.

Danielson, Mary Ann and Mitchell, Nancy (1995) explored the relationship between problem solving and group decision- making technique that; (1) use of the NGT led to a large quantity of ideas generated, but generally less evidence in the group process, leading to and lower satisfaction, confidence and efficiency and (2) observation of UGA groups detected more "piggy backing" or "spring boarding" of ideas among group members during interaction. Findings suggest that the NGT is useful but not optimal for decision making, and that the advantages of both the NGT and UGA structures are enhanced when combined.

Black, Deb (1994) this booklet describes a process for creative class room problem solving that can be adapted to many types of problems. The booklets five sections correspond to five phases of the problem solving process. The five section address; (1) recognizing that an unresolved situation exists as a first stage of problem solving; (2) Identifying the problem; (3) Finding solutions including tools for generating ideas, suggestions for when the process gets stuck, and problem solving with students; (4) Choosing from among alternatives including identifying criteria, and problem solving with students; and (5) Taking action such as looking at the results of the action and working with students in this phase.

Shorndrick, Denise. D et. Al., (1992) Administration of the Test Of Interpersonal problem solving to 46 boys (grades 3 – 4) with learning disabilities (LD) and 46 boys without LD found that LD students had lower scores on Problem Formulation, Consequential thinking, and Total Problem Solving Ability. No group differences were noted on the two measures of creativity.

Isaksen, Scott G. et. Al., (1993) reviewed the trends in research into described the 'Project' which is examined Problem Solving, an ecologically based process model used to define problems, generate ideas, and refine solutions. Research into five dimensions of Problem Solving were proposed; the situational outlook, personal orientation, outcome problem solving processes and the task.

Scheck, Gina D. (1992) made a study on middle school students who were designated as gifted, honoured, or average and divided them into problem solving treatment of comparison groups, and assessed them on problem – solving ability and potential giftedness. Treatment students showed significant gains in problem-solving ability competed with comparison groups, with no significant difference among ability levels.

Clode, Linda (1992) developed an enrichment program for sixth-grade gifted students combined problem- solving with future studies in a way that would simulate real life crisis problem solving. The program involved forecasting problems of the future – requiring evacuation of Earth, assuming roles on a spaceship, and simulating crises as the spaceship travelled to Titan.

Charistensen, Kip W and Martin – Loren (1992) examined how interpersonal cognitive skills, adaptability and critical thinking can be developed through problem solving and co-operative learning in technology education. These skills have been identified as significant needs of the work place as well as for functioning in society.

Dr. Anice James and P. V. Marice (2005) made a study of select Variables as Determinants of Problem – Solving Ability. The investigators of this study assessed the effect of Reasoning and Brain Hemisphericity on Problem Solving Ability of the learners. A random sample of 309 XI and XII standard students who opted for art and science group from 4 higher secondary schools of Vellore constituted the sample. Problem – Solving Ability Test prepared and standardized by Roop Rekha Garg, Mental Health in Arts and Science prepared and standardized by Anuradha Joshi and Bhuban Chandra Mahapatra (1994) and 'SOLAT' Test developed and standardized by Venketaraman (1994) were the tools used for the study. The major findings of the study are, there are significant gender differences in the student's Mental Health and Problem Solving Ability in an arts and science, favouring boys and girls. Mental Health and Gender are foud to be the most significant predictors of Problem Solving Ability in arts and science.

Indira Sharma (2007) made a study on problem solving ability and Mental Health attitude as determinant of academic achievement of higher secondary students. The sample consisted of 309 students of XI and XII Class of Government, Aided and Private selected by multistage random sampling. The tool used was Problem Solving Ability test by s.Mani(2012). The marks of XI and XII class Board Examination were treated as Mental Health score of students. The finding are (I) Higher secondary students have shown average problem solving ability and no difference in problem solving ability of boys and girls, (ii) it was found that the group had average Mental Health and statistically no difference in the Mental Health of Boys and girls.

CONCLUSION

In this chapter, research results of the past investigators are taken into account and denoted so that it may avoid overlapping of the research topic. Also it mentions the significance of variables, their correlation etc, on which the research is done. Based upon these studies, researcher framed the relevant hypotheses and select tools for the further research work.

❒

3

Research Design and Method of Investigation

This chapter gives an overall picture of design of the study, the form of hypotheses to be tested, research tools used for the data collection, reliability and validity of the tools, scoring procedure, pilot study, nature and collection of the sample, a brief description of the procedure adopted for the data collection, and statistical techniques to be employed for the analysis of the data. Hence the present chapter serves as a guide to research, to show how all the major part of the project the objectives, the review of literature, hypotheses and statistical techniques work together to address the central research questions

DESIGN OF THE STUDY

"Choosing a design for a study basically involves selecting the most appropriate technique to solve a particular problem under investigation" (Anderson, Durston and Poole, 1970).

STATEMENT OF PROBLEM

The present study is entitled as "A study on Mental Health and Problem Solving Ability of higher secondary school students"

HYPOTHESES OF THE PROBLEM

The following hypotheses have been framed by the researcher for the present study.

1. The level of mental health of higher secondary school students is moderate in nature.
2. The level of problem solving ability of higher secondary school students is moderate in nature.
3. There is no significant difference in mental health of higher secondary school students with respect to Gender.
4. There is no significant difference in mental health of higher secondary school students with respect to Medium of Learning.
5. There is no significant difference in mental health of higher secondary school students with respect to Type of Management.
6. There is no significant difference in mental health of higher secondary school students with respect to Type of Family.
7. There is no significant difference in mental health of higher secondary school students with respect to Birth Order.
8. There is no significant difference in mental health of higher secondary school students with respect to Father's Educational Qualification.
9. There is no significant difference in mental health of higher secondary school students with respect to Father's Occupation.
10. There is no significant difference in mental health of higher secondary school students with respect to Mother's Educational Qualification.
11. There is no significant difference in mental health of higher secondary school students with respect to Mother's Occupation.
12. There is no significant difference in mental health of higher secondary school students with respect to Family Monthly Income.
13. There is no significant difference in mental health of higher secondary school students with respect to Type of House.
14. There is no significant difference in mental health of higher secondary school students with respect to Parent's Approach on Advice.
15. There is no significant difference in mental health of higher secondary school students with respect to Wake up time.
16. There is no significant difference in Problem Solving Ability of higher secondary school students with respect to Gender.
17. There is no significant difference in Problem Solving Ability of higher secondary school students with respect to Medium of Learning.
18. There is no significant difference in Problem Solving Ability of higher secondary school students with respect to Type of Management.

19. There is no significant difference in Problem Solving Ability of higher secondary school students with respect to Type of Family.
20. There is no significant difference in Problem Solving Ability of higher secondary school students with respect to Birth Order.
21. There is no significant difference in Problem Solving Ability of higher secondary school students with respect to Father's Educational Qualification.
22. There is no significant difference in Problem Solving Ability of higher secondary school students with respect to Father's Occupation.
23. There is no significant difference in Problem Solving Ability of higher secondary school students with respect to Mother's Educational Qualification.
24. There is no significant difference in Problem Solving Ability of higher secondary school students with respect to Mother's Occupation.
25. There is no significant difference in Problem Solving Ability of higher secondary school students with respect to Family Monthly Income.
26. There is no significant difference in Problem Solving Ability of higher secondary school students with respect to Type of House.
27. There is no significant difference in Problem Solving Ability of higher secondary school students with respect to Parent's Approach on Advice.
28. There is no significant difference in Problem Solving Ability of higher secondary school students with respect to Wake up time.
29. There is no relation between Mental Health and Problem Solving ability of higher secondary school students.

METHOD OF THE STUDY

As, the study intends to collect data pertaining mental health and problem solving ability among higher secondary school students, survey method is employed to describe and interpret what exists at presents. The survey methods gather data from a relatively large number of cases at a particular time. It is not concerned with characteristics of individuals as individuals. It is concerned with the statistics that result when data are abstracted from a number of individual cases.

VARIABLES OF THE STUDY

The present investigation includes the following variables.

1. Mental Health - Independent variables
2. Problem Solving Ability - Dependent variables
3. Back ground Variables:

- Gender
- Medium of Learning
- Type of Management
- Type of Family
- Birth Order
- Father's Educational Qualification
- Father's Occupation
- Mother's Educational Qualification
- Mother's Occupation
- Family Monthly Income
- Type of House
- Parents Approach on Advice
- Wake - up Time

TOOLS AND TECHNIQUES USED

To test the hypotheses formulated, the following tools have been used in the present study.

i. Personal data sheet developed by the investigator.
ii. Mental Health Inventory developed and standardized by M. Illayaraja Dr. M. Suresh Kumar (2009) was adopted.
iii. Problem Solving Ability Test developed and Standardized by S. Mani. (2012) adopted.

MENTAL HEALTH INVENTORY

Description of the Inventory

Mental health Inventory was standardised by M. Illayaraja Dr. M. Suresh Kumar (2009). This inventory consists of 60 statements out of which 20 items are positive statement and the remaining 40 statement are negative in nature. The following table shows the nature of the items of mental health index

TABLE: 3.01: Showing the Nature of Items of the Mental Health Inventory

Nature of Statements	Items Number
Positive	1, 2, 5, 8, 9, 10, 16, 17, 27, 31, 34, 35, 38, 44, 45, 46, 54, 58 & 60
Negative	3, 4, 6, 7, 11, 12, 13, 15, 18, 19, 20, 21, 22, 23, 24, 25, 26, 28, 29, 30, 32, 33, 36, 37, 39, 40, 41, 42, 43, 47, 48, 49, 50, 51, 52, 53, 55, 56, 57 & 59

Administration

This questionnaire consists of single statement, which expresses the different way in which students think, feel and behave in life situation. The students were required to select any of the two responses to indicate ability to adjust to one's own social, vocational and environmental demands. The investigator requested the student to give responses frank and said that it would be confidential.

Scoring

Since the questionnaire consists of both positive and negative statement two different patterns of scoring have to be adopted for the types of items. The following table provides guidelines to score the responses given to the categories of items.

TABLE: 3.2: Scoring Key for the Mental Health Inventory

Nature of Statement	**Positive Statement**	**Negative Statement**
Yes	1	0
No	0	1

PROBLEM SOLVING ABILITY TEST

Description of the Test

Problem solving is the framework of pattern within which creative thinking and reasoning take place. It is the ability to think and reasoning on given levels of complexity. People who have learned effective problem solving technique are able to solve the problems at higher levels of complexity than more intelligent people who have no such training.

In general, the state of tension is created in mind when an individual faces a problem. He exercises his greatest effort and uses all his abilities, intelligence, thinking, imagination and observation, etc. some individual are able solve problem sooner than others. It indicates that there are different levels of problem solving ability-ranging from average ability to highest ability-depending upon the difficulty level of problem. The person having average problem solving ability can solve a problem, while high level of ability is required to solve complex problems.

Perhaps man's greatest use of sentence language has been the system that he has developed for its application to problem-solving. It is not language alone but also the way in which he uses language. Two men of ability with language may not be equal in ability to solve problem.

The problem solving is a process of overcoming difficulties that appear to interfere with the attainment of a goal. Simple problem can well be solved by instinctive and habitual behaviours. More difficult problems require a series of solution attempts a degree of understanding and a perception of the relationships between the significant factors of the problems.

It has been found that persons having intelligence and reasoning ability can solve the complex quickly. Therefore, it is necessary that on one hand we should try to develop intelligence and reasoning ability and on the other hand we should the problem solving ability through proper education and training of our young boys and girls.

Administration of the Test

The test administration should ensure that seating arrangement is good. Pupils should get sufficient light and fresh air. There should be sufficient distance between two seats. All the pupils should have pencils and pens. For emergency the tester in a group also have some pencils ready with him. While administering the test in group, not more than 30 pupils should be given the test at a time. The teacher should be at least assisted but a supervisor in the administration of the test. The time limit for the test is only 40 minutes. Therefore, tester should be very peculiar about time. The instruction for the test to the pupils written in the test booklet should be clearly and slowly to the pupils. He should ensure before starting the test that all the pupils have fully understood the instruction.

Scoring Procedure

There are 22 problems in the test. Each problem has four alternative answers. Out of these four answers only one is correct. If the pupils writes the correct answer he should be given one mark, and if he writes a wrong answer zero should be given. In the end all the marks should be added.

Pilot study

"A Pilot study is best thought of as a dress rehearsal. In a pilot study all or part of the plan is tried out to identify unanticipated problems or issues. Beginning researches gain valuable experience from conducting a pilot study and it will boost the quality of one's dissertation"

A Pilot study was conducted to determine the suitability of the tools used in the present investigation. A random sample of 25 students was selected from the pilot study for establishing the Reliability and the Validity.

Reliability and Validity of the Tools

The reliability of a test may be defined as, "the degree of consistency with which the test measures what it measures". A test score is called reliable, when we have a reason to believe it to be stable and trust worthy.

Validity means the ability to produce findings that are in agreement with the conceptual or theoretical values. It refers to the success of the scale in measuring what it means to measure. A test is valid, when it measures truly and accurately the ability or quality one want to measure. Thus, validity means truthfulness of the test.

Mantal Health Inventory

Using split half method, the reliability of the mental health inventory was found to be 0.74. Validity of the mental health index was calculated by finding the square root of the reliability value and it was found to be 0.86, indicating that this tool has high reliability and validity

Problem Solving Ability

In order to establish the reliability of the problem solving ability, the split half reliability method was used. The co-efficient of reliability so obtained indicated that the tool was highly reliable the value is 0.672

The validity of problem solving ability was found out by computing the square root of the reliability co-efficient which worked out to be 0.82

Sample of the Study

The sample of the study was selected by adapting the random sampling method. The total sample size is 300. Four schools were selected for the study under different types of management like Government, Government Aided and Private school in Chennai in Tamil Nadu. The detail of the sample composition is presented below.

TABLE. 3.3: Showing the Details of Sample Selected

Types of Management	Sl. No	Name and place of the school	Male	Female	Total
Government School	1	Government boys and girls higher secondary school, Chennai	50	50	100
Government Aided School	2	Dhanalakshmi boys and girls higher secondary school, Chennai	50	50	100

Private School	3	St.Thomas Matriculation Higher secondary school, Chennai	25	25	100
	4	Sheba Matriculation Higher Secondary School, Chennai	20	30	
	Total				**300**

MAIN STUDY

The validated inventory by M. Illayaraja and Dr.M.Suresh KumarPh.D., mental health inventory and problem solving ability of S.Mani (2012) was made use for the main study to collect the necessary data. The sample for the study is belongs to different types of management of schools. The total sample was selected by applying stratified random sampling method. The investigator has selected 300 samples of the higher secondary school students.

STATISTICAL TECHNIQUES USED

a. Mean

$$\text{Mean } (\overline{x}) = A + \frac{\sum fd}{\sum f} \times i$$

Where,

A = Assumed mean

f = frequency

d = deviation from the assumed mean

I = Class interval

b. Standard Deviation

$$\text{Standard Deviation, SD } (\sigma) = \sqrt{\frac{\sum fd^2}{N} - \left[\frac{\sum fd}{N}\right]^2} \times i$$

Where,

f = Frequency

d = Deviation from the assumed mean

I = Class interval

N = Total frequency

c. 'T' TEST

To continue the significance of difference between means of various measures test is used: 't' ratio is calculated from the relation.

$$\text{T-ratio} = \frac{M_1 \sim M_2}{\sqrt{\frac{\sigma_1^2}{N_1} + \frac{\sigma_1^2}{N_2}}} = \frac{M_1 \sim M_2}{S \in D}$$

Where,

M_1 M_2 = Means of the groups

SED = Standard Error Deviation

d. F-TEST

F- ratio = Variance between the group / Variance within the group Correlation term

$$C = \frac{\sum x_1 + \sum x_2 + \sum x_3}{N}$$

$$BSS = \left(\sum x_1\right)^2 / W_1 + \left(\sum x_2\right)^2 / W_2 + \left(\sum x_3\right)^2 W_3 - C$$

$$TSS = \sum x_1^2 + \sum x_2^2 + \sum x_3^2 - C$$

WSS = TSS - BSS

Where,

x_1, x_2, x_3, are score in different group

C = correction Terms

TSS =Total Sum of Squares

BSS=Between Sum of Squares

WSS =Within Sum of Squares

e. Co-Efficient of Correlation (R)

$$r = \frac{N\sum x \sum y - \sum x \sum y}{\sqrt{\left(N\sum x^2 - \left(\sum x^2\right)\right)\left(N\sum y^2 - \left(\sum y\right)^2\right.}}$$

x, y – Variables,

N – Total strength.

CONCLUSION

Adopting the methods and the procedures discussed earlier in this chapter tests were administered and marked. This chapter outlined the design of the study, the procedure followed and the nature of the sample. It describes the hypotheses to be tested, selection of tools, and the method of administration and scoring procedures. The obtained data were then analyzed using appropriate statistical techniques. The next chapter presents the analysis and interpretation of the data collected in the light of the hypothesis formulated.

❐

4

Analysis and Interpretation of Data

Analysis of data is an important step in quantitative research

According to Mouly (1964) "Research data becomes meaningful in the process of being analyzed and interpreted". The key phase of every thesis is the proper analysis and interpretation of the data.

According to Gay(1976), " Analysis of the data is important as any other component of the research process"

According to Carter V Good, states "The purpose of interpretation is essentially one of stating what the finding conveys? What is their significance? What is the answer to the original problem?

This chapter presents the results obtained from the analysis of data collected from the students of higher secondary schools based on two variables viz., Mental Health and Problem Solving Ability. The data has been subjected to descriptive, inferential and correlation statistics

DESCRIPTIVE ANALYSIS

Hypothesis-1

The level of Mental Health of Higher Secondary School Students is moderate in nature

TABLE. 4.1: Showing the level of Mental Health of Higher Secondary School Students

Variable	Range	Level	Frequency	Percentage
Mental Health	Below 25	Low	82	27.3
	26 to 35	Moderate	140	46.7
	Above 36	High	78	26.0

INFERENCE

From the above table it is known that, more number of students is present in the range between 26 to 35, shows that the level of Mental Health of higher secondary school students is moderate in nature. Hence the hypothesis 1 is accepted.

Hypothesis-2

The level of Problem Solving Ability of higher secondary school students is moderate in nature

TABLE. 4.2: Showing the level of Problem Solving Ability of higher secondary school students

Variable	Range	Level	Frequency	Percentage
Problem Solving Ability	Below 7	Low	89	29.7
	8 to 14	Moderate	127	42.3
	Above 15	High	84	28.0

INFERENCE

From the above table it is known that, more number of students is present in the range between 8 to 14, shows that the level of Problem Solving Ability of higher secondary school students is moderate in nature. Hence the hypothesis 2 is accepted.

DIFFERENTIAL ANALYSIS

Hypothesis-3

There is no significant difference in Mental Health of higher secondary school students with respect to Gender

TABLE. 4.3: Showing the Mean, S.D and C.R value for Mental Health of Higher Secondary School Students Respect to Gender

Variable	Gender	f	Mean	Std Deviation	C.R value	L.S
Mental Health	Male	153	32.99	10.563	0.286	N.S
	Female	147	32.62	12.119		

INFERENCE

From the above table it is observed that the calculated C.R Value (0.286) is lesser than the table value (1.96) at 0.05 level of significance shows that there is no significant difference in Mental health of higher secondary school students with respect to Gender. Hence the hypothesis 3 is accepted.

Hypothesis-4

There is no significant difference in Mental Health of higher secondary school students with respect to Medium of learning

TABLE.4.4: Showing the Mean, S.D and C.R value for Mental Health of Higher Secondary School Students with Respect to Medium of Learning

Variable	Medium of Learning	F	Mean	Std Deviation	C.R value	L.S
Mental Health	Tamil	79	32.89	11.327	0.069	N.S
	English	221	32.78	11.363		

INFERENCE

From the above table it is observed that the calculated C.R Value (0.069) is lesser than the table value (1.96) at 0.05 level of significance shows that there is no significant difference in mental health of higher secondary school students with respect to Medium of Learning.Hence the hypothesis 4 is accepted.

Hypothesis-5

There is no significant difference in Mental Health of higher secondary school students with respect to Type of Management.

TABLE. 4.5: Showing ANOVA for Mental Health of Higher Secondary School Students with Respect to Type of Management

Variables	Source of Variance	Sum of Squares	df	Mean Square	'F' Ratio	L.S
Mental Health	Between Groups	30.978	2	15.489	0.120	N.S
	Within Groups	38381.192	297	129.230		
	Total	**8412.170**	**299**			

INFERENCE

From the above table it is seen that the calculated 'F' value (0.120) is lesser than 'F' Table value (3.03) at 0.05 level of significance. Shows that there is no significant difference in Mental Health of higher secondary school students with respect to Type of Management. Hence, hypothesis 5 is accepted

Hypothesis-6

There is no significant difference in Mental Health of higher secondary school students with respect to Type of Family.

TABLE.4.6: Showing the Mean, S.D and C.R value for Mental Health of Higher Secondary School Students with Respect to Type of Family

Variable	Type of family	F	Mean	Std Deviation	C.R value	L.S
Mental Health	Nuclear	226	32.04	11.025	2.068	0.05
	Joint	74	35.16	11.003		

INFERENCE

From the above table it is observed that the calculated C.R Value (2.068) is higher than the table value (1.96) at 0.05 level of significance. Shows that there is significant difference in mental health of higher secondary school students with respect to type of family. Hence the hypothesis 6 is rejected.

Moreover, students from joint family show higher mental health than nuclear family.

Hypothesis-7

There is no significant difference in Mental Health of higher secondary school students with respect to Birth Order.

TABLE.4.7: Showing ANOVA for Mental Health of Higher Secondary School Students with Respect to Birth Order

Variables	Source of Variance	Sum of Squares	df	Mean Square	'F' Ratio	L.S
Mental Health	Between Groups	139.858	2	69.929	0.543	N.S
	Within Groups	38272.312	297	128.863		
	Total	**38412.170**	**299**			

INFERENCE

From the above table, it is seen that the calculated 'F' Value (0.543) is lesser than table value (3.03) at 0.05 level of significance, so it is inferred that there is no significant difference in Mental Health of higher secondary school students with respect to Birth Order. Hence the hypothesis 7 is accepted

Hypothesis-8

There is no significant difference in Mental Health of higher secondary school students with respect to Father's Educational Qualification.

TABLE.4.8: Showing ANOVA for Mental Health of Higher Secondary School Students with Respect to Father's Educational Qualification

Variables	Source of Variance	Sum of Squares	df	Mean Square	'F' Ratio	L.S
Mental Health	Between Groups	4071.439	2	2035.719	17.606	0.01
	Within Groups	38340.731	297	115.625		
	Total	**38412.170**	**299**			

INFERENCE

From the above table it is seen that the calculated 'F' Value (17.606) is greater than table value (4.68) at (0.01) level of significance, so it is inferred that there is significant difference in Mental Health of higher secondary school students with respect to Father's Educational Qualification.

Further calculation has been made to check the difference among Father's Educational Qualification.

TABLE. 4.8 (A) Showing the Mean, S.D and C.R value for Mental Health of Higher Secondary School Students with Respect to Father's Educational Qualification

Variable	Father's Educational Qualification	F	Mean	Std Deviation	C.R Value	L.S
Mental Health	Illiterate Vs School	43	29.02	8.991	1.566	N.S
		209	31.71	10.495		
	School Vs College	209	31.71	10.495	5.255	0.01
		48	40.98	13.075		
	College Vs Illiterate	48	40.98	13.075	5.024	0.01
		43	29.02	8.991		

INFERENCE

From the above table following inferences have been made.

In the first case, the calculated value (1.566) is lesser than table value (1.96) at 0.05 level of significance, show that there is no significant difference in mental health of higher secondary students whose fathers are Illiterate and have school level educational qualification.

In the second case, the calculated value (5.255) is higher than the table value (2.58) at 0.01 level of significance, show that there is significant difference in mental health of higher secondary school students whose father's have School and College level educational qualification.

In the third case, the calculated value (5.024) is higher than the table value (2.58) at 0.01 level of significance, shows that there is significant difference in mental health of higher secondary school whose father's are Illiterate and have college level educational qualification. Hence, Hypothesis 8 is partially verified

From this verification of mean value students whose father's have college level educational qualification exhibit high mental health than that of other educational status.

Hypothesis-9

There is no significant difference in Mental Health of higher secondary school students with respect to Father's Occupation.

TABLE. 4.9: Showing the Mean, S.D and C.R value for Mental Health of Higher Secondary School Students with Respect to Father's Occupation

Variable	Father's Occupation	F	Mean	Std Deviation	C.R value	L.S
Mental Health	Private	238	32.30	11.139	1.523	N.S
	Govt	62	34.76	11.950		

INFERENCE

From the above table it is observed that the calculated C.R Value (1.523) is lesser than the table value (1.96) at 0.05 level of significance. Shows that there is no significant difference in mental health of higher secondary school students with respect to Father's Occupation. Hence the hypothesis 9 is accepted.

Hypothesis-10

There is no significant difference in Mental Health of higher secondary school students with respect to Mother's Educational Qualification.

TABLE. 4.10: Showing ANOVA for Mental Health of Higher Secondary School Students with Respect to Mother's Educational Qualification

Variables	Source of Variance	Sum of Squares	Df	Mean Square	'F' Ratio	L.S
Mental Health	Between Groups	727.608	2	363.804	2.867	N.S
	Within Groups	37684.562	297	126.884		
	Total	**38412.170**	**299**			

INFERENCE

From the above table it is seen that the calculated 'F' Value (2.867) is lesser than table value (3.03) at 0.05 level of significance, so it is inferred that there is no significant difference in Mental Health of higher secondary school students with respect to Mother's Educational Qualification. Hence the hypothesis 10 is accepted.

Hypothesis-11

There is no significant difference in Mental Health of higher secondary school students with respect to Mother's Occupation.

TABLE. 4.11: Showing ANOVA for Mental Health of Higher Secondary School Students with Respect to Mother's Occupation

Variables	Source of Variance	Sum of Squares	df	Mean Square	'F' Ratio	L.S
Mental Health	Between Groups	36.605	2	18.302	0.142	N.S
	Within Groups	38375.565	297	29.211		
	Total	**38412.170**	**299**			

INFERENCE

From the above table it is seen that the calculated 'F' Value (0.142) is lesser than table value (3.03) at 0.05 level of significance, so it is inferred that there is no significant difference in Mental Health of higher secondary school students with respect to Mother's Occupation. Hence the hypothesis 11 is accepted

Hypothesis-12

There is no significant difference in Mental Health of higher secondary school students with respect to Family Monthly Income.

TABLE.4.12: Showing ANOVA for Mental Health of Higher Secondary School Students with Respect to Family Monthly Income

Variables	Source of Variance	Sum of Squares	df	Mean Square	'F' Ratio	L.S
Mental Health	Between Groups	255.042	2	112.521	0.875	N.S
	Within Groups	38187.128	297	128.576		
	Total	**38412.170**	**299**			

INFERENCE

From the above table it is seen that the calculated 'F' Value (0.875) is lesser than table value (3.03) at 0.05 level of significance, so it is inferred that there is no significant difference in Mental Health of higher secondary school students with respect to Family Monthly Income. Hence the hypothesis 12 is accepted.

Hypothesis-13

There is no significant difference in Mental Health of higher secondary school students with respect to Type of House.

TABLE. 4.13: Showing the Mean, S.D and C.R value for Mental Health of Higher Secondary School Students with Respect to Type of House

Variable	Type of house	F	Mean	Std Deviation	C.R value	L.S
Mental Health	Own	116	33.47	11.341	0.795	N.S
	Rent	184	32.40	11.342		

INFERENCE

From the above table it is observed that the calculated C.R Value (0.795) is lesser than the table value (1.96) at 0.05 level of significance. Shows that there is no significant difference in Mental health of higher secondary school students with respect to Type of House. Hence the hypothesis 13 is accepted.

Hypothesis-14

There is no significant difference in Mental Health of higher secondary school students with respect to Parent's Approach on Advice.

TABLE.4.14: Showing the Mean, S.D and C.R value for Mental Health of Higher Secondary School Students with Respect to Parent's Approach on Advice

Variable	Parent's advice	F	Mean	Std Deviation	C.R value	L.S
Mental Health	Some Times	130	34.85	11.860	2.592	0.01
	Always	162	31.40	10.845		

INFERENCE

From the above table it is observed that the calculated C.R Value (2.592) is higher than the table value (2.58) at 0.01 level of significance. Shows that there is significant difference in mental health of higher secondary school students with respect to Parent's Approach on Advice.Hence the hypothesis 14 is rejected

Moreover, students who get less advice from parents have high mental health then that of students get advice always.

Hypothesis-15

There is no significant difference in Mental Health of higher secondary school students with respect to Wake up Time.

TABLE .4.15: Showing the Mean, S.D and C.R value for Mental Health of Higher Secondary School Students with Respect to wake Up Time

Variable	Wake up Time	F	Mean	Std Deviation	C.R value	L.S
Mental Health	Before 6 A.M	156	33.85	12.215	1.663	N.S
	After 6 A.M	144	31.68	10.218		

INFERENCE

From the above table it is observed that the calculated C.R Value (1.663) is lesser than the table value (1.96) at 0.05 level of significance, shows that there is no significant difference in mental health of higher secondary school students with respect to Wake up time. Hence the hypothesis 15 is accepted

Hypothesis-16

There is no significant difference in Problem Solving Ability of Higher secondary school students with respect to Gender.

TABLE. 4.16: Showing the Mean, S.D and C.R value for Problem Solving Ability of Higher Secondary School Students with Respect to Gender

Variable	Gender	F	Mean	Std Deviation	C.R value	L.S
Problem Solving Ability	Male	153	10.98	5.182	0.066	N.S
	Female	147	10.94	5.682		

INFERENCE

From the above table it is observed that the calculated C.R Value (0.066) is lesser than the table value (1.96) at 0.05 level of significance, shows that there is no significant difference in Problem Solving Ability of higher secondary school students with respect to Gender. Hence the hypothesis 16 is accepted.

Hypothesis-17

There is no significant difference in Problem Solving Ability of higher secondary school students with respect to Medium of learning.

TABLE. 4.17: Showing the Mean, S.D and C.R value for Problem Solving Ability of Higher Secondary School Students with Respect to Medium of Learning

Variable	Medium of Learning	f	Mean	Std Deviation	C.R value	L.S
Problem Solving Ability	Tamil	79	10.82	5.481	0.262	N.S
	English	221	11.01	5.415		

INFERENCE

From the above table it is observed that the calculated C.R Value (0.262) is lesser than the table value (1.96) at 0.05 level of Significance, shows that there is no significant difference in Problem Solving Ability of higher secondary school students with respect to Medium of Learning. Hence the hypothesis 17 is accepted.

Hypothesis-18

There is no significant difference in Problem Solving Ability of higher secondary school students with respect to Type of Management.

TABLE.4.18: Showing ANOVA for Problem Solving Ability of Higher Secondary School Students with Respect to Type of Management

Variables	Source of Variance	Sum of Squares	Df	Mean Square	'F' Ratio	L.S
Problem Solving Ability	Between Groups	30.978	2	15.489	0.120	N.S
	Within Groups	38381.192	297	129.230		
	Total	**38412.170**	**299**			

INFERENCE

From the above table it is seen that the calculated 'F' value (0.120) is lesser than 'F' Table value (3.03) at 0.05 level of Significance, so it is inferred that there is no significant difference in problem solving ability of higher secondary school students with respect to Type of Management.

Hypothesos-19

There is no significant difference in Problem Solving Ability of higher secondary school students with respect to Type of Family.

TABLE. 4.19: Showing the Mean, S.D and C.R value for Problem Solving Ability of Higher Secondary School Students with Respect to Type of Family

Variable	Type of family	f	Mean	Std Deviation	C.R value	L.S
Problem Solving Ability	Nuclear	226	10.60	5.450	2.009	0.05
	Joint	74	12.05	5.229		

INFERENCE

From the above table it is observed that the calculated C.R Value (2.009) is higher than the table value (1.96) at 0.05 level of significance, shows that there is significant difference in Problem Solving Ability of higher secondary school students with respect to type of family. Hence the hypothesis 19 is rejected.

Moreover, students from joint family shows higher problem solving ability than nuclear family.

Hypothesos-20

There is no significant difference in Problem Solving Ability of higher secondary school students with respect to Birth Order.

TABLE 4.20: Showing ANOVA for Problem Solving Ability of Higher Secondary School Students with Respect to Birth Order

Variables	Source of Variance	Sum of Squares	Df	Mean Square	'F' Ratio	L.S
Problem Solving Ability	Between Groups	21.009	2	10.504	0.356	N.S
	Within Groups	8774.511	297	29.544		
	Total	**8795.520**	**299**			

INFERENCE

From the above table it is seen that the calculated 'F' Value (0.356) is lesser than table value (3.03) at 0.05 level of Significance, so it is inferred that there is no significant difference in Problem Solving Ability of higher secondary school students with respect to Birth Order. Hence the hypothesis 20 is accepted

Hypothesos-21

There is no significant difference in Problem Solving Ability of higher secondary school students with respect to Father's Educational Qualification.

TABLE. 4.21: Showing ANOVA for Problem Solving Ability of Higher Secondary School Students with Respect to Father's Educational Qualification

Variables	Source of Variance	Sum of Squares	Df	Mean Square	'F' Ratio	L.S
Problem Solving Ability	Between Groups	66.280	2	33.140	1.128	N.S
	Within Groups	8729.240	297	29.391		
	Total	**8795.520**	**299**			

INFERENCE

From the above table it is seen that the calculated 'F' Value (1.128) is lesser than table value (3.03) at 0.05 level of Significance, so it is inferred that there is no significant difference in Problem Solving Ability of higher secondary school students with respect to Father's Educational Qualification.

Hence the hypothesis 21 is accepted

Hypothesos-22

There is no significant difference in Problem Solving Ability of higher secondary school students with respect to Father's Occupation.

TABLE. 4.22: Showing the Mean, S, D and C.R value for Problem Solving Ability of Higher Secondary School Students with Respect to Father's Occupation

Variable	Father's occupation	F	Mean	Std Deviation	C.R value	L.S
Problem Solving Ability	Private	238	10.73	5.262	1.461	N.S
	Govt	62	11.85	5.967		

INFERENCE

From the above table it is observed that the calculated C.R Value (1.461) is lesser than the table value (1.96) at 0.05 level of Significance, shows that there is no significant difference in problem solving ability of higher secondary school students with respect to Father's Occupation. Hence the hypothesis 22 is accepted

Hypothesos-23

There is no significant difference in Problem Solving Ability of higher secondary school students with respect to Mother's Educational Qualification.

TABLE.4.23: Showing ANOVA for Problem Solving Ability of Higher Secondary School Students with Respect to Mother's Educational Qualification

Variables	Source of Variance	Sum of Squares	Df	Mean Square	'F' Ratio	L.S
Problem Solving Ability	Between Groups	361.955	2	180.977	6.373	0.01
	Within Groups	8433.565	297	28.396		
	Hypothesos-19	8795.520	299			

INFERENCE

From the above table it is seen that the calculated 'F' Value (6.373) is greater than table value (4.68) at 0.01 level of significance, so it is inferred that there is significant difference in Problem Solving Ability of higher secondary school students with respect to Mother's Educational Qualification. Further calculation has been made to check the difference among father's educational qualification.

TABLE.4.23 (A): Showing the Mean, S.D and C.R value for Problem Solving Ability of Higher Secondary School Students with Respect to Mother's Educational Qualification

Variable	Mother's Educational Qualification	F	Mean	Std Deviation	C.R Value	L.S
Problem Solving Ability	Illiterate Vs School	49	9.47	4.277	1.742	N.S
		213	10.85	5.131		
	School Vs College	213	10.85	5.131	2.764	0.01
		38	13.53	7.303		
	College Vs Illiterate	38	13.53	7.303	3.240	0.01
		49	9.47	4.277		

INFERENCE

From the above table following inference have been made.

In the first case, the calculated value (1.742) is lesser than table value (1.96) at 0.05 level of significance, shows that there is no significant difference in problem solving ability of higher secondary students whose mother 'are illiterate and have school level educational qualification.

In the second case, the calculated (2.764) is higher than the table value (2.56) at 0.01 level of significance; show that there is significant difference in Problem Solving Ability of higher secondary school students whose mother's have school and college level educational qualification.

In the third case, the calculated value (3.240) is higher than the expected table value (2.56) at 0.01 level of significance, shows that there is significant difference in Problem Solving Ability of higher secondary school whose mother's are illiterate and have college level educational qualification.

Hence, Hypothesis 23 is partially verified.

From this verification of mean value students whose father's have college level educational qualification exhibit high problem solving ability than that of other educational status.

Hypothesis-24

There is no significant difference in Problem Solving Ability of higher secondary school students with respect to Mother's Occupation.

TABLE.4.24: Showing ANOVA for Problem Solving Ability of Higher Secondary School Students with Respect to Mother's Occupation

Variables	Source of Variance	Sum of Squares	Df	Mean Square	'F' Ratio	L.S
Problem Solving Ability	Between Groups	175.451	2	87.726	3.033	0.05
	Within Groups	8620.068	297	29.024		
	Total	**8795.520**	**299**			

INFERENCE

From the above table it is seen that the calculated 'F' Value (3.033) is greater than table value (3.03) at (0.05) level of significance, so it is inferred that there is significant difference in Problem Solving Ability of higher secondary school students with respect to Mother's Occupation.

Further calculation has been made to check the difference among mother's occupation.

TABLE. 4.24 (A): Showing the Mean, S.D and C.R values for Problem Solving Ability of Higher Secondary School Students with Respect to Mother's Occupation

Variable	Mother's occupation	F	Mean	Std Deviation	C.R Value	L.S
Problem Solving Ability	Private Vs Government	134	10.81	4.919	2.386	0.05
		24	13.54	6.366		
	Government Vs Other	24	13.54	6.366	2.274	0.05
		142	10.66	5.630		
	Other Vs Private	142	10.66	5.630	0.237	N.S
		134	10.81	4.919		

INFERENCE

From the above table following inference have been made.

In the first case, the calculated value (2.386) is higher than table value (1.96) at 0.05 level of significance, show that there is significant difference in problem solving ability of students whose mother is working in private and Government sector.

In the second case, the calculated value (2.274) is higher than the table value (1.96) at 0.05 level of significance; show that there is significant difference in problem solving ability of students whose mother is working in government and other sectors.

In the third case, the calculated value (0.237) is lesser than the expected table value (1.96) at 0.05 level of significance, shows that there is no significant difference in problem solving ability of students whose mother is working in other and private sector. Hence, Hypothesis 24 is partially verified.

From the verification of mean value students whose mother is working in government job have high problem solving ability than that of other sectors.

Hypothesis-25

There is no significant difference in Problem solving Ability of higher secondary school students with respect to Family Monthly Income.

TABLE.4.25: Showing ANOVA for Problem Solving Ability of Higher Secondary School Students with Respect to Family Monthly Income

Variables	Source of Variance	Sum of Squares	Df	Mean Square	'F' Ratio	L.S
Problem Solving Ability	Between Groups	136.869	2	68.434	2.347	N.S
	Within Groups	8658.651	297	29.154		
	Total	**8795.520**	**299**			

INFERENCE

From the above table it is seen that the calculated 'F' Value (2.347) is lesser than table value (3.03) at (0.05) level of significance, so it is inferred that there is no significant difference in Problem Solving Ability of higher secondary school students with respect to Family Monthly Income. Hence the, hypothesis 25 is accepted.

Hypothesis-26

There is no significant difference in Problem Solving Ability of higher secondary school students with respect to Type of House.

TABLE.4.26: Showing the Mean, S.D and C.R value for Problem Solving Ability of Higher Secondary School Students with Respect to Type of House

Variable	Type of house	F	Mean	Std Deviation	C.R value	L.S
Problem Solving Ability	Own	116	11.53	5.554	1.459	N.S
	Rent	184	10.60	5.324		

INFERENCE

From the above table it is observed that the calculated C.R Value (1.459) is lesser than the table value (1.96) at 0.05 level of Significance, shows that there is no significant difference in Problem Solving Ability of higher secondary school students with respect to Type of House. Hence the, hypothesis 26 is accepted

Hypothesis-27

There is no significant difference in Problem Solving Ability of higher secondary school students with respect to Parent's Approach on Advice.

TABLE. 4.27: Showing the Mean, S.D and C.R value for Problem Solving Ability of Higher Secondary School Students with Respect to Parent's Approach on Advice

Variable	Parents approach on advice	F	Mean	Std Deviation	C.R value	L.S
Problem Solving Ability	Some Times	130	11.95	5.512	3.060	0.01
	Always	162	10.02	5.185		

INFERENCE

From the above table it is observed that the calculated C.R Value (3.060) is greater than the table value (2.56) at 0.01 level of significance. Shows that there is significant difference in Problem Solving Ability of higher secondary school students with respect to Parent's Approach on Advice. Hence the, hypothesis 27 is rejected

Moreover, students who get less advice from parents have high problem solving ability than that of students get advice always.

Hypothesis-28

There is no significant difference in Problem Solving Ability of higher secondary school students with respect to Wake up Time.

TABLE. 4.28: Showing the Mean, S.D and C.R value for Problem Solving Ability of Higher Secondary School Students with Respect to Wake Up Time

Variable	Wake up time	F	Mean	Std Deviation	C.R value	L.S
Problem Solving Ability	Before 6 AM	156	12.38	5.379	4.915	0.01
	After 6 AM	144	9.42	5.053		

INFERENCE

From the above table it is observed that the calculated C.R Value (4.915) is higher than the table value (2.56) at 0.01 level of signifance. Shows that there is significant difference in Problem Solving Ability of higher secondary school students with respect to Wake up time. Hence the, hypothesis 28 is rejected.

Moreover, students who wake up before 6 AM will have high problem solving ability than that of other students, wake up after 6 AM.

CORRELATIONAL ANALYSIS

Hypothesis-29

There is no significance relation between Mental Health and Problem Solving Ability of higher secondary school students

TABLE.4.29: Showing the Correlation between Mental Health and Problem Solving Ability of Higher Secondary School Students

Variables	Y	'r' Value	L.S
Mental Health	300	0.161	0.05
Problem Solving Ability	300		

INFERENCE

The above table shows that there is positive correlation between Mental Health and Problem Solving Ability. Hence the, hypothesis 29 is rejected.

CONCLUSION

The analysis and interpretation of data represent the application of deductive and inductive logic to the research process. The data are often classified by division into subgroups and the analyzed and synthesized in such a way that hypothesis may be accepted and rejected. The final result may be a new principle or generalization. Like interpretation of results, the formulation of conclusion and generalization also demands keen observations, wide outlook and power logical thinking. A brief report of the present research study together with major finding and conclusion has been presented in the succeeding chapter.

❒

5

Summary, Findings and Conclusion

This chapter deals with the consolidation of the various findings presented in the previous chapter findings are statements of factual information based upon data analysis. Conclusion is answers to the questions raised or the statements of acceptance or rejection of the hypotheses proposed. In this chapter the researcher deals with the aspects pertaining to the tools used for the investigations, objectives and hypotheses of the study, based on analysis the major findings arrived at, and all finally the educational implication together with suggestion for further research. The aim of the present investigation is to study mental health and problem solving ability among higher secondary school students.

STATEMENT OF THE PROBLEM

"A study on Mental Health and Problem Solving Ability of Higher Secondary School Students".

OBJECTIVES OF THE STUDY

To find out the level of mental health of higher secondary school students.

1. To find out the level of problem solving ability of the higher secondary school students.
2. To find out the significant difference in mental health of the higher secondary school students with respect to Gender.
3. To find out the significant difference in mental health of the higher secondary school students with respect to Medium of learning.
4. To find out the significant difference in mental health of the higher secondary school students with respect to Type of Management.
5. To find out the significant difference in mental health of the higher secondary school students with respect to Type of family.
6. To find out the significant difference in mental health of the higher secondary school students with respect to Birth order.
7. To find out the significant difference in mental health of the higher secondary school students with respect to Father's Educational Qualification.
8. To find out the significant difference in mental health of the higher secondary school students with respect to Father's Occupational.
9. To find out the significant difference in mental health of the higher secondary school students with respect to Mother's Educational Qualification.
10. To find out the significant difference in mental health of the higher secondary school students with respect to Mother's Occupation.
11. To find out the significant difference in mental health of the higher secondary school students with respect to Family monthly income.
12. To find out the significant difference in mental health of the higher secondary school students with respect to Type of house.
13. To find out the significant difference in mental health of the higher secondary school students with respect to Parent's approach on Advice.
14. To find out the significant difference in mental health of the higher secondary school students with respect to Wake up time.
15. To find out the significant difference in problem solving ability of the higher secondary school students with respect to Gender.
16. To find out the significant difference in problem solving ability of the higher secondary school students with respect to Medium of learning.
17. To find out the significant difference in problem solving ability of the higher secondary school students with respect to Type of Management.
18. To find out the significant difference in problem solving ability of the higher secondary school students with respect to Type of family.

19. To find out the significant difference in problem solving ability of the higher secondary school students with respect to Birth Order.
20. To find out the significant difference in problem solving ability of the higher secondary school students with respect to Father's Educational Qualification.
21. To find out the significant difference in problem solving ability of the higher secondary school students with respect to Father's Occupation.
22. To find out the significant difference in problem solving ability of the higher secondary school students with respect to Mother's Educational Qualification.
23. To find out the significant difference in problem solving ability of the higher secondary school students with respect to Mother's Occupation.
24. To find out the significant difference in problem solving ability of the higher secondary school students with respect to Family Monthly Income.
25. To find out the significant difference in problem solving ability of the higher secondary school students with respect to Type of House.
26. To find out the significant difference in problem solving ability of the higher secondary school students with respect to Parent's Approach on advice.
27. To find out the significant difference in problem solving ability of the higher secondary school students with respect to Wake up time.
28. To find out the significant relation between Mental Health and Problem Solving Ability of the higher secondary school students.

HYPOTHESES OF THE STUDY

The following hypotheses have been framed by the researcher for the present study.

1. The level of mental health of higher secondary school students is moderate in nature.
2. The level of problem solving ability of higher secondary school students is moderate in nature.
3. There is no significant difference in mental health of higher secondary school students based on Gender.
4. There is no significant difference in mental health of higher secondary school students based on Medium of Learning.
5. There is no significant difference in mental health of higher secondary school students based on Type of Management.
6. There is no significant difference in mental health of higher secondary school students based on Type of Family

7. There is no significant difference in mental health of higher secondary school students based on Birth Order
8. There is no significant difference in mental health of higher secondary school students based on Father's Educational Qualification
9. There is no significant difference in mental health of higher secondary school students based on Father's Occupation.
10. There is no significant difference in mental health of higher secondary school students based on Mother's Educational Qualification.
11. There is no significant difference in mental health of higher secondary school students based on Mother's Occupation.
12. There is no significant difference in mental health of higher secondary school students based on Family Monthly Income.
13. There is no significant difference in mental health of higher secondary school students based on Type of House.
14. There is no significant difference in mental health of higher secondary school students based on Parent's Approach on Advice.
15. There is no significant difference in mental health of higher secondary school students based on Wake up time.
16. There is no significant difference in Problem Solving Ability of higher secondary school students based on Gender.
17. There is no significant difference in Problem Solving Ability of higher secondary school students based on Medium of Learning.
18. There is no significant difference in Problem Solving Ability of higher secondary school students based on Type of Management.
19. There is no significant difference in Problem Solving Ability of higher secondary school students based on Type of Family.
20. There is no significant difference in Problem Solving Ability of higher secondary school students based on Birth Order.
21. There is no significant difference in Problem Solving Ability of higher secondary school students based on Father's Educational Qualification.
22. There is no significant difference in Problem Solving Ability of higher secondary school students based on Father's Occupation.
23. There is no significant difference in Problem Solving Ability of higher secondary school students based on Mother's Educational Qualification.
24. There is no significant difference in Problem Solving Ability of higher secondary school students based on Mother's Occupation.
25. There is no significant difference in Problem Solving Ability of higher secondary school students based on Family Monthly Income.
26. There is no significant difference in Problem Solving Ability of higher secondary school students based on Type of House.

27. There is no significant difference in Problem Solving Ability of higher secondary school students based on Parent's Approach on Advice.
28. There is no significant difference in Problem Solving Ability of higher secondary school students based on Wake up time.
29. There is no relation between Mental Health and Problem Solving ability of higher secondary school students

SAMPLE OF THE STUDY

The sample of the study was selected by adapting the random sampling method. The total sample size is 300. Four schools were selected for the study under different types of management like Government, Government Aided and Private school in Chennai in Tamil Nadu.

TOOLS USED BY THE INVESTIGATOR

The general category of inquiry forms includes data includes data-gathering instruments through which responds answer questions or respond to statements in writing, 'questionnaire' is used to collect factual information from the target population. In the present study,
The following tools are:

- Personal data sheet developed by the investigator.
- Mental Health developed and standardized by M.Illayaraja Dr. M. Suresh Kumar (2009) was adopted.
- Problem Solving Ability developed and Standardized by S. Mani. (2012) adopted.

MAJOR FINDINGS OF THE STUDY

1. The level of Mental Health of higher secondary school students is moderate in nature.
2. The level of Problem Solving Ability of higher secondary school students is moderate in nature.
3. Male and female students of higher secondary schools do not differ significantly in their mental Health.
4. Tamil and English medium students of higher secondary school do not differ significantly in Mental Health.
5. Government, Government – Aided and Private higher secondary school student do not differ significantly in Mental Health.
6. Nuclear and Joint Family students of higher secondary school differ significantly in mental health.
    - Moreover, students from joint family show higher mental health than nuclear family.

7. Students of higher secondary school do not differ significantly in Mental Health with respect to Birth Order.
8. Higher secondary school students differ significantly in mental health based on Father's Educational Qualification.
    - Students whose father has college level educational qualification exhibit high mental health than of other educational status.
9. Higher secondary school students do not differ significantly in Mental Health based on Father's Occupation.
10. Higher secondary school students do not differ significantly in mental health based on Mother's Educational Qualification.
11. Higher secondary school students do not differ significantly in mental health based on Mother's occupation.
12 Students of higher secondary school do not differ significantly in mental health based on Family monthly income.
13. Students who live in own and rented houses do not differ significantly in mental health.
14. Higher secondary school students differ significantly in mental health with respect to Parent's Approach on Advice.
    - Students who get less advice from parents have high mental health than that of students gets advice always.
15. Students of higher secondary school do not differ significantly in mental health with respect to Wake up Time.
16. Male and female students of higher secondary schools students do not differ significantly in Problem Solving Ability.
17. Tamil and English Medium students of higher secondary school do not differ significantly in Problem Solving Ability.
18. Government, Government Aided and Private higher secondary school student do not differ significantly in Problem Solving Ability.
19. Nuclear and Joint Family students of higher secondary school students do not differ significantly in Problem Solving Ability.
    - Students from joint family shows higher problem solving ability than nuclear family.
20. Students of higher secondary school do not differ significantly in Problem Solving Ability with respect to Birth Order.
21. Higher secondary school students do not differ significantly in Problem Solving Ability based on Father's Educational Qualification
22. Higher secondary school students who not differ significantly in Problem Solving Ability based on Father's Occupation.
23. Higher secondary school students differ significantly in Problem Solving Ability based on Mother's Educational Qualification.

- Student whose mother's have qualification exhibit high problem solving ability than that of other educational status.

24. Higher secondary school students differ significantly in Problem Solving Ability based on Mother's occupation.
    - Students whose mother is working in government job have high problem solving ability than that of other sectors.
25. Students of higher secondary school do not differ significantly in Problem Solving Ability based on Family monthly income.
26. Higher secondary school students who live in own and rented house do not differ significantly in Problem Solving Ability.
27. Higher secondary school students differ significantly in Problem Solving Ability with respect to Parent's Approach on Advice.
    - Students who get less advice from parents have high problem solving ability than that of students get advice always.
28. Students of higher secondary school differ significantly in Problem Solving Ability with respect to Wake up Time.
    - Students who wake up before 6 AM will have high problem solving ability than that of other students, wake up after 6AM.
29. There is significant relation between Mental Health and Problem Solving Ability of higher secondary school students.

EDUCATIONAL IMPLICATIONS

The present study gives the importance of Mental health and Problem Solving Ability among higher secondary school students. This plays an essential role in their academic achievement and in healthy intellectual minds which will helps in promoting their students futures. Therefore, both of them should be improved among the students.

There is significant difference in Mental Health of higher secondary school students with respect to type of family. Joint Family students have high significant difference than Nuclear family because of their mental health. There are many members in the Joint Family with different characteristics. The students have to adjust according to different moods. Therefore the Mental Health of the students will be naturally higher than the others.

There is significant difference in Mental Health of higher secondary school students with respect to Father's Educational Qualification. The student's father's are in different qualification like Illiterate, Schooling and College. Many students father's are completed their college. Degree Holder father's are higher than schooling and Illiterate father's. So there many students Mental Health are higher than the others educational status.

There is significant difference in Mental Health of higher secondary school students with respect to Mother's Educational Qualification. The students

Mother's are in different qualification like Illiterate, Schooling and College. Many students Mother's are completed their Illiterate and Schooling. Illiterate and Schooling Holder Mother's are higher than College Mother's. So there many students Mental Health are higher than the others educational status.

There is significant difference in Mental Health of higher secondary school students with respect to Parent's Approach on Advice. The parents sometimes advice have high significant difference than always parents advice. Many students parents are advice their children's for some times for their future.

There is significant difference in Problem Solving Ability of higher secondary school students with respect to type of family. Joint Family students have high significant difference than Nuclear family because of their Problem Solving Ability. There are many members in the Joint Family with different characteristics. The students have to adjust him / her according to different moods. Therefore the Problem Solving Ability of the students will be naturally higher than the others.

There is significant difference in Problem Solving Ability of higher secondary school students with respect to Mother's Educational Qualification. The students Mother's are in different qualification like Illiterate, Schooling and College. Many students Mother's are completed their Illiterate and Schooling. Illiterate and Schooling Holder Mother's are higher than College Mother's. So there many students Problem Solving Ability are higher than the others educational status.

There is significant difference in Problem Solving Ability of higher secondary school students with respect to Mother's Occupation. The students Mother's are in different occupation like Private, Govt and Other. Many students Mother's are completed their Private and Govt. Private and Govt Holder Mother's are higher than Other Mother's. So there many students Problem Solving Ability are higher than the others educational status.

There is significant difference in Problem Solving Ability of higher secondary school students with respect to Parent's Approach on Advice. The parents sometimes advice have high significant difference than always parents advice. Many students parents are advice their children's for some times for their future.

DELIMITATION OF THE STUDY

This investigation has the following delimitation

1. The sample is limited to 300 students
2. The sample is taken only from Chennai, in Tamil Nadu
3. The sample is higher secondary school students only
4. The sample are taken only from 1 Government School, 1 Government Aided School, 2 Matriculation School.

SUGGESTION FOR THE FURTHER RESEARCH

Following are some of the suggestion put forward by the investigator for further research

1. This study was confirmed with Tamil and English medium higher secondary school students. To make the finding of the study more universal, a comprehensive study of this type involving different standards of students at various levels could be under taken.
2. The study was conducted only in a few selected schools in Chennai, Tamil Nadu. It can be extended to many other schools and in many districts.
3. A comprehensive study can be undertaken among primary, high school, higher secondary school and college students.
4. The study could also be tested on different scholastic groups.
5. The study could also be tested on different groups.

CONCLUSION

The purpose of the study was to study the relationship among the variables viz., Mental Health and Problem Solving Ability. The study is sure to find some usefulness in the field of education and findings of the study can serve as a database for future research.

❐

6

The Problem and its Perspectives

1. We want to do work that makes a difference to me and to my world.
2. We don't want to remember, recall and regurgitate
3. We don't want to learn for the sake of tests
4. We don't want learning made easy; rather, they want it to mean something.
5. We want to learn with the media of our times.
6. We want to do work that is relevant, meaningful and authentic.
7. We want to be engaged intellectually
8. We want stronger relationships with their teachers, with each other and with their
9. Communities locally, provincially, nationally and globally
10. We want teachers to know how we learn, to take into account what we understand and
11. What we misunderstand and use this knowledge as a starting place to guide our continued
12. learning.
13. We want to be able to work with others in the classroom, online and in our community.

14. We want to be able to pick up our information anywhere, anytime
15. We want in-depth learning.
16. We need feedback in time to help us learn and in time do something about it.

EDUCATION

Education is a comprehensive term. As we have seen, educations are bound up with human race. Its boundaries are rich and varied as life itself. Its meaning is as wide as life itself, just as it is difficult to squeeze life in a few words, in the same way; it is difficult to give meaning to or definition to the term 'Education'.

The term "Education" may be understood as Educare and Educere.

Educare: Educare is a Latin word and it means 'to nourish', 'bring up', 'to rise'. This means, educating a child means nourishing or bringing up the child according to certain ends.

Educere: Educere is also a Latin word and it means 'to lead out' 'to draw out'. This means, educating a child implies drawing out what is ingrained in the child or leading him out of darkness into light.

Indian Perspective

1. *In Rigveda, "Education has been understood as something which makes a man self-reliant and selfless".*
2. *In Upanishadas, "Education has been understood as something the end product of which salvation".*
3. *According to Swami Vivekananda, "Education is 'the manifestation of divine perfection already existing in man'. By education he meant drawing out the divine potential already existing in man".*
4. *According to Gurudev Tagore, "Education is that which makes one's life in harmony with all existence and thus enables the mind to find the ultimate truth which gives us the wealth or inner light and love and gives significance to life".*
5. *According to Arubindo, "Education means helping the growing soul to draw out that is in itself".*

Western Perspective

- According to Plato, "Education is the capacity to feel pleasure and pain at the right moment. It develops in the body and in soul of the pupil all the beauty and all perfection which he is capable of".
- According to Aristotle, "Education the creation of a sound mind in a sound body..... it develops man's faculty especially his mind so that he may be able to enjoy the contemplation of supreme truth, goodness and beauty of which perfect happiness essentially consists".

- According to Pestalozzi, "Education is the natural, harmonious and progressive development of man's innate powers".
- According to Froebel, "Education is enfoldment of what is already enfolded in the germ".

LEARNING

Learning is associated with the acquisition of new behavior of modification of old behavior. Different psychologists have defined learning in different ways. Let us discuss some important definitions given by the eminent psychologists.

- According to Skinner, "learning is not acquiring knowledge or skill by mere mechanical repetitions. It is process in which the learner organized different elements and experiences to reach a particular goal".
- According to Morris L. Bigge, "Learning is change in a living individual which is not heralded by genetic inheritance. It may be chance in insights, behavior, perception or motivation or a combination of these".
- According to Garret, "Learning is an organization of behavior. It is he activity by virtue which we organize our responses with new habits".
- Murphy states that "Learning is modification of both behavior and the way of perceiving".
- According to Fischer & Immordino-Yang, (2008), "People learn. Learning is fundamental to human beings. It is the specialization that we use to become fully human"

Learning may be considered finally as the process of constant modifications of behavior through continual with the environment by the individuals. It is an integral aspect of the individuals' development in its widest sense.

Characteristics of Learning

- Learning is a continuous change in behavior. It is a lifelong process.
- It is comprehensive. It affects every aspect of human life.
- Learning is physically, emotionally and cognitively attached with the whole of the person.
- Learning brings changes in the discipline of behavior.
- Learning is development and encouragement. Sometimes it becomes more influential motivator than some direct stimulus such as fear of punishment.

STRATEGY

- According to Oxford (1990), "The strategy concept has come to mean as plan, set or conscious action towards achievement of an objective. They are specific action are taken by the learner to make learning easier, faster, more enjoyable, more self-directed, more effective and more and transferable to new situation".

- According to Ellis (1994), "the concept of 'strategy' is somewhat fuzzy one, not easy to tie down" and brings to light many problems. On the basis of a wide variety of definitions by many researchers, Ellis states that it is open to question whether learning strategies are recognized as behavioral, mental or as both. Oxford (1989), on the other hand, appears to see them essentially behavioral, whereas Weinstein and Mayer (1986) describe them both as behavioral and mental.
- Another difficulty emphasized by Ellis is the nature if the behavior classified as learning strategies. As stated by Stern (Ellis 1994), there is distinction between 'strategies', which are defined as approaches to learning, and 'techniques', which are observable forms of learning (e.g grammar or vocabulary). In general, a strategy is a tool, plan, or method used for accomplishing a task.

LEARNING STRATEGIES

- According to Weinstein and Mayer (1986), "Learning strategies are the behaviors and thoughts that learner engages in during learning that are intended to influence the learner's encoding process".
- According to Chamot (1987), "Learning strategies are techniques, approaches or deliberate actions that students take in order to facilitate the learning, recall of both linguistic and content or information".
- According to Rubin (1987), "Learning strategies are strategies which contribute to the development of the language system which the learner constructs and affect learning directly".
- Hattie et al. (1996) constructed a meta-analysis study on learning strategies, which included over 50 learning-strategies interventions. Their research that the most commonly employed interventions focused on students' memory, organizational skills, motivation, attributions for success, and task-specific strategies such as elaboration and translation. Expected outcomes of learning-strategy interventions mainly involved improved 10 school performance, although some interventions targeted increased positive emotions towards school and learning in general.
- Different taxonomies of learning strategies have been emerging over the past couple of decades. They have been subdivided into:
- Cognitive, meta-cognitive and resource management strategies (Pokay & Blumenfeld, 1990)
- Cognitive, meta-cognitive and motivational skills (Mayer, 1998)
- Cognitive regulation and volition al control (Pintrich & De Groot, 1990).

- It appears that four main categories – cognitive, meta-cognitive, motivational and behavioral strategies – can encompass the variables commonly included as learning I, strategies. Under heading of cognitive strategies, activities that are particular relevant for students' academic outcomes in
- Rehearsal of information and procedures (Eshel & Kohavi 2003; Pintrich & De Groot, 1990; Wolters, 1999) Organization or new knowledge and skills.
- Elaboration/translation of new content (Pintrich & De Groot, 1990; Pokay & Blumenfeld, 1990). Metacognitive strategies found to be useful across subject areas and grade levels which include.
- Knowing one's mental processes (Cardelle-Elawar, 1992; Pintrich 2002; Pokay&Blumenfeld, 1990)
- Planning objectives and monitoring progress (Cardelle-Elawar, 1992; Carretal 1991; Pintrich& De Groot, 1990; Pokay&Blumenfeld, 1990; Weinsterin, Schulte & Palmer, 1987; Wolters, 1999; Zimmerman &Martinez-Pons, 1986).
- Integrating new pieces of information into coherent knowledge representations (Cardelle-Elawar, 1992)
- Evaluating learning process and skills.

Donald Clark "Learning Strategies" or "instructional strategies" are the various methodologies used to involve the learners in the training program, such as questioning during lectures, simulation with CBT, reflection after reading, etc; they are used to obtain the "learning objectives" which are the new behaviors that want your learners to use when they return to their jobs.

The learning strategy is a general guideline for selecting the learning strategy for changing the present behavior to the desired behavior. It is based on Bloom's Taxonomy (learning domains). It runs from the passive learning methods to the more active participation methods, while Bloom's Taxonomy runs from top to bottom, with the lower level behaviors being on top and the higher behaviors being on the bottom. That is, there is a direct correlation in learning.

- Lower levels of behavior can be taught using the more passive learning methods.
- Higher levels of behavior require some sort of action or involvement by the learners.

IMPORTANCE OF LEARNING STRATERGIES

Content knowledge requires mastery of facts and reasoning in the specific field or topic. The process of learning itself reaches beyond content knowledge in encompasses the way a student learns with ever-increasing effectiveness. The improvement of learning, not just content knowledge is an important outcome of postsecondary education. Various researches connected the successful employment of strategic learning to aspects of meta-cognitive awareness and or regulation (Braten&Stomso,2005;Carnell, 2007;Dahlin,1999; Garner,1990; Hanley, 1995; Sunger,2007; Wolters, 1997).

RESARCHES ABOUT LEARNING STRATEGIES

Most of the research and development of learning strategies for students with learning disabilities has come from the researchers and educations affiliated with The University of Kansa, Center for Research on Learning. In general, their research suggests that use of learning strategies can improve student performance in inclusive settings or on grade appropriate tasks. In reading for example, results from a study of the use of the Word Identification Strategy indicated that the number of oral reading errors decreased while reading comprehension scores increased for all students on ability level and grade level materials (Lenz & Hughes, 1990). Another study revealed that the students using the Test Taking Strategy improved average test scores in inclusive classes from 57% to 71% (Hughes & Schumaker, 1991).

Other researchers in the area of learning strategies have also found positive results. For example, Graham, Harris and Colleagues (e.g. Graham, Harris, MacAuthor & Schwartx, 1991) have validated strategies for improving the quality of student compositions, planning process and revisions. Another line of research, Palinesar and Brown (e.g.) successfully tested and replicated reciprocal teaching, a strategy to improve student reading performance.

THE SUB- AREAS OF LEARNING STRATEGIES

The following are the sub areas of Learning Strategies:

Study Strategies

Study strategies are behaviors specifically focused on reviewing and learning material, such as habitual use of mnemonics and other memory aids. These are study strategies that significantly enhance a student's ability to encode and retrieve information (Scruggs & Mastropieri, 1992).

Note-taking and Listening Skills

Note-taking skills and text-marking strategies are specific learning strategies associated with the ability to distinguish between important and no important information. Research examines the utility of note taking both from the perspective of concurrent information processing and forth purpose of review at alters time. Effective note taking involves reconstructing information in a way that is most meaningful to the learner (Porte, 2001).The usefulness of instruction in specific note-taking strategies for the purpose of improving academic performance generally has been supported (Kiewra & Benton, 1985; Shrager & Mayer, 1989; Wade & Trathen, 1989).

Reading and Comprehension Strategies

Samuels (1989) characterizes reading as an "active, goal-directed, problem-solving process in which the reader's task is to construct meaning from information contained in the text". Comprehension strategies include such behaviors as previewing texts, self-quizzing, and mapping ideas (Miranda, Villaescusa, & Vidal-Abarca, 1997; Paris & Oka, 1989). Although instruction in this area is considered essential to academic success, it appears that very little instructional time is focused on it. Comprehension strategies are arguably the most important of learning strategies, and their mastery becomes increasingly necessary as a child progresses through school.

Writing and Research Skills

Like reading and comprehension, writing and research skills are required for academic success as a child progresses through school. This area includes the ability to gather information from a variety of resources, develop an organized plan, integrate ideas, make appropriate revisions, and complete increasingly complex research tasks in a library or other archived information to rage source. Children's instruction in this area must go beyond traditional library skills instruction, which primarily taught students the use of the Dewey decimal system, to include the use of other resources such as those available on the Internet or audio / video materials.

Test-Taking Strategies

Test-taking strategies are specific strategies manifested as actual behaviors used while taking a test. Eliminating unlikely choices and learning how to allocate time between difficult versus easy items are examples of test-taking strategies. Initial information processing and preparative study activities are excluded from this area. Instruction in test-taking strategies has been shown to be helpful for any student, but particularly for such special populations as minority students or those for who English is their second language (Hughes, 1993; Johns & VanLeirsburg, 1992; Scruggs & Mastropieri, 1986; Scruggs & Tolfa, 1985).

Organizational techniques

Organizational techniques are specific strategies used to organize learning materials, ranging from preparation before each class to systematic recording of daily assignments. Basic techniques for categorizing and arranging learning tasks can be taught to students in preparation for more complex organizational tasks (Slade, 1986).

Time Management

Time management is a meta-cognitive technique that involves recognizing the most efficient ways to use time. This skill is often neglected until a student enters college, when he or she leaves behind parental supervision and at the same time confronts more choices as to how time will be spent. Mastery of time management skills in high school or earlier can have a strong impact on a student's motivation to complete tasks. This skill contributes to a sense of control and eases transition to progressively less structured learning situations.

PROBLEMS FACED BY HIGHER SECONDARY STUDENTS

Students all over the world face a number of problems. This is very much true in the case of India also. The student community is affected by lot of problems. Lack of quality education, the thread of unemployment, absence of adequate opportunities, the politicization and criminalization of academic life, rampant corruption and nepotism and a host of such factors dishearten the students and sometimes lead to law and order problems. As students are the future citizens of the world, every country should shoulder the responsibility of providing an immaculate environment to the students. Only then they can come up with some amicable solution. All such negativeness can be effectively controlled, with the aid of participation right from the parents to the policy makers of education.

- Personal Issues
- Few personal issues faced by students are:
- Loneliness
- Depression
- Grief
- Anger
- Stress
- parenting problems
- relationship problems
- suicide bereavement
- surviving sexual abuse
- family violence

Students' personal problems include the academic and non-academic aspects. Moser and Moser (1963) believe general problems of personal nature as found in the school, college and university students besides the academic achievement problems are lack of social aptitudes, romantic involvements, problems of finance, undesirable habits and lack of self-sufficiency.

There are many issues which plagues our youths day after day. Issues such as peer pressure are becoming a major threat to our youths. Our youths, they want to fit in and so they do whatever it takes to fit in or be accepted. Hardly anyone likes to be different; so instead of standing out, our youths try their hardest to fit in. Our youths must realize the need to stay true to themselves by being who they are rather than being who everyone wants them to be or who their peers want them to be. Poverty is another issue which can have a lot of negative effects on our youths. Coming from poor families, our youths especially the males may see the need to take control by doing whatever it takes to generate an income for the family. The females may become "Slack" doing whatever is required to provide for them. Though poverty should not be a reason for such actions, it does contribute to the decisions made by our youths. Under pressure it's hard to think straight and sound so our youths make bad decisions which they later regret. At the time of making such decision, it seems like that's the only decision available to make.

What we must understand is that our youth face numerous challenges and so they need guidance; they need someone who's willing to listen, understand and relate to them. Someone who won't be quick to judge but to listen; someone who won't be quick to condemn but ready to offer words of advice. Though many youths may react unappreciative to the advice, some do take it into consideration and even do what was said.

A lack of proper parenting may also contribute negatively to the growth and development of our youths especially in the case where they have been abused. In some situations both parents may be working and becomes too busy to spend time with their child/children or the parents experience problems which cause them to divorce. Though this may not be the case for everyone, children who grow without both parents struggle while children who witness the breakdown of the family through divorce may find it hard to overcome what has taken place to the family. It therefore lacks the love, guidance and proper parenting that both parents usually bring to the table.

A rise in hormones: hormones begin to act up during teenage years and some of our youths become eager to experiment with the feelings and so they get caught up in sexual activities. This results in a number of our females becoming pregnant in their teenage years.

Lack of communication and the decline in being ambitious. For some reason, our youths find great difficulty in communicating with other peers and adults effectively. They go about it the wrong way or they do not know how to put what they feel into words. What's worse is the decline in ambition. Many of our youths seem to be happy with receiving whatever life throws at them that they no longer see the need to set goals nor work to achieve them .Maybe this is so because nothing in life comes easy so they back away from the hard work; but doesn't this mean the harder you work towards your goals the greater the feeling?

There are many more issues which affect the lives of our youths. What our youths need to realize is that although they are faced with numerous struggles and obstacles, they have what it takes to overcome them. Each child is unique; each child is made differently; each child is blessed and so they must realize how blessed they are and accept the fact that life is filled with challenges .They must also realize that in order to overcome these challenges they must be positive, dedicated and determined. They must realize the need to be equipped with everything positive to achieve success. Furthermore, they must realize that in everything they do, they need God.

A young person's family history has a significant influence on the way they behave, function, and relate to people. Family is often thought of as a person's immediate relatives, but can include others who have significant influence, both positive and negative, on shaping who we are and how we see others, the world and ourselves.

FAMILY RISK AND PROTECTIVE FACTORS

There are many family risk factors that can influence a young person's level of engagement in health risk behaviors. Some factors will be entrenched characteristics of a young person's life that cannot be modified. These include:

- Low birth weight
- Premature birth
- Less than two years between siblings
- Family size
- "Difficult" temperament

Early childhood experiences, e.g. malnutrition, poverty, parenting style. Other risk factors may be amenable to change through intervention, such as current exposure to abuse. In addition, protective factors may or may not have existed in a young person's background. Interventions should have a goal of modifying available risk factors and enhancing available protective factors, to the extent possible. This requires an understanding of historical events that will continue to impact on a young person's health and wellbeing, and ways in which we can increase the number of protective factors in a young person's life to try and offset these risk factors.

FAMILY PROBLEM

Children in intact families tend to exhibit better emotional and psychological well-being and are less likely to exhibit behavioral problems such as school violence, juvenile delinquency and substance abuse. In addition, they tend to have higher grades and are less likely to be sexually active.

Paternal Relationship: Family structure is related to youths' relationships with their fathers. Adolescents living in intact families reported, on average, having closer relationships with their fathers compared to peers living in blended families or in divorced or never-married single parent families, controlling for adolescents' age, race, gender, and family income. This was true among youth in their early adolescence. Among youth in their middle adolescence, those living in intact families reported, on average, feeling closer to their fathers than peers in never-married or divorced single-parent families, but no more so than peers in blended families.

Emotional Distress: Adolescents who live in intact families are less likely to experience emotional or psychological problems. Controlling for a host of factors including adolescents' age, gender, race/ethnicity, family income, and relationships with their mothers and fathers, adolescents living in intact families tended to report lower levels of psychological distress (e.g., how often they feel sad, tense, lonely, excited, happy) than peers in living blended families (i.e., mothers were in a remarriage or a cohabiting relationship).

Violence at Home

One of the main reasons that children become violent is because they are exposed to violence in their own homes, whether it is directed towards them or towards others.

Violence at home can be of a physical nature, or it can be expressed verbally or through neglect and abandonment. Abusive homes and violent neighborhoods are stronger predictors of adult violent behavior than violence in the media. Most abusive parents were physically or sexually abused as children.

SOCIAL ISSUES

A social issue (also called a social problem or a social illness) refers to an issue that influences and is opposed by a considerable number of individuals within a society. It is often the consequence of factors extending beyond an individuals control and local geographical environment.

Social issues encompass issues that a small to representative group of people within a society disagree with or find undesirable. A social issue is also known as a social problem.

In some cases, a social issue is the source of a conflicting opinion on the grounds of what is perceives as a morally just personal life or societal order.

A number of social problems crop up in the period of adolescence. The social contacts of the person expand from infancy to maturity. In infancy a child's social contacts are with one person, usually its mother. From the early childhood onwards the mother-child relationship normally expands as the child comes into contact with the other members of family.

When the child moves outside his family circle, he establishes contact with other children of his own age. When he takes admission in the school the peer group expands because now the child is free to choose his own friends and associates.

Here he meets his teacher. As he enters adolescence he becomes a part of the gag, whatever be the stage of development of other people from his social environment. Adolescence is the stage of development which produces a number of problems for the person. These problems arise out of the adolescent's adjustment with following social groups:

1. Family;
2. School;
3. Associates of one's own sex; and
4. Associates of the other sex.

Social Problems Arose by the Parents:

During adolescent years the boy or girl tends to develop interests for groups outside the family. The youngsters commonly have misgivings about the changes that are taking place in their interests. On the one hand, they feel joy in being dependent upon their parents and on the other; the experiences with their peers are also pleasant. The peer group attracts them a greater force, because it offers them esteem and status which is either lacking in the family or is not got there at all.

Parents generally complicate the problem by placing demands on the adolescent sons or daughters. When they come to know that the relationship between them and their children is about to change, when they find that their children are becoming more rebellious, less responsive, and less involved in the life of the family they feel threatened.

Every father or mother thinks that his son or daughter is a psychological extension of himself, and when the adolescent slips along into the outside world, he or she feels that he or she is losing a part of himself or herself. As the adolescent becomes more independent he needs not so much care, direction, and attention of his parents, which parents still think necessary for his existence and well-being.

Social problems which have a root in the relationship between the adolescent and his parents arise because the two do not understand each other sympathetically. The parents believe in' the efficacy of greater control and direction.

The adolescent wants more independence but he also wants his parents to tell him what to do. The parents want to give more direction and control but at the same time require him to think and act for himself. There is dilemma, and the inconsistency is not soluble and therefore it creates difficulties for both.

The mutual problems should be discussed by the parents and the adolescents frankly. It is very unfortunate what whenever the two parties try to clarify the issues through discussions heated arguments are advanced by each to defend its own point of view.

The adolescent who is in conflict with the family tries to seek social satisfaction outside the home, but he does get sufficient success in his attempt. If he wants to become successful outside the family he should have emotional support and acceptance within the family.

Problems of Adjustment with the School

The average adolescent tries to run away from home, though economically and vocationally he is yet not able to leave it. It is the school where he can be away from home for a particular length of time in the day.

It is in the school also where he can mix with associates in the study-hall, in the classroom, on the playground and on the streets. If the school does not organize social gatherings like excursions, outings, trips, and if there is no arrangement for social development, the adolescent does not find the school a satisfactory place. Consequently, he becomes a truant.

If the school wants that the pupils should find joy and satisfaction, pleasure and happiness it should organize social activities in its premises. These activities, if wisely directed, tend to develop social maturity in the adolescents. Maximum participation in curricular activities like evening games and sports, plays and dramatics and student councils will inculcate better social interests, skills and attitudes.

Social Problems of Adjustment with Associates of One's Own Sex

Why does a boy belonging to upper class or higher caste family not like to mix with the one of lower class family? Why is a particular boy not popular? Why does a boy like a particular boy and not others? These are some of the problems raised when the adolescent tries to mix with the associates of his own sex.

So long as he is a child he does not have such problems. Children of different socioeconomic status work and play with each other. But the social distance increases in the adolescence period. Upper class boys do not like to make friendship with boys of lower class.

In the society of adolescents there are many who are not popular, who do not belong, and who are occasional. It is strange to find isolates everywhere. Isolates are boys and girls who regard others their best friends but are disregarded by them. The adolescents who are thus rejected become quarrelsome or unduly sensitive. On the other hand, those who are liked seem to be cheerful, humorous and lively.

Social Problems of Adjustment with the Other Sex

The adolescence is the stage when interest in the other sex is developed as a result of certain physical developments. The perennial topics of conversation among boys or among girls are sex and the opposite sex.

They try to learn about sex from each other; often, they do help each other but such help is fraught with difficulties. Hence, there is a need for sex education at this stage. It is this stage when the youngsters try to discover the other sex. At first the boys and girls do not know what to make of each other and how to get along together.

The boy now sees the neighbor girl in a new way. She is now really a different person from what she was when both of them were of twelve-year's age. If he develops healthy relations with her he is in a happy position. If he does not achieve a satisfactory adjustment to the other sex, he may have difficulties in marriage. He may have other social problems also.

The boy who cannot establish happy relations with girls may withdraw from their associations. If he becomes too interested in the other sex and goes too far he may cause scandal. If the adolescent boy withdraws from association with girls he will become mentally unhealthy. Marriage becomes either impossible or likely to be unhappy for the introverted youngster who does not have healthy normal associations with the other sex.

Adolescent girls try to attract adolescent boys. The increasingly do thing which may catch and sustain the attention of the other sex. They are more active because of their earlier sex maturity.

Many girls, who find the boys of their own age sexually not so mature and responsive, try to seek attention from older boys. As sex maturity among boys and girls occurs at different ages, in a complicated and rapidly changing social situation the adolescents find it difficult to make social adjustment with the other sex.

Education and Social Maturity

The teacher who has to guide the adolescent facing social problems will have to understand the social liabilities and assets. He has to find out the relationships between the adolescent on the one hand and his parents, the peer group, and the school on the other.

The teacher has to make a close study of the quiet, commonplace youngster who is rejected by his group or the other sex. If she teacher wants to understand the adolescents and develop them socially he may do the following.

1. Know the settings and backgrounds of the adolescents.
2. Make an appraisal for their social status.
3. Plan a broad social program to meet the needs of all.
4. Teach them an informal applied Social Psychology directly or indirectly.

The first step in helping the adolescent achieve social maturity is to gather information about his settings and backgrounds. It is, therefore, necessary that the teacher should try to find out whether or not a particular boy or girl takes part in social activities, whether or not he or she belongs to a team, a society, or a council. Early or late maturing, higher or lower socio-economic status of the family may be influencing his or her social maturity.

The teacher has to investigate the causes of social maladjustment. He should then plan a social program comprehensive enough to meet the needs of all adolescents. As some of the problems arise in the school environment, he may produce good social atmosphere in the school for adequate social development. But most of the social problems arise out of the school, in the family, in the group, in the relations with the other sex.

To solve these problems an active cooperation of the parents and the society has to be sought so that desirable social adjustment may be fostered. Regular P.T.A. meetings, conferences between parents and adolescents, healthy associations of one sex with the other, active participation by both boys and girls in the school and community functions may go a long way in helping the adolescents achieve social maturity.

The teacher his subject; the boys or girls learn it. But of greater importance than teaching and learning of the particular subject in the classroom is the development of social maturity. The first thing needed for that is a good-humored, relaxed, friendly, social climate in the class.

Where socialized activity program as group games, scouting and guiding, debates and dramatics, run regularly and where students take part in them freely, social maturity is developed as desired. Social adjustment or social maturity may be developed through a direct or indirect instruction in informal applied social psychology.

Bullying Online and At School

- Bullying is an ongoing pattern of harassment and abuse. It can be done directly by physical or verbal attacks or indirectly by exclusion, spreading rumors, etc.
- Cyber bullying is a growing problem among Middle and High School aged students. While it also occurs among College-aged students, for the most part young people have matured past cyber bullying at that point.
- If a child feels he or she is being cyber bullied, you must accept it as cyber bullying. In all cases of bullying, it is up to the victim, not the adult, to determine whether bullying is taking place
- Bullies seek power through aggression and direct their attacks at vulnerable victims. In-person bullies often lose their popularity in high school and have a high likelihood of having a criminal record as adults.
- Girls are more likely than boys to be cyber bullies, due to the verbal (nonphysical) nature of online communication.

Girls' Bullying is Focused on Social Exclusion

- 1 in 5 kids report being bullied or bullying. Every 7 minutes, a child is bullied in the school setting.
- While most teachers believe they always intervene in face-to-face bullying, only 25% of students report they have received teachers' help when they needed it.
- Cyber bullying is, in many ways, a larger problem than face-to face bullying, for several reasons: Adults and peers are often not in a position to intervene, and victims' hurt is not visible as useful feedback for the bullies to experience as a "reality check." It is far too easy for cyber bullies to convince themselves they are merely "joking." Some are surprised at the harm they cause, because the abuse did not feel "real."
- Those who are bullied sometimes learn to perpetuate the problem and become bullies themselves, simultaneously or concurrently. This is the cycle of victim-perpetrator that catches so many children and adults.

Violent Culture

- Numerous researches have established the undeniable relationships between militarism, sexism, racism and violence within the culture.
- Principally, there is no difference between the state of mind that seeks to resolve international conflicts by force and the state of mind that seeks to resolve interpersonal or familial conflicts by force and the misuse of power.

- There is a direct link between the way in which we use power with our children, our significant others, our neighbors and our environment and what we teach our children about violence.
- Subtle coercion or verbal abuse may also be experienced and observed by children as a form of violence.
- Cultures in which young children regularly receive loving touch have lower incidents of violent crimes.
- Research done with psychiatrically hospitalized adolescents demonstrated a significant reduction of violent and sexual acting out when staff increased the use on non-sexual, affectionate touch with the teens.
- Fear and violent behavior have a direct correlation. Monitor media news presentations that capitalize on creating fear through undue sensationalism and manipulative means.

Teen Suicide

- Suicide is the third leading cause of death for adolescents and young adults.
- Young males are much more likely to commit suicide than their female peers.
- Female adolescents are more likely to attempt suicide than their male peers.
- Female Hispanic students are more likely to attempt suicide than all other students.
- American Indian/Alaskan Native male adolescents have the highest suicide rate.
- Myths and Faulty Beliefs about Suicidal Teens
- Once a teenager decides to kill himself, nothing can stop him.
- Young people talk about suicide mostly to get attention, therefore the best thing to do is to ignore the person.
- If we ask a young person if they are thinking about suicide, we run the danger of putting the idea of suicide in their mind.
- When a person tries to commit suicide and fails, the pain and shame will deter another attempt.
- Since depression is often a common sign of suicidal behavior, once the depression has subsided, the suicidal teen is out of danger.
- Because suicide may "run" in families it cannot be prevented.

A social problem is a condition that at least some people in a community view as being undesirable. Everyone would agree about some social problems, such as murders and DWI traffic deaths. Other social problems may be viewed as such by certain groups of people. Teenagers who play loud music in a public park obviously do not view it as a problem, but some other people may consider it an undesirable social condition. Some nonsmokers view smoking as an undesirable social condition that should be banned or restricted in public buildings.

Every newspaper is filled with stories about undesirable social conditions. Examples include crime, violence, drug abuse, and environmental problems. Such social problems can be found at the local, state, national and international levels.

There are many social problems that teenagers go through. Drugs and Teenagers Drug use is the increasing problem among teenagers in today's high schools. Most drug use begins in the preteen and teenage years, these years most crucial in the maturation process. During these years adolescents are faced with difficult tasks of discovering their self-identity, clarifying their sexual roles, assenting independence, learning to cope with authority and searching for goals that would give their lives meaning. Drugs are readily, adolescents are curious and venerable, and there is peer pressure to experiment, and there us a temptation to escape from conflicts. The use of drugs by teenagers is the result of a combination of factors such as peer pressure, curiosity, and availability. Drugs addiction among adolescents in turn leads to depression and suicide.

One of the most important reasons of teenage drug usage is peer pressure. Peer pressure represents social influences that effect adolescents, it can have a positive or a negative effect, depending on person's social group and one can follow one path of the other. We are greatly influenced by the people around us.

According to the staff of government, MohdAzuanHussin, said that, one of the most devastating side effects of drug addiction and abuse is depression. Depression is the result of chemical imbalance, environmental influence, or a combination of both. Using heavy and very highly addictive drugs as heroin, cocaine, opium and many others will cause sudden mood changes, deterioration of the immune system, nervous breakdowns, unusual flares of temper and many other side effects. Besides physical side effects, drug addiction can create problems in a person's social circles. The person may run into many conflicts with his family and friends, resulting in desire for isolation. This in turn will create more problems since the person will have no social support. Furthermore, drug addiction is a financial strain especially for teenagers. When a person is addicted to drugs he will do anything to obtain money to fulfill his needs. Drug addiction is the results of 3 "I's". Teenagers may think of their problems as Inescapable, Interminable and Intolerable. Life may seem bleak and miserable. Seeing no way out feeling lonely and no prospects for improvement leads to depression. This can further lead to attempted suicide.

PERSONAL ISSUES VERSUS SOCIAL ISSUES

Personal issues are those that individuals deal with themselves and within a small range of their peers and relationships. On the other hand, social issues attribute to values cherished by widespread society.

The line between a personal issue and a public issue may be subjective; however, when a large enough sector of society is affected by an issue, it becomes a social issue.

Based on the theoretical framework, the researcher has undertaken the present study to find the effect of certain personal and social problems of the students in enhancing learning strategies in order to improve their performance in academic arena.

STATEMENT OF THE PROBLEM

The problem of the research is entitled as *"A critical study on the learning strategies in relation to certain personal and social issues among higher secondary students"*.

OPERATIONAL DEFINITIONS OF THE TERMS USED

Learning Strategies

A set of steps to accomplish a particular task, such as taking a test, comprehending, text and writing a story to make learning more meaningful. In the present study, it is measured by Learning Strategy Inventory, constructed and validated by Kathy Stroud and Ceil Reyonolds (2000).

Personal Issues and Social Issues

Personal issues are those that individuals deal with themselves and within a small range of their peers and relationships. On the other hand, social issues attribute to values cherished by widespread society.

A social issue is also called a social problem or a social illness refers to an issue that influences and is opposed by a considerable number of individuals within a society. It is often the consequence of factors extending beyond an individuals control and local geographical environment.

In the present study, it is assessed by Youth Problem Inventory prepared by Dr. M Varma (2004).

Higher Secondary Students

In the present study, students studying in XI grade are considered as Higher Secondary Students.

OBJECTIVES OF THE STUDY

The following objectives have been set in the present study:

1. To find out the levels of Learning Strategies along with its dimensions among Higher Secondary Students.
2. To find the levels of learning of youth problems in Toto and all its dimensions among Higher Secondary Students.
3. To find whether there are any significant difference in the Learning Strategies along with its dimensions, youth problems in Toto and all its dimensions among Higher Secondary Students with regard to
   - Gender (Male / Female)
   - Academic Stream (Arts / Science)
   - Medium of Instruction (English / Tamil)
   - Type of Family (Joint / Nuclear)
   - Birth Order (First Born / Middle Born / Last Born)
   - Parental Monthly Income (below Rs.10,000/between Rs10,000 and Rs25,000/above Rs.25,000)
4. To find whether there is any significant correlation between Learning Strategies along with its dimensions and Youth Problem along with its dimensions among Higher Secondary Students.

NEED OF THE STUDY

Education is important for everyone to lead a successful life, especially for the students in higher secondary school level and their progress in education marks and criteria for choosing their future studies. Hence the higher secondary school level is said to be a crucial stage in the academic life of a student. It is said to be a foundation stage for college and further learning and to establish successful career. Every student should enlighten with right way to attain an interest in the field of education. Higher secondary school students are mostly adolescents. Adolescence age is highly critical period in the life of all the students to choose their own interest in the field of education. The impact of personal problems is an important one among the students', especially for higher secondary school students. The importance of the present study is to focus mainly on the higher secondary school students' personal problems, social issues and the learning strategies and also to know its relations.

In the present day many factors affect student's learning. These factors are socio-economic background, type of school and other personal variables, study habits, etc.; the teacher uses variety of strategy to convey information to students to students to accomplish their tasks.

One's influence on process in pursuit of excellence will tend to be one's perception of how to achieve success. The learning strategies help to acquire knowledge and personal enlightenment. The learning strategized students perform higher than other students in academics. It provides additional support for the evaluation of the curriculum and instruction at all levels of educational progress. It increases the explicit presentation of learning or process strategized behavior of positively students.

DELIMITIATIONS

The study has the following delimitations:

- Geographically, sample area selected was Chennai, Tamil Nadu.
- Six schools were selected at random, of which two were Aided Schools, two were Government Schools and the remaining were Private Schools.
- The present study intended to assess the Learning Strategies; but not to increase the level of Learning Strategies.
- 302 Higher Secondary Student were considered in the present study.

SUMMARY

In this chapter, the overview of the problem, the objectives, need and significance of the study are discussed. The next chapter deals with the review of the related literature related to the problem.

❐

7

Review of the Related Literature

It is necessary for a research worker to acquire up to date information about what has been taught and done in the particular area, from which the tends to take up a research problem which enables him to investigate the problem through proper channel.

Study of the related literature includes locating, reading and evaluating reports of research as well as reports of casual observation and opinion that are related to the individual planned research project. The survey of Related Literature implies locating studying of published articles research abstracts etc., which provides ideas, theories, and explanations on hypothesis valuable in formulating the problem.

According to Monly (1963), "Review of related studies promotes a greater understanding of the problem and its crucial aspects ensure the avoidance of unnecessary duplication".

According to George J. Mouly (1970), "The review of literature promotes a greater understanding of the problem and its crucial aspects and ensures the avoidance of unnecessary duplication; it provides comparative data on the basis of which to evaluate and interpret the significance of one's findings, and in addition, contributes to the scholarship of the investigator".

According to Best (1963), A familiarity with literature in any problem area helps the students to discover what is already known, attempted methods, promising solutions and disappointing problems that remain to be solved.

IMPORTANCE OF REVIEW OF RELATED LITERATURE

It provides a background for the development of present study. This part of dissertation gives evidence for the researcher's knowledge about the field.

The result of the review provide the data used in research. The findings of the previous research work help the researcher to have an insight to the present study and thus save time.

The review of related literature helps the researchers to convert his hypothesis to the specific and concise one. It provides further orientation to the problem as well as eliminates the possibilities of unnecessary duplicate of efforts value information on research techniques may be gained from the reports of previous research wide.

In searching related literature, the researcher should note certain important elements:

1. Reports of closely related studies that have been investigated.
2. Design of the study, including procedures employed and data-gathering instruments used.
3. Population that was sampled: sampling methods employed.
4. Variables that were defined.
5. Extraneous variables that could have affected the findings.
6. Faults that could have been avoided.
7. Recommendations for further research.

STUDIES RELATED TO LEARNING STRATEGIES

Dowson and Martin (1997), demonstrates the use of cone generic measurement mile in assessing and improving the variety of scales comprising of Goals Orientation and Learning Strategies Survey (GOALS-S), and it also illustrates the use of f cross-validation as a way; to assess the stability of the GOALS-S scales. Three academic goals, four social goals, three cognitive strategies, and three meta-cognitive strategies were defined and operationalized in the developed GOAL-S instrument. Preliminary factor analyses were used to refine the measure. Its 13 scales were tested with 380 Australian Urban students. Once collected, data from a randomly chosen sub sample (half the original sample) were subjected to confirmatory factor analysis using 13 separate one-factor congeneric models. Modified models that showed sufficient fit in the first half were tested with the second half of the sample. The initia modeling process supported the construct validity of only four of the original scales, but relatively minor modifications resulted in considerably better fit for the other nine scales. Results also demonstrate support for the reliability of at least eight of the GOALS-S scales.

Shih et.al (1998) reported the results of a study designed to examine how student with different learning styles functioned in World Wide Web-based courses offered by project BIO at low state University in the Fall of 1997, and to determine what factors influenced their learning. The objectives of the study were to identify; the demographic characteristics of the students by learning styles; how students' learning strategies, patterns of learning, achievement and selected variables. The population for this study was 99 students taking two non-major introductory courses. These two Web-based courses were stand alone courses in which most course materials and resources were accessed and delivered by the internet. An online questionnaire that included a learning strategies scale, patterns of learning scale, and demographic questions was designed and posted on the Web. A total of 78 students also took the Group Embedded Figures Test (GEFT), learning styles test. Total data were collected on 74 students. Results indicated that learning styles, patterns of learning toward Web-based instruction, and student characteristics did not have an effect on Web-based learning achievement.

Geiser (1999) examined the effects of traditional versus learning-style-responsive study strategies on eighth grader's mathematics achievement, frequency of studying and attitudes. Found that students applying learning-style responsive strategies had significantly higher mathematics achievement and attitude scores than the students using traditional strategies. No differences were found in frequency of studying for tests.

Fuchs et al., (2000) described the Peer-Assisted Learning Strategies (PALS) program for developing reading skills in grades 2-6. It notes a 3rd grade teacher's perspective and reports on research and development efforts supporting use of PALS reading with students with learning disabilities. Noted is the recent extension of PALS reading downwards into kindergarten and 1st grade and upright into high school.

Olivares and Gabraiela (2002) investigated the effort of learning strategies in writing achievement in an intermediate-advanced college-level Spanish writing course and examine the influence of the students' native language and textbook on these strategies; subjects were a class of 20 students that compromised nine first language and 11 foreign/second language speakers. The Strategy Inventory of Language Learning provided an estimate of learning strategies.

Chen (2002) did research on 197 business students using MSLQ and comparing self-regulated strategies in lecture versus hands-on computer lab. Effort regulation had a positive effect, peer learning a negative effect on learning computer concepts in lectures. Prior computer experience has no effect. Data were inconclusive effective strategies in hands-on lab.

Shih and Gamon (2002) described students in web-based courses (n=74) completed the Group Embedded Figures Test and an online questionnaire on learning strategies and patterns. They used strategies to determine important ideas from lectures and memorize key concepts. They used online features more for checking grades than communicating with the class. Learning strategies accounted for one-fourth of achievement.

Tuckman (2003) determined the effectiveness of teaching students the use of specific learning and motivation strategies and sub strategies to meet the cognitive and motivational demands of college. Findings indicate that training in learning and motivation strategy use contributed to GPA improvement.

Sabbation (2004) familiarized teachers with the concept of graphic organizers as an effective comprehension strategy, presents a research-based rationale for their use with students with learning disabilities, and introduces graphic organizers as a tool for helping students with learning disabilities make sense of wide variety of textual information.

Ward and Lee (2004) compared the effectiveness of problem-based learning (PBL) versus lecture-based instruction (LBI) in high school foods and nutrition classes. Two classes were randomly assigned to the PBL group, while the remaining two were assigned to LBI group. A pretest was administered. During the semester, LBI students received course content primarily through lectures. PBL students received situations or problems and utilized various resources to problem-solve. A posttest was administered. The "t" test for independent samples showed no significant difference in mean gains ("p"=0.203) on test scores between PBL students and LBI students.

Kim (2005) investigated the 76 six graders were divided into two groups. The experimental group was taught using the constructivist approach while the control group was taught using traditional approach. A total of 40 hours over nine weeks was used to implement the experiment. The instruments used were as follows; mathematics tests administered by the teacher, self-concept inventory, learning strategies inventory and a classroom environment survey. The results are constructivist teaching is more effective than traditional teaching in terms of academic achievement; constructivist teaching is not effective in relation to self-concept and learning strategy, but had some effect on motivation, anxiety towards learning and self-monitoring; a constructivist environment was preferred to a traditional classroom.

Chen and Dwyer (2006) employed as major components for designing and implementing educational and training learning environments. However, the design and development of hypertext materials are still heavily based on deficiencies in hypermedia research, one of the most cited and applied instructional theories, Charles Reigeluth's Elaboration Theory (ET), is the target of investigation in this study. Elaboration Theory prescribes that instruction start with an epitome that teaches a few simple, general ideas in order to link to the learner's prior knowledge. The purpose of this study:

- Determine whether Elaboration-Theory-based hypertext, designed by using instructional strategies proposed by Reigeluth, was effective in facilitating student achievement of different education objective;
- Determine whether different Elaboration-Theory-based hypertexts (the one with the two Elaboration-Theory strategies versus the one with the five Elaboration-theory strategies) were equally effective in facilitating students' achievement of different educational objectives;
- Determine whether the students with different prior knowledge levels (high and low) achieve differently on different educational objectives in the same hypertext environment;
- Determine whether a significant interaction exist between Elaboration-Theory-based hypertext and learner' level of prior knowledge.

Findings reveal that students' play a crucial role in influencing their learning achievement. It was also found that Elaboration-Theory-based hypertexts employing instructional strategies are superior to linear hypertext in enhancing students' achievement of factual and conceptual knowledge.

Chiu et al (2007) examined whether strategies of memorization, transfer through elaboration, and meta-cognition accounted for reading science and mathematics achievement across 34 countries. 158,848 fifteen-year-old completed a reading literacy test and 88,590 completed a mathematics test. We analyzed the data using multiple level regressions of Rasch-estimated test scores and modeled difference across countries and across schools. Students who reported using memorization strategies often scored lower in all the subjects. Transfer through elaboration was not significantly linked to any achievement scores. Lastly, students reporting greater use of meta-cognitive strategies often scored higher. Compared to students in individualistic societies, to achievement scores of students in collective cultures were linked more strongly to schoolmates; use of meta-cognitive strategies. These results highlight how cultural contexts can moderate the links between adolescents; learning strategies and their academic achievement.

Marat (2007) examined student's and teacher's efficiency in use of learning strategies in mathematics, and the relationship with achievement. The second phase of multi-method doctoral study, ninety-two students and ten teachers from diverse secondary school were surveyed on efficacy in use of learning strategies, and the factors they perceived as facilitating or inhibiting the use of learning strategies in the classroom context. The findings are contextualized within a multi-methods frame work comprising two research projects. The cumulative findings bring to light illusory-efficacy in sizeable number of student's participants who did not achieve, highlighting the importance of true efficacy and learning strategies to reduce disparities and enhance achievement.

Liem (2008) adopted a combination of expectancy-value and achievement goal theories, this study examined the role of self-efficacy, task value, and achievement goals in student's learning strategies, task disengagement, peer relationship, and English achievement outcome. A sample of 1475 years-9 students participated in the study. A structural equation model showed that while task value predicted only mastery goals, self-efficacy predicted each of the three types of achievement goal. Mastery and performance – approach goals were both positive predictors of deep learning and peer relationship. Mastery goals were also negatively associated with surface learning. In contrast, performance-avoidance goals were positive predictor of surface learning and task engagement but a negative predictor of peer relationship. On the whole, findings suggest that like mastery goals, performance-approach goals can generate adaptive outcomes.

Adele (2008) investigated the effects of three teaching strategies (cooperative learning, problem solving and conventional) on junior secondary school students' achievement in social studies. The result of the study also indicated that the effect to teaching strategies was gender sensitive. Discussion or conclusion: The findings of the study are highly significant and relevant. These results have implications for curriculum planning, teacher training and retraining programmer and classroom practice.

Hsieh and Dwyer (2009) examined the instructional effectiveness of different online reading strategies for students identified as possessing different learning styles, either internal or external Locus of control styles, on test measuring different learning objectives. Participants were 169 undergraduate students, randomly assigned to four online reading treatments: none, rereading strategy, keyword strategy and question and answer strategy. Immediately after interacting with their respective instructions, students received four individual criterion measures. Analysis indicated and insignificant interaction between learning styles and treatment type: however, comprehension test reflect a significant main effect for students receiving the online rereading treatment. ($F = 3.09$, $df = 3/169$, $P = 0.03$), with an effect size of 0.04. The rereading treatment also appears to be more significantly more effective than the control for the comprehension test. Results indicate that not all types of reading strategies are equally effective in facilitating different types of learning objectives. The results indicate that, even though different reading strategies may be structurally different, they are functionally identical for raising questions relative to the cost and amount of time required for student interaction.

STUDIES RELATED TO YOUTH PROBLEM

According to Spielberger (as cited in Puskar, Ren, & Bernardo, 2008), there are two aspects of anger: state anger and trait anger. State anger is an emotional response to a provoking incident, while trait anger tends to occur more frequently in some individuals than others. Trait anger may occur in situations where most people would not respond in the same manner. Anger in adolescents is associated with many problems, including aggression.

According to Novaco (as cited in Taylor, Novaco, Gillmer, & Thorne, 2002), though it does not always lead to aggression, anger is often a precursor to aggression, particularly very intense anger, as this type of anger can decrease a person's ability to control his or her behavior.

Individuals express anger differently and for different reasons. Most people think of aggression as the physical expression of anger, though it is possible to express anger in nonviolent ways as well. Physical violence, however, is more visible and tends to result in more critical outcomes. The National Center for Education Statistics (2010) reported that approximately 1.9 million crimes occurred in elementary and secondary schools throughout the nation, meaning about 40 students per 1,000 were victims of some type. These statistics do not include bullying or cyber-bullying, which are also serious types of aggression. In 2009, 28 percent of students ages 12-18 reported feeling bullied by one or more of their peers (Institute of Educational Sciences, n.d.). Anger has also been linked to other serious problems, such as depression, suicide, and substance abuse (Daniel, Goldston, Erkanli, Franklin, & Mayfield, 2009). Problems of this magnitude often affect a student's ability to meet their full potential..

Deffenbacher, Lynch, Oetting, and Kemper (1996) suggest that individuals with high trait anger are more likely to have interpersonal problems, academic difficulties, and conflict in their jobs. When students believe they have the necessary resources to deal with difficulties, they are more likely to make wise choices. If, on the other hand, they feel that they cannot face a problem, they may make poor choices.

According to Csibi&Csibi (2011), some studies have shown that girls often use avoidance when dealing with stressful situations, which causes emotional tension. Eventually, that tension must be released in some way, such as aggression towards their peers. This can lead to further interpersonal problems, which may have been the initial cause of the stress.

In order for educators and counselors to effectively serve adolescents and identify solutions for preventing these outcomes, it is important for them to be aware of the factors that can contribute to the expression of anger. Perceived social support, emotion regulation, family environment, and personality are some of the contributing factors (Puskar, et al., 2008; Turblad, Grann, &

Lichtenstein, 2006; Sanz, Garcia-Vera, & Magan, 2010). Fortunately, there are several school-based programs that have shown promise in addressing some of the core issues related to anger. An awareness of the available programs in the field as well as the task of evaluating and researching their effectiveness are crucial steps in addressing the problem of anger. If schools and mental health professionals can address the problem at an early age, perhaps it will prevent more serious problems during adulthood.

Leff et al (2010) assert that there are two main types of aggression: physical and relational. Physical aggression tends to be more overt, like hitting or pushing others. It Relational aggression is less overt and does not involve direct contact with others, but it can be just as damaging as physical aggression. In fact, Crick and Grotpeter (as cited in Leff et al., 2010), refer to it as relational aggression because those who perpetrate this type of aggression seek to undermine others' attempts to build or maintain relationships, whether it is through subtle things like spreading rumors or outright bullying. Society often sends the message that adolescents must look or behave a certain way in order to build and maintain friendships. For those who fit into that mold, it is easier to experience relational success, but for those who are different, they often times face taunting and torment from their peers.

(Kalish& Kimmel, 2010). Bullying is all too common in many schools today and can results in terrible tragedies like suicide, or even worse. Most of the infamous school shootings that have occurred in recent years have been carried out by young men who had been consistently singled out by their peers for quite some time.

Kalish and Kimmel (2010) believe that boys in our schools today are socialized to believe they should not back down when they are provoked and, if they do, they risk losing their masculine identity. This sends the message that it is okay to use violence when they feel masculinity has been threatened. In other words, bullying can lead victims to resort to violence as a way to end the abuse and take revenge on the perpetrators

Bullying does not always lead to aggressive responses, nor do those who respond to others in an aggressive manner do so because they have been bullied (Crick & Dodge, 1996). While bullying is an intentional pattern of harassing behavior, some individuals act aggressively in response to a one time frustrating or provoking incident, which is called reactive aggression. Others use aggression not because they believe they have been wronged, but because they believe it will get them what they want, which is called proactive aggression.

Aggression is not the only problem associated with anger. Anger and depression are also correlated. Depression is a serious issue because it affects an individual's quality of life, as well as his or her ability to make decisions and participate in daily activities. Depression is also serious because it can sometimes lead to suicide. In a study by Withers and Kaplan (1987), over two-thirds of the participants reported symptoms of depression prior to a suicide attempt. The characteristics of depression that are related to suicide attempts in adults, however, are not the same as those that can lead to suicide in adolescents. Hopelessness is a strong indicator for suicide attempts in adults, but less so in adolescents. A sense of self-worth and capability for responding to stress relate more strongly to suicide attempts in adolescents than in adults (Cole, 1989). Tsuaie et al (as cited in Puskar et al., 2008) found that those who do not cope well with negative life events tend to react with anger more often and are also more likely to become depressed, or commit suicide. Some of the negative life events that frequently occur prior to a suicide attempt are disagreements with family, friends, significant others, and conflicts in the workplace (Withers & Kaplan, 1987).

Though it may be more obvious that depression and suicide are linked, studies have also found links between anger and suicide. After controlling for depression and substance abuse, in addition to previous suicide attempts, Daniel et al (2009), found that high trait anger scores and outward expression of anger were correlated with increased suicide attempts in males. For females, however, the suicide risk increased as trait anger scores and outward expression of anger scores decreased, but only if the study participants had a history of depression. Despite these gender differences in how anger can affect an individual's likelihood to experience depression and suicide, it is clear that anger affects both genders in a negative manner.

According to Kothari commission (1964-66) "Wastage and Stagnation" are the symptoms ailment due to which there is absence of proper relationship between life and attraction for children to be in School". Truancy is the exclusively professional concern of teachers for educational welfare. The range of people who could be involved in a treatment decision is very broad; they include teachers, parents, educational welfare officers, educational Psychologists, Social workers, magistrates, and psychiatrists. What type of action will be taken depends on a number of factors and the definition of the child's problem and largely depends on the profession in which he/she is involved.

Truancy may also results in juvenile delinquency. There are many types of delinquent acts; truancy is included under the act of "Tendency to escape". A truant student finds himself like a prisoner in jail. Everything at school seems mechanical. He runs from the situation i.e. truancy from school and running from home.

Some of the studies related to truancy are discussed below:

Ferguson in 1952 conducted a study on Glasgow-School leavers and produced the results that truants did more detected crimes than regular school attending students.

FranciesA.Muller (1958) tried to compare truancy with the classroom disorders. He states that unhappiness, unsuccessfulness is responsible for making a child, a truant, and physical conditions also affect the truancy rate. Home and community environment play an important role in the development of the child. He observes that truancy is the result of classroom disorders, home problems, such as grade retardation, reading disability and personality problems.

Chauhan N.S. (1978) did the comparative study of truants and non truants. Most of the characteristics of delinquency arise out of truancy. Truancy results in delinquency. The phenomenon of truancy appears to be grounded in none accepting to school as extensions of home.

Bahuguna B.D (1980) made a study of cause of irregular attendance in a few selected schools of Delhi. The investigator concludes that truancy is due to following causes: Poor Achievement, Poverty and in some cases early marriage and poor study atmosphere, Dislike for teacher and curriculum, Administrative Laxity.

Sharma T.R (1981) made a survey of the problem of truancy among high school students. He observed that truants are mostly boys and they are generally quite healthy. Main contributing factors are uneducated.

Father, illiterate mother, overcrowded houses, bad economic conditions, low intelligence, and bad company. Parmel Yadav (1988) did his investigation on finding all the causes of truancy of the students of reward. The main causes which strike most were: family cause, academic cause, economic cause, social cause, natural calamities defective teaching and miscellaneous cause. To reduce the truancy rate, Parents and teachers should be guided properly.

Mangal S.K. (1997) in the first Edition of his book "Our Life And Psychology" gave some factors which are responsible for truancy:-

- Weak physical health of child
- Undeveloped mental health of the child
- Non-cooperative behaviour of teachers
- Indiscipline prevalent in the school.
- Lack of interesting and co curricular activities
- Social and emotional maladjustment

The main report of sixth All India Educational Survey by N.C.E.R.T,(1999) shows that Per student expenditure in all types of schools (in Rs.) in Haryana is 893.19 While in Government schools per student expenditure (in Rs.) is 865.46.Truancy is one of the hindrance in proper utilization of this expenditure.

Hardre and Reeve (2003) find that a combination of three factors successfully predicted that 27% of the variation in attitude towards dropping out. One of those factors alone school performance predicts17% of the variation in drop out intentions

Mac Gillivary& Mann-Erickson, (2006) find that truant youth contribute significantly to the incidence of daytime crime. Data from National incidence reporting system indicate that the number of crimes committed by school hours exceed those after school.

M.V.R Raju and Digumarati Bhaskara Rao (2007) in their book "Behavioral problems of school children" states that, the influencing factors for these behavioral problems are socio economic background, television, cinema, and defective child rearing practices.

The global school based survey (2008) by SterSiziya,Adamen. S. Mulla & Emmoanuel Rudatsirikira finds that, Truancy was associated with lower school grade, having been victim of bullying, having gone hungry sometimes because of lack of food at home and less parental observation. They found that adolescent who reported parental supervision and support were less likely to be truant than those who lacked social support.

According to Talukdar &Talukdar (2008) many studies have been conducted on problems of adolescents and various factors influencing adolescent behavior. Conflict between parents, mother's low level of education, lack of support from parents, negligence by parents, adverse affect of television viewing giving rise to unfulfilled unrealistic demands, exposure to peers who smoke, drink or use drugs, their social status in modern society, etc. were some of the important factors found to be responsible for development of problem behavior in adolescents. Problem behaviors in adolescents give rise to symptoms such as frustration, obstinacy, aggressiveness, impulsiveness, violent behavior, antisocial behavior, etc. Faulty lifestyle is responsible for some behavioral problems in adolescents. It is essential to assess the problems of adolescents so that appropriate measures can be taken for proper management. It can contribute towards prevention of neurotic problems to some extent and help adolescents to develop their behavior for the greater benefit of the society.

There are certain problems that typically confront the adolescent and demand difficult answers of him. First is the need for achieving heterosexual compatibility- that is emotional, intellectual, and social compatibility free of distorting sexual overtones. A second problem confronting the adolescent is the acquisition of an ability to tolerate "aloneness". A third problem is how to use one's leisure time. A fourth problem that must be resolved by the adolescent before he can be considered mature is the acquisition of a relatively stable value system on which to base his behavior (Lambert et al., 1972).

The real problems of adolescence center on emotional, social, moral and economic problems. Most adolescents solve their problems by slow degrees during the ages from twelve to twenty one. The adolescent with severe conflicts and violent reactions is so much more dramatic than the boy or girl who develops slowly without fireworks overemphasized as the period of storm and stress (Cole, 1948)

According to Chaube (2002), it has been indicated earlier that with the onset of adolescence there come many physical and mental changes in the individual. These two types of changes are accompanied by many other changes in the individual who feels all these changes but he fails to understand the causes of the same. He does not understand why his voice has become heavy and hoarse. The innocent and bright look on his face is no more there. He shows keenness in reading various books and watching movies. He develops a desire to participate more in social activities. These new desires pose problems of adjustment in the new environment. If these problems are not solved, the adolescent is bound to develop inner conflicts. His mental peace is disturbed. The burden of solving this problems lie on the adolescent. Some of his problems are such that they are against the wishes of the parents. The adolescent also appears to defy the discipline which the guardian wants to impose on him. The problems of boys relate more to economic independence and information connected with the opposite sex. The problems of girls relate mostly to efforts for making their appearance more attractive. These problems make the problems of their adjustment in their environment more difficult.

Talukdar, N. N., & Talukdar, M.C. (2008). Adjustment Problem of Adolescent Students.(i). to find out the level of adjustment of male and female adolescent students in the areas namely home, health, social, emotional and educational. (ii). to identify the major factors responsible for adjustment problems in adolescents. The study was conducted on 200 adolescent students – 100 male and 100 female of class XI & XII, aged 16 – 19 years to assess their level of adjustment in the areas namely home, health, social, emotional and educational. Adjustment Inventory for College Students (AICS) developed by A.K.P. Sinha and R. P. Singh (1995) was used for the study. Overall adjustment of male students was found to be better than female students. Social adjustment was average in both the groups. The results also revealed unsatisfactory adjustment of female adolescents in different areas under study. Emotional adjustment of both the groups was unsatisfactory. Many factors identified in the study were thought to be responsible for adjustment problems in the adolescents like overprotection, lack of love and affection at home, lack of interest in studies, day dreaming, sleep disturbance, etc.

CONCLUSION

The survey of related literature has helped the investigator to have a clear perspective of the problem chosen for the present investigation. The review of the related literature has enabled the investigator to formulate relevant objectives and hypotheses for the present study. Further, based on the review of a suitable methodology and well planned procedure for the present investigation could be adopted and it is dealt in the succeeding chapter.

❐

8

Research Design and Methodology

In the modern society research has become an important activity for its very progress. Research produces new knowledge which takes the society forward. It enables to find solutions to problems and resolve conflicts in the society.

Research has been defined as, "A studious inquiry or Examination; especially critical and exhaustive investigation or experimental having for its aim the discovery of new facts and their correct interpretation, the revision of accepted conclusions, theories or laws in the light of newly discovered facts or partial applications of new revised conclusions, theories or laws" (Webster, 1981).

Develop new scientific tools, concepts and theories which would facilitate reliable and valid study of human behavior in decision making. (Aggarvan and Diwan, 1997).

The research process can be "Viewed as the overall scheme of scientific activities which the scientists engage in order to produce knowledge; it is a paradigm of scientific enquiry" (Frankfort – Nachimas & Nachmmias, 1992). Scientific activities satisfy the criteria of logical verification. The knowledge produced thus is provable both through reason experience or observation.

Research design in a catalogue of various phases and facts relating to the formulation of a research effort. It is an arrangement of the essential condition for collection and analysis of data in a term that aims to combine relevance to research purpose with economy in the procedure.

This chapter gives an overall picture of the design of the study, the form of hypotheses to be tested, research tools used for the collection of data, the reliability and validity of the tools, pilot study, nature and collection of the sample, a brief description of the procedure adopted for the data collection, scoring and statistical techniques to be employed for the analysis of the data.

HYPOTHESES OF THE STUDY

The following hypotheses have been set in the present study:

1. The levels of Learning Strategies along with its dimensions among Higher Secondary Students are average in nature.
2. The levels of youth problems in toto and all its dimensions among Higher Secondary Students are average in nature.
3. There is no significant difference in Learning Strategy among Higher Secondary Students with regard to
    - Gender (Male / Female)
    - Academic Stream (Arts / Science)
    - Medium of Instruction (English / Tamil)
    - Type of Family (Joint / Nuclear)
    - Birth Order (First Born / Middle Born / Last Born)
4. Parental Monthly Income (below Rs.10,000/between Rs10,000 and Rs25,000/above Rs.25,000)
5. There is no significant difference in Study Strategy – a dimension of Learning Strategy among Higher Secondary Students with regard to
    - Gender (Male / Female)
    - Academic Stream (Arts / Science)
    - Medium of Instruction (English / Tamil)
    - Type of Family (Joint / Nuclear)
    - Birth Order (First Born / Middle Born / Last Born)
6. Parental Monthly Income (below Rs.10, 000/between Rs10,000 and Rs25,000/above Rs.25,000)
7. There is no significant difference in Note-Taking/Listening – a dimension of Learning Strategy among Higher Secondary Students with regard to
    - Gender (Male / Female)
    - Academic Stream (Arts / Science)

- Medium of Instruction (English / Tamil)
- Type of Family (Joint / Nuclear)
- Birth Order (First Born / Middle Born / Last Born)
- Parental Monthly Income (below Rs.10,000/between Rs10,000 and Rs 25,000/above Rs.25,000)

8. There is no significant difference in Reading/Comprehension– a dimension of Learning Strategy among Higher Secondary Students with regard to
    - Gender (Male / Female)
    - Academic Stream (Arts / Science)
    - Medium of Instruction (English / Tamil)
    - Type of Family (Joint / Nuclear)
    - Birth Order (First Born / Middle Born / Last Born)
9. Parental Monthly Income (below Rs.10,000/between Rs10,000 and Rs25,000/above Rs.25,000)
10. There is no significant difference in Writing/Research Skills– a dimension of Learning Strategy among Higher Secondary Students with regard to
    - Gender (Male / Female)
    - Academic Stream (Arts / Science)
    - Medium of Instruction (English / Tamil)
    - Type of Family (Joint / Nuclear)
    - Birth Order (First Born / Middle Born / Last Born)
11. Parental Monthly Income (below Rs.10,000/between Rs10,000 and Rs25,000/above Rs.25,000)
12. There is no significant difference in Test-Taking Strategy – a dimension of Learning Strategy among Higher Secondary Students with regard to
    - Gender (Male / Female)
    - Academic Stream (Arts / Science)
    - Medium of Instruction (English / Tamil)
    - Type of Family (Joint / Nuclear)
    - Birth Order (First Born / Middle Born / Last Born)
13. Parental Monthly Income (below Rs.10, 000/between Rs10, 000 and Rs25,000/above Rs.25,000)
14. There is no significant difference in Organizational techniques – a dimension of Learning Strategy among Higher Secondary Students with regard to

- Gender (Male / Female)
- Academic Stream (Arts / Science)
- Medium of Instruction (English / Tamil)
- Type of Family (Joint / Nuclear)
- Birth Order (First Born / Middle Born / Last Born)

15. Parental Monthly Income (below Rs.10,000/between Rs10,000 and Rs25,000/above Rs.25,000)
16. There is no significant difference in Time Management – a dimension of Learning Strategy among Higher Secondary Students with regard to

    - Gender (Male / Female)
    - Academic Stream (Arts / Science)
    - Medium of Instruction (English / Tamil)
    - Type of Family (Joint / Nuclear)
    - Birth Order (First Born / Middle Born / Last Born)

17. Parental Monthly Income (below Rs.10,000/between Rs10,000 and Rs25,000/above Rs.25,000)
18. There is no significant difference in Youth Problems among Higher Secondary Students with regard to

    - Gender (Male / Female)
    - Academic Stream (Arts / Science)
    - Medium of Instruction (English / Tamil)
    - Type of Family (Joint / Nuclear)
    - Birth Order (First Born / Middle Born / Last Born)

19. Parental Monthly Income (below Rs.10,000/between Rs10,000 and Rs25,000/above Rs.25,000)
20. There is no significant difference in Personal Problems and Over Sensitivity – a dimension of Youth Problem among Higher Secondary Students with regard to

    - Gender (Male / Female)
    - Academic Stream (Arts / Science)
    - Medium of Instruction (English / Tamil)
    - Type of Family (Joint / Nuclear)
    - Birth Order (First Born / Middle Born / Last Born)

21. Parental Monthly Income (below Rs.10,000/between Rs10,000 and Rs25,000/above Rs.25,000)
22. There is no significant difference in Family issues – a dimension of Youth Problem among Higher Secondary Students with regard to

- Gender (Male / Female)
- Academic Stream (Arts / Science)
- Medium of Instruction (English / Tamil)
- Type of Family (Joint / Nuclear)
- Birth Order (First Born / Middle Born / Last Born)

23. Parental Monthly Income (below Rs.10,000/between Rs10,000 and Rs25,000/above Rs.25,000)
24. There is no significant difference in School issues – a dimension of Youth Problem among Higher Secondary Students with regard to
    - Gender (Male / Female)
    - Academic Stream (Arts / Science)
    - Medium of Instruction (English / Tamil)
    - Type of Family (Joint / Nuclear)
    - Birth Order (First Born / Middle Born / Last Born)
25. Parental Monthly Income (below Rs.10,000/between Rs10,000 and Rs25,000/above Rs.25,000)
26. There is no significant difference in Social Issues – a dimension of Youth Problem among Higher Secondary Students with regard to
    - Gender (Male / Female)
    - Academic Stream (Arts / Science)
    - Medium of Instruction (English / Tamil)
    - Type of Family (Joint / Nuclear)
    - Birth Order (First Born / Middle Born / Last Born)
27. Parental Monthly Income (below Rs.10,000/between Rs10,000 and Rs25,000/above Rs.25,000)
28. There is no significant correlation between Learning Strategies along with its dimensions and youth problems along with its dimensions.

METHOD OF STUDY

As the study intends to collect data pertaining to Learning strategy and Youth problems. The normative method is employed to describe and interpret what exist at present. It involves some type of comparison or contrast and attempts to discover relationship between the existing non-manipulated variables.

TOOLS USED IN THE STUDY

To collect the pertinent data for the present investigation, standardized tools have been employed to quantify the variables involved in the study.

The investigator has used the following tools for the data collection.

TABLE.8.1: Showing the Details of the Tools used in the Present Study

S.No	Research Tools	Author
1.	Learning Strategy Inventory(2000)	Kathy Stroud & Cecil Reynolds
2.	Youth Problem Inventory(2004)	Dr. (Mrs.) M. Verma

DESCRIPTION, ADMINISTRATION AND SCORING PROCEDURE OF THE TOOLS USED IN THE PRESENT STUDY

Learning Strategy Inventory

Description

The Learning Strategy Inventory (APPENDIX-A)was constructed by KATHY STROUD, and CECIL REYNOLDS (2000), was used. It consists of 7 dimensions and 52 questions. The dimensions are Study Strategy, Note-Taking / Listening, Reading / Comprehension, Writing / Research Skills, Test –Taking Strategy, Organizational Technique and Time Management. There are no negative questions. Four point scale is used. They are Never true, sometimes true, often true and almost always true.

TABLE.8.2: Showing the Items Pertaining to Different Dimensions of Learning Strategy

Name of the tool	Total number of items	Dimensions	Total no: of items dimension wise
SMALSI	52	Study Strategy	9 items (1-9)
		Note-Taking / Listening	8 items (10-17)
		Reading / Comprehension	5 Items (18–22)
		Writing / Research Skills	6 items (23-28)
		Test –Taking Strategy	6 items (29-34)
		Organizational Technique	11 items (35-45)
		Time Management	7 items (46-52)

Administration

Before the administration of the test, the following instructions were given to the students. "Each of the following has four alternatives. Choose one of the alternatives you consider the best. Mark your answer in the form of a tick (√) only on the place provided against each statement. Give your response without fear and answer all the questions. Your responses would be kept confidential and used only for research purposes".

Scoring

In the learning strategy inventory, the responses almost always true (AAT) was awarded 3 points; often true (OT) was awarded 2 points; sometimes true (ST) was awarded 1 point; never true (NT) was awarded 0 point. The maximum score possible was 156 and the minimum score was zero. The sum of points for all the statements was considered as the total score.

Youth Problem Inventory

DESCRIPTION

The Youth Problem Inventory (APPENDIX-B) was constructed and standardized by Dr. (Mrs.) M. Varma (2004) and it provides four separate problems that are faced by adolescence students. The Youth Problem Inventory consists of 80 questions. There are no negative questions. Three point scales namely true, partially true and false are used.

TABLE.8.3: Showing the Items Pertaining to Different Dimensions of Youth Problems

Name of the tool	Total no: of items	Dimensions	Total no: of items dimension wise
Youth Problem Inventory	80	Area A – Family problems	31 statements
		Area B – School problems	20 statements
		Area C – Social problems	5 statements
		Area D – Personal problems and Over sensitivity	24 statements

ADMINISTRATION

Necessary instructions were given to the subjects before administering the inventory. The subjects were asked to read each statement carefully and record their responses by putting a (√) mark to the appropriate responses. The subjects were asked to answer all the statements, without omitting any. Responses were obtained in the booklet itself. There is no time limit; but they were asked to complete as early as possible.

SCORING

The respondents were provided with three alternatives true, partially true and false. The score 2, 1and 0 were given to each responses true, partially true and false respectively. Low scores reserve to less problematic students and high scores indicate problematic students.

PILOT STUDY

Before finalizing the final form of the tools and collection of data for the main study, a pilot study was done in October 2014. It was conducted among 50 students to establish reliability and validity of the tools used in the study.

ESTABLISHING RELIABILITY

The reliability of a test may be defined as the degree of consistency with which the test measures what it measures.

Learning Strategy Inventory

To compute the reliability of learning strategy inventory, Split half method was employed. The reliability was computed and it was found to be 0.89, using Spearman Brown formula, indicating the tool to be highly reliable.

Youth Problem Inventory

To compute the reliability of youth problem inventory, odd even method was employed, the reliability was computed and found to be 0.81, using the Spearman Brown formula, indicating the tool to be highly reliable.

ESTABLISHING VALIDITY

Validity is concerned with the integrity of the conclusions that are generated from a piece of research. The index of reliability is sometimes taken as a measure of validity.

Learning Strategy Inventory

The validity of learning strategy inventory was found out by computing the square root of the reliability co-efficient which worked out to be 0.94, indicating that the tool is highly valid.

Youth Problem Inventory

The validity of youth problem inventory was found out by computing the square root of the reliability coefficient which worked out to be 0.90. It shows that the validity of the youth problem inventory is high.

MAIN STUDY

The invigilator had adopted Survey Method in the present study in Nivember 2014. The invigilator has designed the above mentioned tools to measure the Learning strategy and Youth problems of the adolescence students. In order to administer the tools, the investigator got permission from the Heads of the institutions well in advance and approached the teachers with clear instructions to get along with the tools. The list of schools where the invigilator administered the tools is given below.

TABLE.8.3: Showing the Details of the Composition of the Sample in the Present Study

Type of Schools	Name of the Schools	Boys	Girls	Total
Government	Government Higher Secondary School Perungulathur, Chennai-600 063	27	23	50
	Government Higher. Secondary School Perungulathur, Chennai-600 063	25	27	52
Government Aided	Kamaraj Higher Secondary School Ayanavaram, Chennai-600 023	23	27	50
	W.P.A Higher Secondary School Ayanavaram, Chennai-600 023	35	15	50
Private	M.C.C Metric Higher Secondary School Chetpet, Chennai-600 031	30	20	50
	C.S.I Bain Metric Higher Secondary School Kilpauk, Chennai-600 010	0	50	50
Total		**140**	**162**	**302**

STATISTICAL TECHNIQUES USED

The following statistical techniques were used in the present study

i. Mean

$$\text{Mean}(\bar{X}) = A + \frac{\sum fd}{\sum f} \times i$$

Where,

A = Assumed mean

f = frequency

d = deviation from the assumed mean

i = Class interval

ii. Standard Deviation

$$\text{Standard Deviation, } SD(\sigma) = \sqrt{\frac{\sum fd^2}{N} - \left[\frac{\sum fd}{N}\right]^2} \, xi$$

Where,

f = Frequency

d = Deviation from the assumed mean

I = Class interval

N = Total frequency

iii. 't' TEST

To check the significance of difference between means of various measures, 't' test is used: 't' ratio is calculated from the relation.

$$\text{t-ratio} = \frac{M_1 \sim M_2}{\sqrt{\frac{\sigma_1^2}{N_1} + \frac{\sigma_1^2}{N_2}}} = \frac{M_1 \sim M_2}{S \in D}$$

Where,

= Means of the groups

SED = Standard Error Deviation

iv. F-TEST

F- Ratio = Variance between the group / Variance within the group Correlation term

$$C = \frac{\sum r_1 + \sum r_3 + \sum x_3}{N}$$

$$BSS = (\Sigma x_1)^2 / W_1 + (\Sigma x_2)^2 / W_2 + (\Sigma x^3)^2 / W_3 - c$$

$$TSS = \sum x_1^2 + \sum x_2^2 + \sum x_3^2 + C$$

WSS = TSS - BSS

Where,

x_1, x_2, x_3, score in different group

C = correction Term

TSS = Total Sum of Squares

BSS = Between Sum of Squares

WSS = Within Sum of Squares

v. Coefficient of Correlation (r)

$$r = \frac{n\left(\sum xy\right) - \left(\sum x\right)\sum y}{\sqrt{\left[n\sum x^2 - \left(\sum x\right)^2\right]\left[n\sum y^2 - \left(\sum y\right)^2\right]}}$$

x, y – Variables,
N- Total strength.

CONLUSION

Adopting the methods and the procedures discussed earlier in this chapter, tests were administered and scored. This chapter outlined the design of the study, the procedure followed and the nature of the sample. It described the hypotheses to be tested, selection of tools, and the method of administration and scoring procedures. The obtained data were then analyzed, using appropriate statistical techniques. The next chapter presents the analysis and interpretation of the data collected in the light of the hypotheses formulated.

❐

9

Statistical Analysis and Interpretation of Data

Research consists of systematic observation and description of the characteristic of properties for the purpose of discovering relationship, starting with the description of the measures of the variables and goes on to the higher levels of statistical analysis. The data collected is carefully edited, systematically classified and tabulated, scientifically analyzed and interpreted and rationally concluded.

Thus, in the present study, the data collected with regard to the Learning Strategy and Youth Problem of Higher Secondary School students in Chennai were analyzed with reference to the objectives and hypotheses of the study. The data have been subjected to the following statistical analysis namely percentile, descriptive, differential and correlation. The results of statistical analysis have been summarized and tabulated.

CATEGORISATION OF THE SAMPLE BASED ON THE VARIABLES OF THE STUDY

Categories of the sample based on learning strategies along with its dimensions

The sample has been classified on the basis of Learning Strategies along with its dimensions of Higher secondary Students into three categories (low, medium and high), as indicated in the following table.

TABLE.9.1: Showing the levels of Learning Strategies along with its Dimensions

Sl.No	Learning Strategies and its Dimensions	Categories	Range	Frequency	Percentage
1.	Study Strategy	Low	0-11	59	19.5
		Moderate	12-18	163	54.0
		High	19-high	80	26.5
2.	Note-taking/ Listening	Low	0-9	77	25.5
		Moderate	10-16	141	46.7
		High	17-high	84	27.8
3.	Reading/ Comprehension	Low	0-7	100	33.1
		Moderate	8-14	190	62.9
		High	15-high	12	4.0
4.	Writing/ Research Skill	Low	0-8	115	38.1
		Moderate	9-16	184	60.9
		High	17-high	3	1.0
5.	Test-taking Strategy	Low	0-9	32	10.6
		Moderate	10-18	156	51.7
		High	19-high	114	37.7
6.	Organizational Technique	Low	0-10	39	12.9
		Moderate	11-20	184	60.9
		High	20-high	79	26.2
7.	Time Management	Low	0-6	53	17.5
		Moderate	7-12	160	53.0
		High	13-high	89	29.5
8	Learning strategies in toto	Low	0-65	48	15.9
		Moderate	66-102	159	52.6
		High	103-139	95	31.5

INFERENCE

From the table it is clear that the levels of Learning Strategies and its dimensions among Higher Secondary students are moderate in nature.

Hence hypothesis I stating that "The levels of Learning Strategies along with its dimensions among Higher Secondary Students are average in nature" is accepted.

Categories of the sample based on youth problems along with its dimensions

The sample has been classified on the basis of Youth Problem along with its dimensions of higher secondary students into three categories (low, medium and high), as indicated in the following table.

TABLE.9.2: Showing the levels of Youth Problem along with its Dimensions

Sl.No	Youth Problem and its Dimensions	Categories	Range	Frequency	Percentage
1.	Personal Problem and Oversensitivity	Low	0-16	183	60.6
		Moderate	17-32	108	35.8
		High	33-high	11	3.6
2.	Family Issues	Low	0-21	188	62.3
		Moderate	22-42	104	34.4
		High	43-high	10	3.3
3.	School Issues	Low	0-13	198	65.6
		Moderate	14-26	94	31.1
		High	27-high	10	3.3
4.	Social Issues	Low	0-3	204	67.5
		Moderate	4-6	81	26.8
		High	7-high	17	5.6
5.	Total	Low	0-47	160	53
		Moderate	48-92	130	43
		High	93-136	12	4

INFERENCE

From the table it is clear that the levels of Youth Problem and its dimensions among Higher Secondary students are low in nature.

Hence hypothesis II stating that "The levels of youth problems in toto and all its dimensions among Higher Secondary Students are average in nature" is rejected.

(a) Influence of Gender on Learning Strategy Among Higher Secondary Students

The scores related to learning strategy of Male and Female Higher Secondary Students have been computed and details are furnished in the following table.

TABLE.9.3: Showing the Significant Difference between the mean Scores of learning Strategy among Higher Secondary Students with Respect to Gender

Variable	Gender	No of cases	Mean	S.D	Critical Ratio	L.S
Learning Strategy	Males	137	83.2628	21.237	5.13	0.01
	Females	165	96.0727	22.052		

INFERENCE

From the table, it is clear that the obtained C.R value (5.13) is higher than the table value (2.58) at 0.01 level. Therefore there is significant difference between the mean scores of Learning strategy among Higher Secondary Students with respect to Gender.

It is also noted that the female students have significantly higher Learning Strategy than their counterparts.

Hence the hypothesis – III (a) stating that "There is no significant difference between the mean scores of Learning Strategy among Higher Secondary students with respect to Gender" is rejected.

(b) Influence of Academic Streams on Learning Strategy

The scores related to learning strategy of Arts and Science streams among Higher Secondary Students have been computed and details are furnished in the following table.

TABLE 904: Showing the Significant Difference between the mean Scores of Learning Strategy with Respect to their Academic Stream

Variable	Academic Stream	No: of cases	Mean	S.D	Critical Ratio	L.S
Learning Strategy	Arts	151	88.2252	22.556	1.57	N.S
	Science	151	92.2980	22.480		

INFERENCE

From the table, it is clear that the obtained C.R value (1.57) is lower than the table value (1.96) at 0.05 level. Therefore there is no significant difference between the mean scores of learning strategy with respect to Academic Stream among Higher Secondary Students.

Hence the hypothesis – III (b) stating that "There is no significant difference between the mean scores of Learning strategy among Higher Secondary students with respect to Academic Stream" is accepted.

(c) Influence of Medium of Instruction on Learning Strategy

The scores related to Learning strategy of English and Tamil medium Higher Secondary Students have been computed and details are furnished in the following table.

TABLE.9.5: Showing the Significant Difference between the mean Scores of Learning Strategy with Respect to Medium of Instruction

Variable	Medium of Instruction	No of cases	Mean	S.D	Critical Ratio	L.S
Learning strategy	English	210	85.6524	21.382	5.59	0.01
	Tamil	92	100.7826	21.780		

INFERENCE

From the table, it is clear that the obtained C.R value (5.59) is higher than the table value (2.58) at 0.01 level. Therefore there is significant difference between the mean scores of learning strategy with respect to Medium of Instruction.

It is also noted that the Tamil medium students have significantly higher Learning Strategy than their counterparts.

Hence the hypothesis – III (c) stating that "There is no significant difference between the mean scores of learning strategy among Higher Secondary students with respect to Medium of Instruction" is rejected.

(d) Influence of Type of Family on Learning Strategy

The scores related to Learning Strategy of students hailing from joint and nuclear families have been computed and details are furnished in the following table.

TABLE.9.6: Showing the Significant Difference between the mean Scores of Learning strategy with Respect to Type of Family

Variable	Type of family	No of cases	Mean	S.D	Critical Ratio	L.S
Learning Strategy	Joint	86	87.8837	24.477	1.10	N.S
	Nuclear	216	91.2083	21.756		

INFERENCE

From the table, it is clear that the obtained C.R value (1.10) is lower than the table value (1.96) at 0.05 level. Therefore there is no significant difference between the mean scores of learning strategy with respect to Type of family.

Hence the hypothesis – III (d) stating that "There is no significant difference between the mean scores of Learning strategy among Higher Secondary students with respect to Type of Family" is accepted.

(e) Influence of Birth Order on Learning Strategy

The scores related to Learning strategy among Higher Secondary Students with respect to Birth Order (first born/ middle born/ last born) have been computed and details are furnished in the following table.

TABLE.9.7: ANOVA showing the Significant Difference between the mean Scores of Learning Strategy with Respect to Birth Order

Variable		df	Sum of Squares	Mean Squares	F Ratio	L.S
Learning Strategy	Between Groups	2	222.3486	111.1743	.2171	**N.S**
	Within Groups	299	153145.9859	512.1939		
	Total	301	153368.3344			

INFERENCE

From the table, it is clear that the obtained 'F' value (.2171) is lower than the table value (3.03) at 0.05 level. Therefore there is no significant difference between the mean scores of learning strategy with respect to Birth Order.

Hence the hypothesis – III (e) stating that "There is no significant difference between the mean scores of Learning strategy among Higher Secondary students with respect to Birth Order" is accepted.

(f) Influence of Parental Monthly Income on Learning Strategy

The scores related to learning strategy among Higher Secondary Students with respect to Parental Monthly Income (below Rs.10,000/ between Rs.10,000 and Rs.25,000 / above Rs.25,000) have been computed and details are furnished in the following table.

TABLE.9.8: ANOVA Showing the Significant Difference between the mean Scores of Learning Strategy with Respect to Parental Monthly Income

Variable		df	Sum of Squares	Mean Squares	F Ratio	L.S
Learning Strategy	Between Groups	2	18032.5258	9016.2629	19.9198	0.01
	Within Groups	299	135335.8086	452.6281		
	Total	301	153368.3344			

INFERENCE

From the table, it is clear that the obtained 'F' value (19.9198) is higher than the table value (4.68) at 0.01 level. Therefore there is significant difference between the mean scores of learning strategy with respect to Parental Monthly Income.

So, further analysis has been done to find the significant difference between the groups.

TABLE.9.9: Showing the Multiple Comparisons of the mean Scores of Learning Strategy with Respect to Parental Monthly Income

Variable	Parental Monthly Income	N	Mean	S.D	Critical Ratio	L.S
Learning Strategy	Below Rs.10,000 Vs	142	97.9014	22.325	3.74	0.01
	Between Rs.10,000 and Rs.25,000	90	86.8889	21.591		
	Below Rs.10,000 Vs	142	97.9014	22.325	6.49	0.01
	Above Rs.25,000	70	79.1000	18.482		
	Between Rs.10,000 and Rs.25,000 Vs	90	86.8889	21.591	2.77	0.01
	above Rs.25,000	70	79.1000	18.482		

INFERENCE

In the First case from the table, it is clear that the obtained C.R value (3.74) is higher than the table value (2.58) at 0.01 level. Therefore there is significant difference between the mean scores of learning strategy among students whose Parental Monthly Income is Below Rs.10, 000 and whose Parental Monthly Income is between Rs.10, 000 and Rs.25, 000.

In the Second case from the table, it is clear that the obtained C.R value (6.49) is higher than the table value (2.58) at 0.01 level. Therefore there is significant difference between the mean scores of learning strategy among students whose Parental Monthly Income is Below Rs.10, 000 and whose Parental Monthly Income is Above Rs.25, 000.

In the Third case from the table, it is clear that the obtained C.R value (2.77) is higher than the table value (2.58) at 0.01 level. Therefore there is significant difference between the mean scores of Learning strategy among students whose Parental Monthly Income is Between Rs.10, 000 and Rs.25,000 and whose Parental Monthly Income is Above Rs.25,000.

Moreover students whose parental income is below Rs.10,000 have shown significantly higher learning strategy than the other two groups.

Hence the hypothesis – III (f) stating that "There is no significant difference between the mean scores of Learning strategy among Higher Secondary students with respect to Parental Monthly Income" is rejected.

(a) Influence of Gender on Study Strategy-A Dimension of Learning Strategy

The scores related to Study Strategy – a dimension of learning strategy of Male and Female Higher Secondary Students have been computed and details are furnished in the following table.

TABLE.9.10: Showing the Significant Difference between the mean Scores of Study Strategy – a Dimension of learning Strategy with Respect to Gender

Variable	Gender	No of cases	Mean	S.D	Critical Ratio	L.S
Study Strategy	Males	137	14.1314	4.372	3.92	0.01
	Females	165	16.0727	4.042		

INFERENCE

From the table, it is clear that the obtained C.R value (3.92) is higher than the table value (2.58) at 0.01 level. Therefore there is significant difference between the mean scores of Study Strategy – a dimension of learning strategy with respect to Gender. It is also noted that the female students have significantly higher study strategy than their counterparts.

Hence the hypothesis – IV (a) stating that "There is no significant difference between the mean scores of Study Strategy – a dimension of learning strategy among Higher Secondary students with respect to Gender" is rejected.

(b) Influence of Academic Streams on Study Strategy-A Dimension of Learning Strategy

The scores related to Study Strategy – a dimension of learning strategy of Arts and Science streams among Higher Secondary Students have been computed and details are furnished in the following table.

TABLE.9.11: Showing the Significant Difference between the mean Scores of Study Strategy – a Dimension of learning Strategy with Respect to Academic Stream

Variable	Academic Stream	No of cases	Mean	S.D	Critical Ratio	L.S
Study Strategy	Arts	151	14.9669	4.312	0.91	N.S
	Science	151	15.4172	4.287		

INFERENCE

From the table, it is clear that the obtained C.R value (0.91) is lower than the table value (1.96) at 0.05 level. Therefore there is no significant difference between the mean scores of Study Strategy – a dimension of learning strategy with respect to Academic Stream.

Hence the hypothesis – IV (b) stating that "There is no significant difference between the mean scores of Study Strategy – a dimension of learning strategy among Higher Secondary students with respect to Academic Stream" is accepted.

(c) Influence of Medium of Instruction on Study Strategy- A Dimension of Learning Strategy

The scores related to Study Strategy – a dimension of learning strategy of English and Tamil medium Higher Secondary Students have been computed and details are furnished in the following table.

TABLE.9.12: Showing the Significant Difference between the mean Scores of Study Strategy – a Dimension of Learning Strategy with Respect to Medium of Instruction

Variable	Medium of Instruction	No of cases	Mean	S.D	Critical Ratio	L.S
Study Strategy	English	210	14.5095	4.084	4.17	0.01
	Tamil	92	16.7500	4.389		

INFERENCE

From the table, it is clear that the obtained C.R value (4.17) is higher than the table value (2.58) at 0.01 level. Therefore there is significant difference between the mean scores of Study Strategy – a dimension of learning strategy with respect to Medium of Instruction.

It is also noted that the Tamil medium students have significantly higher study strategy than their counterparts.

Hence the hypothesis – IV (c) stating that "There is no significant difference between the mean scores of Study Strategy – a dimension of learning strategy among Higher Secondary students with respect to Medium of Instruction" is rejected.

(d) Influecne of Type of Family on Study Strategy-A Dimension of Learning Strategy

The scores related to Study Strategy – a dimension of learning strategy of students hailing from joint and nuclear families have been computed and details are furnished in the following table.

TABLE.9.13: Showing the Significant Difference between the mean Scores of Study Strategy – a Dimension of learning Strategy with Respect to Type of Family

Variable	Type of family	No of cases	Mean	S.D	Critical Ratio	L.S
Study Strategy	Joint	86	14.3488	4.500	2.10	0.05
	Nuclear	216	15.5278	4.178		

INFERENCE

From the table, it is clear that the obtained C.R value (2.10) is higher than the table value (1.96) at 0.05 level. Therefore there is significant difference between the mean scores of Study Strategy – a dimension of learning strategy with respect to Type of family. It is also noted that the students from Nuclear family have significantly higher study strategy than their counterparts.

Hence the hypothesis – IV (d) stating that "There is no significant difference between the mean scores of Study Strategy – a dimension of learning strategy among Higher Secondary students with respect to Type of Family" is rejected.

(e) Influence of Birth Order on Study Strategy-A Dimension of Learning Strategy

The scores related to Study Strategy – a dimension of learning strategy among Higher Secondary Students with respect to Birth Order (first born/ middle born/ last born) have been computed and details are furnished in the following table.

TABLE.9.14: ANOVA Showing the Significant Difference between the mean Scores of Study Strategy – a Dimension of learning Strategy with Respect to Birth Order

Variable		df	Sum of Squares	Mean Squares	F Ratio	L.S
Study Strategy	Between Groups	2	16.2292	8.1146	.4376	N.S
	Within Groups	299	5544.6317	18.5439		
	Total	301	5560.8609			

INFERENCE

From the table, it is clear that the obtained 'F' value (.4376) is lower than the table value (3.03) at 0.05 level. Therefore there is no significant difference between the mean scores of Study Strategy – a dimension of learning strategy with respect to Birth Order.

Hence the hypothesis – IV (e) stating that "There is no significant difference between the mean scores of Study Strategy – a dimension of learning strategy among Higher Secondary students with respect to Birth Order" is accepted.

(f) Influence of Parental Monthly Income on Study Strategy- A Dimension of Learning Strategy

The scores related to Study Strategy – a dimension of learning strategy among Higher Secondary Students with respect to Parental Monthly Income (below Rs.10,000/ between Rs.10,000 and Rs.25,000 / above Rs.25,000) have been computed and details are furnished in the following table.

TABLE.9.15: ANOVA Showing the Significant Difference between the mean Scores of Study Strategy – a Dimension of learning Strategy with Respect to Parental Monthly Income

Variable		df	Sum of Squares	Mean Squares	F Ratio	L.S
Study Strategy	Between Groups	2	476.5612	28.2860	14.0129	0.01
	Within Groups	299	5084.2998	17.0043		
	Total	301	5560.8609			

INFERENCE

From the table, it is clear that the obtained 'F' value (14.0129) is higher than the table value (4.68) at 0.01 level. Therefore there is significant difference between the mean scores of Study Strategy – a dimension of learning strategy with respect to Parental Monthly Income. So, further analysis has been done to find the significant difference between the groups.

TABLE.9.16: Showing the Multiple Comparisons of the mean Scores of Study Strategy – a Dimension of learning Strategy with Respect to Parental Monthly Income

Variable	Parental Monthly Income	N	Mean	S.D	Critical Ratio	L.S
Study Strategy	Below Rs.10,000 Vs Between Rs.10,000 and Rs.25,000	142	16.3169	4.141	2.33	0.05
		90	15.0111	3.987		
	Below Rs.10,000 Vs Above Rs.25,000	142	16.3169	4.414	5.54	0.01
		70	13.1429	3.657		
	Between Rs.10,000 and Rs.25,000 Vs above Rs.25,000	90	15.0111	3.987	3.09	0.01
		70	13.1429	3.657		

INFERENCE

In the First case, from the table, it is clear that the obtained C.R value (2.33) is higher than the table value (1.96) at 0.05 level. Therefore there is significant difference between the mean scores of Study Strategy – a dimension of learning strategy among students whose Parental Monthly Income is Below Rs.10, 000 and whose Parental Monthly Income is Between Rs.10, 000 and Rs.25, 000.

In the Second case from the table, it is clear that the obtained C.R value (5.54) is higher than the table value (2.58) at 0.01 level. Therefore there is significant difference between the mean scores of Study Strategy – a dimension of learning strategy among students whose Parental Monthly Income is Below Rs.10, 000 and whose Parental Monthly Income is Above Rs.25, 000.

In the Third case from the table, it is clear that the obtained C.R value (3.09) is higher than the table value (2.58) at 0.01 level. Therefore there is significant difference between the mean scores of Study Strategy – a dimension of learning strategy among students whose Parental Monthly Income is Between Rs.10, 000 and Rs.25,000 and whose Parental Monthly Income is Above Rs.25,000.

Moreover it is also noted that students whose parental monthly income is below Rs10,000 have exhibited significantly higher study strategy than the other two groups.

Hence the hypothesis – IV (f) stating that "There is no significant difference between the mean scores of Study Strategy – a dimension of learning strategy among Higher Secondary students with respect to Parental Monthly Income" is rejected.

(a) Influence of Gender on Note-Taking/Listening- A Dimension of Learning Strategy

The scores related to Note-taking/Listening – a dimension of learning strategy of Male and Female Higher Secondary Students have been computed and details are furnished in the following table.

TABLE.9.17: Showing the Significant Difference between the mean Scores of Note-Taking/ Listening – a Dimension of learning Strategy with Respect to Gender

Variable	Gender	No of cases	Mean	S.D	Critical Ratio	L.S
Note-taking/ listening	Males	137	11.8686	4.597	3.96	0.01
	Females	165	14.0424	4.922		

INFERENCE

From the table, it is clear that the obtained C.R value (3.96) is higher than the table value (2.58) at 0.01 level. Therefore there is significant difference between the mean scores of Note-taking/ Listening – a dimension of learning strategy with respect to Gender.

It is also noted that the female students have significantly higher Note-taking/Listening strategy than their counterparts.

Hence the hypothesis – V (a) stating that "There is no significant difference between the mean scores of Note-taking/Listening – a dimension of learning strategy among Higher Secondary students with respect to Gender" is rejected.

(b) Influence of Academic Streams on Note-Taking/Listening-A Dimension of Learning Strategy

The scores related to Note-taking / Listening – a dimension of learning strategy of Arts and Science streams among Higher Secondary Students have been computed and details are furnished in the following table.

TABLE.9.18: Showing the Significant Difference between the mean Scores of Note-Taking / Listening – a Dimension of learning Strategy with Respect to Academic Stream

Variable	Academic Stream	No of cases	Mean	S.D	Critical Ratio	L.S
Note-taking/ Listening	Arts	151	13.0000	4.817	0.20	N.S
	Science	151	13.1126	4.979		

INFERENCE

From the table, it is clear that the obtained C.R value (0.20) is lower than the table value (1.96) at 0.05 level. Therefore there is no significant difference between the mean scores of Note-taking/listening – a dimension of learning strategy with respect to Academic Stream.

Hence the hypothesis – V (b) stating that "There is no significant difference between the mean scores of Note-taking/ Listening – a dimension of learning strategy among Higher Secondary students with respect to Academic Stream" is accepted.

(c) Influence of Medium of Instruction on Note-taking/Listening-A Dimension of Learning Strategy

The scores related to Note-taking/Listening – a dimension of learning strategy of English and Tamil medium Higher Secondary Students have been computed and details are furnished in the following table.

TABLE .9.19: Showing the Significant Difference between the mean Scores of Note-Taking / Listening – a Dimension of learning Strategy with Respect to Medium of Instruction

Variable	Medium of Instruction	No of cases	Mean	S.D	Critical Ratio	L.S
Note-taking/ Listening	English	210	11.9048	4.461	6.40	0.01
	Tamil	92	15.6848	4.833		

INFERENCE

From the table, it is clear that the obtained C.R value (6.40) is higher than the table value (2.58) at 0.01 level. Therefore there is significant difference between the mean scores of Note-taking/Listening – a dimension of learning strategy with respect to Medium of Instruction. It is also noted that the Tamil medium students have significantly higher Note-taking/ Listening than their counterparts.

Hence the hypothesis – V (c) stating that "There is no significant difference between the mean scores of Note-Taking/Listening – a dimension of learning strategy among Higher Secondary students with respect to Medium of Instruction" is rejected.

(d) Influence of Type of Family on Note-Taking/Listening- A Dimension of Learning Strategy

The scores related to Note-taking/listening – a dimension of learning strategy of students hailing from joint and nuclear families have been computed and details are furnished in the following table.

TABLE.9.20: Showing the Significant Difference between the mean Scores of Note-Taking/ Listening – a Dimension of learning Strategy with Respect to Type of Family

Variable	Type of family	No of cases	Mean	S.D	Critical Ratio	L.S
Note-taking/ listening	Joint	86	13.2442	5.430	0.39	N.S
	Nuclear	216	12.9815	4.671		

INFERENCE

From the table, it is clear that the obtained C.R value (0.39) is lower than the table value (1.96) at 0.05 level. Therefore there is no significant difference between the mean scores of Note-taking/ listening – a dimension of learning strategy with respect to Type of family.

Hence the hypothesis – V (d) stating that "There is no significant difference between the mean scores of Note-taking/ listening – a dimension of learning strategy among Higher Secondary students with respect to Type of Family" is accepted.

(e) Influence of Birth Order

INFLUENCE OF BIRTH ORDER ON NOTE-TAKING/LISTENING-A DIMENSION OF LEARNING STRATEGY

The scores related to Note-taking/Listening – a dimension of learning strategy among Higher Secondary Students with respect to Birth Order (first born/ middle born/ last born) have been computed and details are furnished in the following table.

TABLE 9.21: ANOVA Showing the Significant Difference between the mean Scores of Note-Taking/Listening – a Dimension of learning Strategy with Respect to Birth Order

Variable		df	Sum of Squares	Mean Squares	F Ratio	L.S
Note-taking/ Listening	Between Groups	2	5.7131	2.8565	.1187	N.S
	Within Groups	299	7194.3300	24.0613		
	Total	301	7200.0430			

INFERENCE

From the table, it is clear that the obtained 'F' value (.1187) is lower than the table value (3.03) at 0.05 level. Therefore there is no significant difference between the mean scores of Note-taking/Listening – a dimension of learning strategy with respect to Birth Order.

Hence the hypothesis – V (e) stating that "There is no significant difference between the mean scores of Note-taking/listening – a dimension of learning strategy among Higher Secondary students with respect to Birth Order" is accepted.

(f) Influence of Parental Monthly Income on Note-Taking/Listening-A Dimension of Learning Strategy

The scores related to Note-taking/Listening – a dimension of learning strategy among Higher Secondary Students with respect to Parental Monthly Income (below Rs.10,000/ between Rs.10,000and Rs.25,000 / above Rs.25,000) have been computed and details are furnished in the following table.

TABLE.9.22: ANOVA Showing the Significant Difference between the mean Scores of Note-Taking/Listening – a Dimension of learning Strategy with Respect to Parental Monthly Income

Variable		df	Sum of Squares	Mean Squares	F Ratio	L.S
Note-taking/ Listening	Between Groups	2	935.7068	467.8534	22.3309	0.01
	Within Groups	299	6264.3362	20.9510		
	Total	301	7200.0430			

INFERENCE

From the table, it is clear that the obtained 'F' value (22.3390) is higher than the table value (4.68) at 0.01 level. Therefore there is significant difference between the mean scores of Note-taking/Listening – a dimension of learning strategy with respect to Parental Monthly Income. So, further analysis has been done to find the significant difference between the groups.

TABLE .9.23: Showing the Multiple Comparisons of the mean Scores of Note-Taking/Listening – a Dimension of learning Strategy with Respect to Parental Monthly Income

Variable	Parental Monthly Income	N	Mean	S.D	Critical Ratio	L.S
Note-taking/ Listening	Below Rs.10,000 Vs Between Rs.10,000 and Rs.25,000	142	14.8830	4.825	4.71	0.01
		90	11.9000	4.616		
	Below Rs.10,000 Vs Above Rs.25,000	142	14.8803	4.825	6.48	0.01
		70	10.8429	3.966		
	Between Rs.10,000 and Rs.25,000 Vs above Rs.25,000	90	11.9000	4.616	1.56	N.S
		70	10.8429	3.966		

INFERENCE

In the First case from the table, it is clear that the obtained C.R value (4.71) is higher than the table value (2.58) at 0.01 level. Therefore there is significant difference between the mean scores of Note-taking/Listening – a dimension of learning strategy among students whose Parental Monthly Income is Below Rs.10, 000 and whose Parental Monthly Income is Between Rs.10, 000 and Rs.25, 000.

In the Second case from the table, it is clear that the obtained C.R value (6.48) is higher than the table value (2.58) at 0.01 level. Therefore there is significant difference between the mean scores of Note-taking/Listening – a dimension of learning strategy among students whose Parental Monthly Income is Below Rs.10, 000 and whose Parental Monthly Income is Above Rs.25, 000.

In the Third case from the table, it is clear that the obtained C.R value (1.56) is lower than the table value (1.96) at 0.05 level. Therefore there is no significant difference between the mean scores of Note-taking/Listening – a dimension of learning strategy among students whose Parental Monthly Income is Between Rs.10, 000 and Rs.25,000 and whose Parental Monthly Income is Above Rs.25,000

Moreover the students whose parental monthly income is below Rs.10,000 have higher mean scores of note-taking / listening than the other two groups which is statistically significant.

Hence the hypothesis – V (f) stating that "There is no significant difference between the mean scores of Note-taking/Listening – a dimension of learning strategy among Higher Secondary students with respect to Parental Monthly Income" is partially verified.

(a) Influence of Gender on Reading/Comprehension-A Dimension of Learning Strategy

The scores related to Reading/Comprehension – a dimension of learning strategy of Male and Female Higher Secondary Students have been computed and details are furnished in the following table.

TABLE.9.24: Showing the Significant Difference between the mean Scores of Reading/ Comprehension – a Dimension of learning Strategy with Respect to Gender

Variable	Gender	No of cases	Mean	S.D	Critical Ratio	L.S
Reading/ Comprehension	Males	137	8.4745	3.234	3.54	0.01
	Females	165	9.8000	3.245		

INFERENCE

From the table, it is clear that the obtained C.R value (3.54) is higher than the table value (2.58) at 0.01 level. Therefore there is significant difference between the mean scores of Reading/Comprehension – a dimension of learning strategy with respect to Gender. It is also noted that the female students have significantly higher Reading/Comprehension strategy than their counterparts.

Hence the hypothesis – VI (a) stating that "There is no significant difference between the mean scores of Reading/Comprehension – a dimension of learning strategy among Higher Secondary students with respect to Gender" is rejected.

(b) Influence of Academic Streams on Reading/Comprehension-A Dimension of Learning Strategy

The scores related to Reading/ Comprehension – a dimension of learning strategy of Arts and Science streams among Higher Secondary Students have been computed and details are furnished in the following table.

TABLE.9.25: Showing the Significant Difference between the mean Scores of Reading/ Comprehension – a Dimension of learning Strategy with Respect to Academic Stream

Variable	Academic Stream	No of cases	Mean	S.D	Critical Ratio	L.S
Reading/ Comprehension	Arts	151	8.9536	3.213	1.29	N.S
	Science	151	9.4437	3.380		

INFERENCE

From the table, it is clear that the obtained C.R value (1.29) is lower than the table value (1.96) at 0.05 level. Therefore there is no significant difference between the mean scores of Reading/Comprehension – a dimension of learning strategy with respect to Academic Stream.

Hence the hypothesis – VI (b) stating that "There is no significant difference between the mean scores of Reading/ Comprehension – a dimension of learning strategy among Higher Secondary students with respect to Academic Stream" is accepted.

(c) Influence of Medium of Instruction on Reading/Comprehension-A Dimension of Learning Strategy

The scores related to Reading/Comprehension – a dimension of learning strategy of English and Tamil medium Higher Secondary Students have been computed and details are furnished in the following table.

TABLE.9.26: Showing the Significant Difference between the mean Scores of Reading/ Comprehension – a Dimension of learning Strategy with Respect to Medium of Instruction

Variable	Medium of Instruction	No of cases	Mean	S.D	Critical Ratio	L.S
Reading/ Comprehension	English	210	8.4714	3.228	6.43	0.01
	Tamil	92	10.8587	2.846		

INFERENCE

From the table, it is clear that the obtained C.R value (6.43) is higher than the table value (2.58) at 0.01 level. Therefore there is significant difference between the mean scores of Reading/Comprehension – a dimension of learning strategy with respect to Medium of Instruction. It is also noted that the Tamil medium students have significantly higher Reading/Comprehension than their counterparts.

Hence the hypothesis – VI (c) stating that "There is no significant difference between the mean scores of Reading/Comprehension – a dimension of learning strategy among Higher Secondary students with respect to Medium of Instruction" is rejected.

(d) Influence of Type of Family on Reading/Comprehension- A Dimension of Learning Strategy

The scores related to Reading/comprehension – a dimension of learning strategy of students hailing from joint and nuclear families have been computed and details are furnished in the following table.

TABLE.9.27: Showing the Significant Difference between the mean Scores of Reading/ Comprehension – a Dimension of learning Strategy with Respect to Type of Family

Variable	Type of family	No of cases	Mean	S.D	Critical Ratio	L.S
Reading/ Comprehension	Joint	86	8.7093	3.626	1.53	N.S
	Nuclear	216	9.3935	3.150		

INFERENCE

From the table, it is clear that the obtained C.R value (1.53) is lower than the table value (1.96) at 0.05 level. Therefore there is no significant difference between the mean scores of Reading/Comprehension – a dimension of learning strategy with respect to Type of family.

Hence the hypothesis – VI (d) stating that "There is no significant difference between the mean scores of Reading/Comprehension – a dimension of learning strategy among Higher Secondary students with respect to Type of Family" is accepted.

(e) Influence of Birth Order on Reading/Comprehension- A Dimension of Learning Strategy

The scores related to Reading/Comprehension – a dimension of learning strategy among Higher Secondary Students with respect to Birth Order (first born/ middle born/ last born) have been computed and details are furnished in the following table.

TABLE.9.28: ANOVA Showing the Significant Difference between the mean Scores of Reading/ Comprehension – a Dimension of learning Strategy with Respect to Birth Order

Variable		df	Sum of Squares	Mean Squares	F Ratio	L.S
Reading/ Com-prehension	Between Groups	2	18.0441	9.0221	.8270	N.S
	Within Groups	299	3262.0354	10.9098		
	Total	301	3280.0795			

INFERENCE

From the table, it is clear that the obtained 'F' value (.8270) is lower than the table value (3.03) at 0.05 level. Therefore there is no significant difference between the mean scores of Reading/Comprehension – a dimension of learning strategy with respect to Birth Order.

Hence the hypothesis – VI (e) stating that "There is no significant difference between the mean scores of Reading/Comprehension – a dimension of learning strategy among Higher Secondary students with respect to Birth Order" is accepted.

(f) Influence of Parental Monthly Income on Reading/ Comprehension-A Dimension of Learning Strategy

The scores related to Reading/Comprehension – a dimension of learning strategy among Higher Secondary School Students with respect to Parental Monthly Income (below Rs.10,000/ between Rs.10,000 and Rs.25,000 / above Rs.25,000) have been computed and details are furnished in the following table.

TABLE.9.29: ANOVA Showing the Significant Difference between the mean Scores of Reading/Comprehension – a Dimension of learning Strategy with Respect to Parental Monthly Income

Variable		df	Sum of Squares	Mean Squares	F Ratio	L.S
Reading/ Comprehension	Between Groups	2	387.4042	193.7021	20.0219	0.01
	Within Groups	299	2892.6753	9.6745		
	Total	301	3280.0795			

INFERENCE

From the table, it is clear that the obtained 'F' value (20.0219) is higher than the table value (4.68) at 0.01 level. Therefore there is significant difference between the mean scores of Reading/Comprehension – a dimension of learning strategy with respect to Parental Monthly Income.

So, further analysis has been done to find the significant difference between the groups.

TABLE.9.30: Showing the Multiple Comparisons of the mean Scores of Reading/Comprehension – a Dimension of learning Strategy with Respect to Parental Monthly Income

Variable	Parental Monthly Income	N	Mean	S.D	Critical Ratio	L.S
Reading/ Comprehension	Below Rs.10,000 Vs Between Rs.10,000 and Rs.25,000	142	10.2871	3.145	3.31	0.01
		90	8.8333	3.312		
	Below Rs.10,000 Vs Above Rs.25,000	142	10.2871	3.145	6.67	0.01
		70	7.4714	2.749		
	Between Rs.10,000 and Rs.25,000 Vs above Rs.25,000	90	8.8333	3.312	2.84	0.01
		70	7.4714	2.749		

INFERENCE

In the First case from the table, it is clear that the obtained C.R value (3.31) is higher than the table value (2.58) at 0.01 level. Therefore there is significant difference between the mean scores of Reading/Comprehension – a dimension of learning strategy among students whose Parental Monthly Income is Below Rs.10, 000 and whose Parental Monthly Income is Between Rs.10, 000 and Rs.25, 000.

In the Second case from the table, it is clear that the obtained C.R value (6.67) is higher than the table value (2.58) at 0.01 level. Therefore there is significant difference between the mean scores of Reading/Comprehension – a dimension of learning strategy among students whose Parental Monthly Income is Below Rs.10, 000 and whose Parental Monthly Income is Above Rs.25, 000.

In the Third case from the table, it is clear that the obtained C.R value (2.84) is higher than the table value (2.58) at 0.01 level. Therefore there is significant difference between the mean scores of Reading/Comprehension – a dimension of learning strategy among students whose Parental Monthly Income is Between Rs.10, 000 and Rs.25,000 and whose Parental Monthly Income is Above Rs.25,000.

Moreover, students whose parental monthly income is below Rs. 10,000 have significantly higher level of Reading / Comprehension than the other two groups.

Hence the hypothesis – VI (f) stating that "There is no significant difference between the mean scores of Reading/Comprehension – a dimension of learning strategy among Higher Secondary students with respect to Parental Monthly Income" is rejected.

(a) Influence of Gender on Writing/Research Skill- A Dimension of Learning Strategy

The scores related to Writing/Research Skill – a dimension of learning strategy of Male and Female Higher Secondary Students have been computed and details are furnished in the following table.

TABLE.9.31: Showing the Significant Difference between the mean Scores of Writing/Research Skill – a Dimension of learning Strategy with Respect to Gender

Variable	Gender	No of cases	Mean	S.D	Critical Ratio	L.S
Writing/ Research Skill	Males	137	9.1606	3.396	1.09	N.S
	Females	165	9.5939	3.481		

INFERENCE

From the table, it is clear that the obtained C.R value (1.09) is lower than the table value (1.96) at 0.05 level. Therefore there is no significant difference between the mean scores of Writing/Research Skill – a dimension of learning strategy with respect to Gender.

Hence the hypothesis – VII (a) stating that "There is no significant difference between the mean scores of Writing/ Research Skill – a dimension of learning strategy among Higher Secondary students with respect to Gender" is accepted.

(b) Influence of Academic Streams on Writing/Research Skill- A Dimension of Learning Strategy

The scores related to Study Writing/ Research Skill – a dimension of learning strategy of Arts and Science streams among Higher Secondary Students have been computed and details are furnished in the following table.

TABLE.9.32: Showing the Significant Difference between the mean Scores of Writing/ Research Skill – a Dimension of learning Strategy with Respect to Academic Stream

Variable	Academic Stream	No of cases	Mean	S.D	Critical Ratio	L.S
Writing/ Research Skill	Arts	151	9.1656	3.082	1.17	N.S
	Science	151	9.6291	3.768		

INFERENCE

From the table, it is clear that the obtained C.R value (1.17) is lower than the table value (1.96) at 0.05 level. Therefore there is no significant difference between the mean scores of Writing/Research Skill – a dimension of learning strategy with respect to Academic Stream.

Hence the hypothesis – VII (b) stating that "There is no significant difference between the mean scores of Writing / Research Skill– a dimension of learning strategy among Higher Secondary students with respect to Academic Stream" is accepted.

(c) Influence of Medium of Instruction on Writing/Research Skill-A Dimension of Learning Strategy

The scores related to Writing/ Research Skill – a dimension of learning strategy of English and Tamil medium Higher Secondary Students have been computed and details are furnished in the following table.

TABLE.9.33: Showing the Significant Difference between the mean Scores of Writing/Research Skill – a Dimension of learning Strategy with Respect to Medium of Instruction

Variable	Medium of Instruction	No: of cases	Mean	S.D	Critical Ratio	L.S
Writing/ Research skill	English	210	8.9238	3.456	3.81	0.01
	Tamil	92	10.4783	3.178		

INFERENCE

From the table, it is clear that the obtained C.R value (3.81) is higher than the table value (2.58) at 0.01 level. Therefore there is significant difference between the mean scores of Writing/Research Skill – a dimension of learning strategy with respect to Medium of Instruction.

It is also noted that the Tamil medium students have significantly higher Writing/Research Skill than their counterparts.

Hence the hypothesis – VII (c) stating that "There is no significant difference between the mean scores of Writing/Research Skill – a dimension of learning strategy among Higher Secondary students with respect to Medium of Instruction" is rejected.

(d) Influence of Type of Family on Writing/Research Skill- A Dimension of Learning Strategy

The scores related to Writing/Research Skill – a dimension of learning strategy of students hailing from joint and nuclear families have been computed and details are furnished in the following table.

TABLE.9.34: Showing the Difference between the mean Scores of Writing/Research Skill – a Dimension of learning Strategy with Respect to Type of Family

Variable	Type of family	No of cases	Mean	S.D	Critical Ratio	L.S
Writing/ Research Skill	Joint	86	9.0930	3.596	0.94	N.S
	Nuclear	216	9.5185	3.383		

INFERENCE

From the table, it is clear that the obtained C.R value (0.94) is lower than the table value (1.96) at 0.05 level. Therefore there is no significant difference between the mean scores of Writing/Research Skill – a dimension of learning strategy with respect to Type of family.

Hence the hypothesis – VII (d) stating that "There is no significant difference between the mean scores of Writing/Research Skill – a dimension of learning strategy among Higher Secondary students with respect to Type of Family" is accepted.

(e) Influence of Birth Order on Writing/Research Skill - A Dimension of Learning Strategy

The scores related to Writing/Research Skill – a dimension of learning strategy among Higher Secondary Students with respect to Birth Order (first born/ middle born/ last born) have been computed and details are furnished in the following table.

TABLE.9.35: ANOVA Showing the Significant Difference between the mean Scores of Writing/ Research Skill – a Dimension of learning Strategy with Respect to Birth Order

Variable		df	Sum of Squares	Mean Squares	F Ratio	L.S
Writing/ Research Skill	Between Groups	2	1.1203	.5601	.0469	N.S
	Within Groups	299	3569.1976	11.9371		
	Total	301	3570.3179			

INFERENCE

From the table, it is clear that the obtained 'F' value (.0469) is lower than the table value (3.03) at 0.05 level. Therefore there is no significant difference between the mean scores of Writing/Research Skill – a dimension of learning strategy with respect to Birth Order.

Hence the hypothesis – VII (e) stating that "There is no significant difference between the mean scores of Writing/Research Skill – a dimension of learning strategy among Higher Secondary students with respect to Birth Order" is accepted.

(f) Influence of Parental Monthly Income on Writing/Research Skill-A Dimension of Learning Strategy

The scores related to Writing/Research Skill – a dimension of learning strategy among Higher Secondary Students with respect to Parental Monthly Income (below Rs.10,000/ between Rs.10,000 and Rs.25,000 / above Rs.25,000) have been computed and details are furnished in the following table.

TABLE. 9.36: ANOVA Showing the Significant Difference between the mean Scores of Writing/ Research Skill – a Dimension of learning Strategy with Respect to Parental Monthly Income

Variable		df	Sum of Squares	Mean Squares	F Ratio	L.S
Writing/ Research Skill	Between Groups	2	249.9981	1124.9959	11.2561	0.01
	Within Groups	299	3320.3260	11.1048		
	Total	301	3570.3179			

INFERENCE

From the table, it is clear that the obtained 'F' value (11.2561) is higher than the table value (4.68) at 0.01 level. Therefore there is significant difference between the mean scores of Writing /Research Skill – a dimension of learning strategy with respect to Parental Monthly Income.

So, further analysis has been done to find the significant difference between the groups.

TABLE.9.37: Showing the Multiple Comparisons of the mean Scores of Writing/Research Skill – a Dimension of learning Strategy with Respect to Parental Monthly Income

Variable	Parental Monthly Income	N	Mean	S.D	Critical Ratio	L.S
Writing/ Research Skill	Below Rs.10,000 Vs Between Rs.10,000 and Rs.25,000	142	10.2817	3.278	2.77	0.01
		90	9.0556	3.299		
	Below Rs.10,000 Vs Above Rs.25,000	142	10.2817	3.278	4.49	0.01
		70	8.0429	3.483		
	Between Rs.10,000 and Rs.25,000 Vs above Rs.25,000	90	9.0556	3.299	1.87	N.S
		70	8.0429	3.483		

INFERENCE

In the First case from the table, it is clear that the obtained C.R value (2.77) is higher than the table value (2.58) at 0.01 level. Therefore there is significant difference between the mean scores of Writing/Research Skills – a dimension of learning strategy among students whose Parental Monthly Income is Below Rs.10, 000 and whose Parental Monthly Income is Between Rs.10, 000 and Rs.25, 000.

In the Second case from the table, it is clear that the obtained C.R value (4.49) is higher than the table value (2.58) at 0.01 level. Therefore there is significant difference between the mean scores of Writing/Research Skills – a dimension of learning strategy among students whose Parental Monthly Income is Below Rs.10, 000 and whose Parental Monthly Income is Above Rs.25, 000.

In the Third case from the table, it is clear that the obtained C.R value (1.87) is lower than the table value (1.96) at 0.05 level. Therefore there is no significant difference between the mean scores of Writing/Research Skills – a dimension of learning strategy among students whose Parental Monthly Income is Between Rs.10, 000 and Rs.25,000 and whose Parental Monthly Income is Above Rs.25,000.

Moreover the students whose parental monthly income is below Rs.10,000 have exhibited significantly higher writing/research skill than the other two groups.

Hence the hypothesis – VII (f) stating that "There is no significant difference between the mean scores of Writing/Research Skills – a dimension of learning strategy among Higher Secondary students with respect to Parental Monthly Income" is partially verified.

(a) Influence of Gender on Test-Taking Strategy-A Dimension of Learning Strategy

The scores related to Test-taking strategy – a dimension of learning strategy of Male and Female Higher Secondary Students have been computed and details are furnished in the following table.

TABLE.9.38: Showing the Significant Difference between the mean Scores of Test-Taking Strategy – a Dimension of learning Strategy with Respect to Gender

Variable	Gender	No of cases	Mean	S.D	Critical Ratio	L.S
Test-taking-Strategy	Males	137	14.9270	4.758	5.08	0.01
	Females	165	17.7576	4.905		

INFERENCE

From the table, it is clear that the obtained C.R value (5.08) is higher than the table value (2.58) at 0.01 level. Therefore there is significant difference between the mean scores of test-Taking Strategy – a dimension of learning strategy with respect to Gender. It is also noted that the female students have significantly higher Test-taking Strategy than their counterparts.

Hence the hypothesis – VIII (a) stating that "There is no significant difference between the mean scores of Test-Taking Strategy – a dimension of learning strategy among Higher Secondary students with respect to Gender" is rejected.

(b) Influence of Academic Streams on Test-Taking Strategy-A Dimension of Learning Strategy

The scores related to Test-taking Strategy – a dimension of learning strategy of Arts and Science streams among Higher Secondary Students have been computed and details are furnished in the following table.

TABLE. 9.39: Showing the Significant Difference between the mean Scores of Test-Taking Strategy – a Dimension of learning Strategy with Respect to Academic Stream

Variable	Academic Stream	No of cases	Mean	S.D	Critical Ratio	L.S
Test-taking Strategy	Arts	151	15.6623	5.081	2.83	0.01
	Science	151	17.2848	4.868		

INFERENCE

From the table, it is clear that the obtained C.R value (2.83) is higher than the table value (2.58) at 0.01 level. Therefore there is significant difference between the mean scores of Test-taking Strategy – a dimension of learning strategy with respect to Academic Stream. It is also noted that the Science students have significantly higher Test-taking Strategy than their counterparts.

Hence the hypothesis – VIII (b) stating that "There is no significant difference between the mean scores of Test-taking Strategy – a dimension of learning strategy among Higher Secondary students with respect to Academic Stream" is rejected.

(c) Influence of Medium of Instruction on Test-Taking Strategy-A Dimension of Learning Strategy

The scores related to Test-taking strategy – a dimension of learning strategy of English and Tamil medium Higher Secondary Students have been computed and details are furnished in the following table.

TABLE.9.40: Showing the Significant Difference between the mean Scores of Test-Taking Strategy – a Dimension of learning Strategy with Respect to Medium of Instruction

Variable	Medium of Instruction	No of cases	Mean	S.D	Critical Ratio	L.S
Test-taking strategy	English	210	15.8381	4.786	3.23	0.01
	Tamil	92	17.9239	5.304		

INFERENCE

From the table, it is clear that the obtained C.R value (3.23) is higher than the table value (2.58) at 0.01 level. Therefore there is significant difference between the mean scores of Test-taking Strategy – a dimension of learning strategy with respect to Medium of Instruction.

It is also noted that the Tamil medium students have significantly higher Test-taking strategy than their counterparts.

Hence the hypothesis – VIII (c) stating that "There is no significant difference between the mean scores of Test-taking strategy – a dimension of learning strategy among Higher Secondary students with respect to Medium of Instruction" is rejected.

(d) Influence of Type of Family on Test-Taking Strategy-A Dimension of Learning Strategy

The scores related to Test-taking strategy – a dimension of learning strategy of students hailing from joint and nuclear families have been computed and details are furnished in the following table.

TABLE.9.41: Showing the Significant Difference between the mean Scores of Test-Taking Strategy – a Dimension of learning Strategy with Respect to Type of Family

Variable	Type of family	No of cases	Mean	S.D	Critical Ratio	L.S
Test-taking strategy	Joint	86	15.8837	5.374	1.23	N.S
	Nuclear	216	16.7083	4.884		

INFERENCE

From the table, it is clear that the obtained C.R value (1.23) is lower than the table value (1.96) at 0.05 level. Therefore there is no significant difference between the mean scores of test-taking strategy – a dimension of learning strategy with respect to Type of family.

Hence the hypothesis – VIII (d) stating that "There is no significant difference between the mean scores of Test-taking strategy – a dimension of learning strategy among Higher Secondary students with respect to Type of Family" is accepted.

(e) Influence of Birth Order on Test-Taking Strategy-A Dimension of Learning Strategy

The scores related to Test-Taking Strategy – a dimension of learning strategy among Higher Secondary Students with respect to Birth Order (first born/ middle born/ last born) have been computed and details are furnished in the following table.

TABLE.9.42: ANOVA Showing the Significant Difference between the mean Scores of Test-Taking Strategy – a Dimension of learning Strategy with Respect to Birth Order

Variable		df	Sum of Squares	Mean Squares	F Ratio	L.S
Test-Taking Strategy	Between Groups	2	88.7445	44.3723		
	Within Groups	299	7536.5436	25.2058	1.7604	N.S
	Total	301	7625.2881			

INFERENCE

From the table, it is clear that the obtained 'F' value (1.7604) is lower than the table value (3.03) at 0.05 level. Therefore there is no significant difference between the mean scores of Test-Taking Strategy – a dimension of learning strategy with respect to Birth Order.

Hence the hypothesis – VIII (e) stating that "There is no significant difference between the mean scores of Test-Taking Strategy – a dimension of learning strategy among Higher Secondary students with respect to Birth Order" is accepted.

(f) Influence of Parental Monthly Income on Test-Taking Strategy-A Dimension of Learning Strategy

The scores related to Test-taking Strategy – a dimension of learning strategy among Higher Secondary Students with respect to Parental Monthly Income (below Rs.10,000/ between Rs.10,000 and Rs.25,000 / above Rs.25,000) have been computed and details are furnished in the following table.

TABLE.9.43: ANOVA Showing the Significant Difference between the mean Scores of Test-Taking Strategy – a Dimension of learning Strategy with Respect to Parental Monthly Income

Variable		df	Sum of Squares	Mean Squares	F Ratio	L.S
Test-taking Strategy	Between Groups	2	334.9728	167.4864		
	Within Groups	299	7290.3153	24.3823		
	Total	301	7625.2881		6.8692	0.01

INFERENCE

From the table, it is clear that the obtained 'F' value (6.8692) is higher than the table value (4.68) at 0.01 level. Therefore there is significant difference between the mean scores of Test-taking Strategy – a dimension of learning strategy with respect to Parental Monthly Income. So, further analysis has been done to find the significant difference between the groups.

TABLE.9.44: Showing the Multiple Comparisons of the mean Scores of Test-Taking Strategy – A Dimension of learning Strategy with Respect to Parental Monthly Income

Variable	Parental Monthly Income	N	Mean	S.D	Critical Ratio	L.S
Test-taking Strategy	Below Rs.10,000 Vs Between Rs.10,000 and Rs.25,000	142	17.4366	4.872	1.70	N.S
		90	16.2667	5.266		
	Below Rs.10,000 Vs Above Rs.25,000	142	17.4366	4.872	3.86	0.01
		70	14.7857	4.625		
	Between Rs.10,000 and Rs.25,000 Vs above Rs.25,000	90	16.2667	5.266	1.90	N.S
		70	14.7857	4.625		

INFERENCE

In the First case from the table, it is clear that the obtained C.R value (1.70) is lower than the table value (1.96) at 0.05 level. Therefore there is no significant difference between the mean scores of Test-taking Strategy – a dimension of learning strategy among students whose Parental Monthly Income is Below Rs.10, 000 and whose Parental Monthly Income is Between Rs.10, 000 and Rs.25, 000.

In the Second case from the table, it is clear that the obtained C.R value (3.86) is higher than the table value (2.58) at 0.01 level. Therefore there is significant difference between the mean scores of Test-taking Strategy – a dimension of learning strategy among students whose Parental Monthly Income is Below Rs.10, 000 and whose Parental Monthly Income is Above Rs.25, 000.

In the Third case from the table, it is clear that the obtained C.R value (1.90) is lower than the table value (1.96) at 0.05 level. Therefore there is no significant difference between the mean scores of Test-taking Strategy – a dimension of learning strategy among students whose Parental Monthly Income is Between Rs.10, 000 and Rs.25,000 and whose Parental Monthly Income is Above Rs.25,000.

Hence the hypothesis – VIII (f) stating that "There is no significant difference between the mean scores of Test-taking Strategy – a dimension of learning strategy among Higher Secondary students with respect to Parental Monthly Income" is partially verified.

(a) Influence of Gender on Organisational Technique-A Dimension of Learning Strategy

The scores related to Organizational Technique – a dimension of learning strategy of Male and Female Higher Secondary Students have been computed and details are furnished in the following table.

TABLE.9.45: Showing the Significant Difference between the mean Scores of Organizational Technique – a Dimension of learning Strategy with Respect to Gender

Variable	Gender	No of cases	Mean	S.D	Critical Ratio	L.S
Organizational Technique	Males	137	15.7372	5.686	3.40	0.01
	Females	165	17.8848	5.197		

INFERENCE

From the table, it is clear that the obtained C.R value (3.40) is higher than the table value (2.58) at 0.01 level. Therefore there is significant difference between the mean scores of Organizational Technique – a dimension of learning strategy with respect to Gender.

It is also noted that the female students have significantly higher Organizational Technique than their counterparts. Hence the hypothesis – IX (a) stating that "There is no significant difference between the mean scores of Organizational Technique – a dimension of learning strategy among Higher Secondary students with respect to Gender" is rejected.

(b) Influence of Academic Streams onOrganizational Technique-A Dimension of Learning Strategy

The scores related to Organizational technique – a dimension of learning strategy of Arts and Science streams among Higher Secondary Students have been computed and details are furnished in the following table.

TABLE.9.46: Showing the Significant Difference between the mean Scores of Organizational Techniques – a Dimension of learning Strategy with Respect to Academic Stream

Variable	Academic Stream	No of cases	Mean	S.D	Critical Ratio	L.S
Organizational Technique	Arts	151	16.6424	5.892	0.84	N.S
	Science	151	17.1788	5.127		

INFERENCE

From the table, it is clear that the obtained C.R value (0.84) is lower than the table value (1.96) at 0.05 level. Therefore there is no significant difference between the mean scores of Organizational Technique – a dimension of learning strategy with respect to Academic Stream.

Hence the hypothesis – IX (b) stating that "There is no significant difference between the mean scores of Organizational Technique– a dimension of learning strategy among Higher Secondary students with respect to Academic Stream" is accepted.

(c) Influence of Medium of Instruction on Organizational Technique-A Dimension of Learning Strategy

The scores related to Organizational Technique – a dimension of learning strategy of English and Tamil medium Higher Secondary Students have been computed and details are furnished in the following table.

TABLE.9.47: Showing the Significant Difference between the mean Scores of Organizational Technique– a Dimension of learning Strategy with Respect to Medium of Instruction

Variable	Medium of Instruction	No of cases	Mean	S.D	Critical Ratio	L.S
Organizational technique	English	210	16.1048	5.391	3.91	0.01
	Tamil	92	18.7500	5.396		

INFERENCE

From the table, it is clear that the obtained C.R value (3.91) is higher than the table value (2.58) at 0.01 level. Therefore there is significant difference between the mean scores of Organizational technique – a dimension of learning strategy with respect to Medium of Instruction.

It is also noted that the Tamil medium students have significantly higher Organizational technique than their counterparts.

Hence the hypothesis – IX (c) stating that "There is no significant difference between the mean scores of Organizational technique – a dimension of learning strategy among Higher Secondary students with respect to Medium of Instruction" is rejected.

(d) Influence of Type of Family on Organizational Technique-A Dimension of Learning Strategy

The scores related to Organizational Technique – a dimension of learning strategy of students hailing from joint and nuclear families have been computed and details are furnished in the following table.

TABLE.9.48: Showing the Significant Difference between the mean Scores of Organizational Technique – a Dimension of learning Strategy with Respect to Type of Family

Variable	Type of family	No of cases	Mean	S.D	Critical Ratio	L.S
Organizational technique	Joint	86	17.2558	5.975	0.65	N.S
	Nuclear	216	16.7731	5.336		

INFERENCE

From the table, it is clear that the obtained C.R value (0.65) is lower than the table value (1.96) at 0.05 level. Therefore there is no significant difference between the mean scores of Organizational Technique – a dimension of learning strategy with respect to Type of family.

Hence the hypothesis – IX (d) stating that "There is no significant difference between the mean scores of Organizational Technique – a dimension of learning strategy among Higher Secondary students with respect to Type of Family" is accepted.

(e) Influence of Birth Order on Organizational Technique- A Dimension of Learning Strategy

The scores related to Organizational Technique – a dimension of learning strategy among Higher Secondary Students with respect to Birth Order (first born/ middle born/ last born) have been computed and details are furnished in the following table.

Table.9.49: ANOVA Showing the Significant Difference between the mean Scores of Organizational Technique – a Dimension of learning Strategy with Respect to Birth Order

Variable		df	Sum of Squares	Mean Squares	F Ratio	L.S
Organizational Technique	Between Groups	2	80.1525	40.0763	1.3182	N.S
	Within Groups	299	9090.4335	30.4028		
	Total	301	9170.5861			

INFERENCE

From the table, it is clear that the obtained 'F' value (1.3182) is lower than the table value (3.03) at 0.05 level. Therefore there is no significant difference between the mean scores of Organizational Technique – a dimension of learning strategy with respect to Birth Order.

Hence the hypothesis – IX (e) stating that "There is no significant difference between the mean scores of Organizational Technique – a dimension of learning strategy among Higher Secondary students with respect to Birth Order" is accepted.

(f) Influence of Parental Monthly Income on Organizational Technique-A Dimension of Learning Strategy

The scores related to Organizational Technique – a dimension of learning strategy among Higher Secondary Students with respect to Parental Monthly Income (below Rs.10,000/ between Rs.10,000 and Rs.25,000 / above Rs.25,000) have been computed and details are furnished in the following table.

TABLE. 9.50: ANOVA Showing the Significant Difference between the mean Scores of Organizational Technique – a Dimension of learning Strategy with Respect to Parental Monthly Income

Variable		df	Sum of Squares	Mean Squares	F Ratio	L.S
Organizational Technique	Between Groups	2	418.8784	209.4392	7.1554	0.01
	Within Groups	299	8751.7076	29.2699		
	Total	301	9170.5861			

INFERENCE

From the table, it is clear that the obtained 'F' value (7.1554) is higher than the table value (4.68) at 0.01 level. Therefore there is significant difference between the mean scores of Organizational Technique – a dimension of learning strategy with respect to Parental Monthly Income.

So, further analysis has been done to find the significant difference between the groups.

TABLE.9.51: Showing the Multiple Comparisons of the mean Ccores of Organizational Technique – a Dimension of learning Strategy with Respect to Parental Monthly Income

Variable	Parental Monthly Income	N	Mean	S.D	Critical Ratio	L.S
Organizational Technique	Below Rs.10,000 Vs Between Rs.10,000 and Rs.25,000	142	18.1197	5.397	2.57	0.05
		90	16.2000	5.625		
	Below Rs.10,000 Vs Above Rs.25,000	142	18.1197	5.397	3.60	0.01
		70	15.3714	5.148		
	Between Rs.10,000 and Rs.25,000 Vs above Rs.25,000	90	16.2000	5.625	0.97	N.S
		70	15.3714	5.148		

INFERENCE

In the First case from the table, it is clear that the obtained C.R value (2.57) is higher than the table value (1.96) at 0.05level. Therefore there is significant difference between the mean scores of Organizational Technique – a dimension of learning strategy among students whose Parental Monthly Income is Below

Rs.10, 000 and whose Parental Monthly Income is Between Rs.10, 000 and Rs.25, 000.

In the Second case from the table, it is clear that the obtained C.R value (3.60) is higher than the table value (2.58) at 0.01 level. Therefore there is significant difference between the mean scores of Organizational Technique – a dimension of learning strategy among students whose Parental Monthly Income is Below Rs.10, 000 and whose Parental Monthly Income is Above Rs.25, 000.

In the Third case from the table, it is clear that the obtained C.R value (0.97) is lower than the table value (1.96) at 0.05 level. Therefore there is no significant difference between the mean scores of Organizational Technique – a dimension of learning strategy among students whose Parental Monthly Income is Between Rs.10, 000 and Rs.25,000 and whose Parental Monthly Income is Above Rs.25,000.

Students whose parental monthly income is below Rs.10, 000 have significantly higher organizational technique than the other two groups.

Hence the hypothesis – IX (f) stating that "There is no significant difference between the mean scores of Organizational Technique – a dimension of learning strategy among Higher Secondary students with respect to Parental Monthly Income" is partially verified.

(a) Influence of Gender on Time Management-A Dimension of Learning Strategy

The scores related to Time Management – a dimension of learning strategy of Male and Female Higher Secondary Students have been computed and details are furnished in the following table.

TABLE.9.52: Showing the Significant Difference between the mean Scores of Time Management – a Dimension of learning Strategy with Respect to Gender

Variable	Gender	No of cases	Mean	S.D	Critical Ratio	L.S
Time Management	Males	137	9.2555	3.937	3.60	0.01
	Females	165	10.9758	3.830		

INFERENCE

From the table, it is clear that the obtained C.R value (3.60) is higher than the table value (2.58) at 0.01 level. Therefore there is significant difference between the mean scores of Time Management – a dimension of learning strategy with respect to Gender.

It is also noted that the female students have significantly higher Time Management than their counterparts.

Hence the hypothesis – X (a) stating that "There is no significant difference between the mean scores of Time Management – a dimension of learning strategy among Higher Secondary students with respect to Gender" is rejected.

(b) Influence of Academic Streams on Time Management-A Dimension of Learning Strategy

The scores related to Time Management – a dimension of learning strategy of Arts and Science streams among Higher Secondary Students have been computed and details are furnished in the following table.

TABLE.9.53: Showing the Significant Difference between the mean Scores of Time Management – a Dimension of learning Strategy with Respect to Academic Stream

Variable	Academic Stream	No of cases	Mean	S.D	Critical Ratio	L.S
Time Management	Arts	151	10.0000	4.007	0.86	N.S
	Science	151	10.3907	3.929		

INFERENCE

From the table, it is clear that the obtained C.R value (0.86) is lower than the table value (1.96) at 0.05 level. Therefore there is no significant difference between the mean scores of Time Management – a dimension of learning strategy with respect to Academic Stream.

Hence the hypothesis – X (b) stating that "There is no significant difference between the mean scores of Time Management– a dimension of learning strategy among Higher Secondary students with respect to Academic Stream" is accepted.

(c) Influence of Medium of Instruction on Time Management-A Dimeansion of Learning Strategy

The scores related to Time Management – a dimension of learning strategy of English and Tamil medium Higher Secondary Students have been computed and details are furnished in the following table.

TABLE.9.54: Showing the Significant Difference between the mean Scores of Time Management – a Dimension of learning Strategy with Respect to Medium of Instruction

Variable	Medium of Instruction	No of cases	Mean	S.D	Critical Ratio	L.S
Time Management	English	210	10.0095	4.093	1.29	N.S
	Tamil	92	10.6196	3.646		

INFERENCE

From the table, it is clear that the obtained C.R value (1.29) is lower than the table value (1.96) at 0.05 level. Therefore there is no significant difference between the mean scores of Time Management – a dimension of learning strategy with respect to Medium of Instruction.

Hence the hypothesis –X (c) stating that "There is no significant difference between the mean scores of Time Management – a dimension of learning strategy among Higher Secondary students with respect to Medium of Instruction" is accepted.

(d) Influence of Type of Family on Time Management-A Dimension of Learning Strategy

The scores related to Time Management – a dimension of learning strategy of students hailing from joint and nuclear families have been computed and details are furnished in the following table.

TABLE.9.55: Showing the Significant Difference between the mean Scores of Time Management – a Dimension of learning Strategy with Respect to Type of Family

Variable	Type of family	No of cases	Mean	S.D	Critical Ratio	L.S
Time Management	Joint	86	9.5814	3.966	1.70	N.S
	Nuclear	216	10.4398	3.949		

INFERENCE

From the table, it is clear that the obtained C.R value (1.70) is lower than the table value (1.96) at 0.05 level. Therefore there is no significant difference between the mean scores of Time Management – a dimension of learning strategy with respect to Type of family.

Hence the hypothesis – X (d) stating that "There is no significant difference between the mean scores of Time Management – a dimension of learning strategy among Higher Secondary students with respect to Type of Family" is accepted.

(e) Influence of Birth Order on Time Management-A Dimension of Learning Strategy

The scores related to Time Management – a dimension of learning strategy among Higher Secondary Students with respect to Birth Order (first born/ middle born/ last born) have been computed and details are furnished in the following table.

TABLE.9.56: ANOVA Showing the Significant Difference between the mean Scores of Time Management – a Dimension of learning Strategy with Respect to Birth Order

Variable		df	Sum of Squares	Mean Squares	F Ratio	L.S
Time Management	Between Groups	2	82.4669	41.2335	.2171	N.S
	Within Groups	299	4653.0066	15.5619		
	Total	301	4735.4735			

INFERENCE

From the table, it is clear that the obtained 'F' value (.2171) is lower than the table value (3.03) at 0.05 level. Therefore there is no significant difference between the mean scores of Time Management – a dimension of learning strategy with respect to Birth Order.

Hence the hypothesis – X (e) stating that "There is no significant difference between the mean scores of Time Management – a dimension of learning strategy among Higher Secondary students with respect to Birth Order" is accepted.

(f) Influence of Parental MOnthly Income on Time Management-A Dimension of LEarning Strategy

The scores related to Time Management – a dimension of learning strategy among Higher Secondary Students with respect to Parental Monthly Income (below Rs.10,000/ between Rs.10,000 and Rs.25,000 / above Rs.25,000) have been computed and details are furnished in the following table.

TABLE.9.57: ANOVA Showing the Significant Difference between the mean Scores of Time Management – a Dimension of learning Strategy with Respect to Parental Monthly Income

Variable		df	Sum of Squares	Mean Squares	F Ratio	L.S
Time Management	Between Groups	2	115.8560	57.9280	3.7493	0.05
	Within Groups	299	4619.6175	15.4502		
	Total	301	4735.4735			

INFERENCE

From the table, it is clear that the obtained 'F' value (3.7493) is higher than the table value(3.03) at 0.05 level. Therefore there is significant difference between the mean scores of Time Management – a dimension of learning strategy with respect to Parental Monthly Income. So, further analysis has been done to find the significant difference between the groups.

TABLE.9.58: Showing the Multiple Comparisons of the mean Scores of Time Management – a Dimension of learning Strategy with Respect to Parental Monthly Income

Variable	Parental Monthly Income	N	Mean	S.D	Critical Ratio	L.S
Time Management	Below Rs.10,000 Vs	142	10.8380	3.733	2.59	0.01
	Between Rs.10,000 and Rs.25,000	90	9.4667	4.081		
	Below Rs.10,000 Vs	142	10.8380	3.733	1.73	N.S
	Above Rs.25,000	70	9.8286	4.121		
	Between Rs.10,000 and	90	9.4667	4.081	0.55	N.S
	Rs.25,000 Vs above Rs.25,000	70	9.8286	4.121		

INFERENCE

In the First case from the table, it is clear that the obtained C.R value (2.59) is higher than the table value (2.58) at 0.01 level. Therefore there is significant difference between the mean scores of Time Management – a dimension of learning strategy among students whose Parental Monthly Income is Below Rs.10, 000 and whose Parental Monthly Income is Between Rs.10, 000 and Rs.25, 000.

In the Second case from the table, it is clear that the obtained C.R value (1.73) is lower than the table value (1.96) at 0.05 level. Therefore there is no significant difference between the mean scores of Time Management – a dimension of learning strategy among students whose Parental Monthly Income is Below Rs.10, 000 and whose Parental Monthly Income is Above Rs.25, 000.

In the Third case from the table, it is clear that the obtained C.R value (0.55) is lower than the table value (1.96) at 0.05 level. Therefore there is no significant difference between the mean scores of Time Management – a dimension of learning strategy among students whose Parental Monthly Income is Between Rs.10, 000 and Rs.25,000 and whose Parental Monthly Income is Above Rs.25,000.

Hence the hypothesis – X (f) stating that "There is no significant difference between the mean scores of Time Management – a dimension of learning strategy among Higher Secondary students with respect to Parental Monthly Income" is partially verified.

(a) Influence of Gender on Youth Problem among Higher Secondary Students

The scores related to Youth Problem of Male and Female Higher Secondary Students have been computed and details are furnished in the following table.

TABLE.9.59: Showing the Significant Difference between the mean Scores of Youth Problem among Higher Secondary Student with Respect to Gender

Variable	Gender	No of cases	Mean	S.D	Critical Ratio	L.S
Youth Problem	Males	137	49.6204	27.841	1.05	N.S
	Females	165	46.5576	21.422		

INFERENCE

From the table, it is clear that the obtained C.R value (1.05) is lower than the table value (1.96) at 0.05 level. Therefore there is no significant difference between the mean scores of Youth Problem among Higher Secondary Students with respect to Gender.

Hence the hypothesis – XI (a) stating that "There is no significant difference between the mean scores of Youth Problem among Higher Secondary students with respect to Gender" is accepted.

(b) Influence of Academic Streams on Youth Problem among Higher Secondary Students

The scores related to Youth Problem of Arts and Science streams among Higher Secondary Students have been computed and details are furnished in the following table.

TABLE.9.60: Showing the Significant Difference between the mean Scores of Youth Problem with Respect to Academic Stream

Variable	Academic Stream	No of cases	Mean	S.D	Critical Ratio	L.S
Youth Problem	Arts	151	46.1060	27.088	1.30	N.S
	Science	151	49.7881	21.647		

INFERENCE

From the table, it is clear that the obtained C.R value (1.30) is lower than the table value (1.96) at 0.05 level. Therefore there is no significant difference between the mean scores of Youth Problem among Higher Secondary Students with respect to Academic Stream.

Hence the hypothesis – XI (b) stating that "There is no significant difference between the mean scores of Youth Problem among Higher Secondary students with respect to Academic Stream," is accepted.

(c) Influence of Medium of Instruction on Youth Problem among Higher Secondary Students

The scores related to Youth Problem of English and Tamil medium Higher Secondary School Students have been computed and details are furnished in the following table.

TABLE.9.61: Showing the Significant Difference between the mean Scores of Youth Problem with Respect to Medium of Instruction

Variable	Medium of Instruction	No of cases	Mean	S.D	Critical Ratio	L.S
Youth Problem	English	210	46.9429	22.594	0.98	N.S
	Tamil	92	50.2391	28.515		

INFERENCE

From the table, it is clear that the obtained C.R value (0.98) is lower than the table value (1.96) at 0.05 level. Therefore there is no significant difference between the mean scores of Youth Problem among Higher Secondary Students with respect to Medium of Instruction.

Hence the hypothesis – XI (c) stating that "There is no significant difference between the mean scores of Youth Problem among Higher Secondary students with respect to Medium of Instruction" is accepted.

(d) Influence of Type of Family on youth Problem among Higher Secondary Students

The scores related to Youth Problem of students hailing from joint and nuclear families have been computed and details are furnished in the following table.

TABLE.9.62: Showing the Significant Difference between the mean Scores of Youth Problem with Respect to Type of Family

Variable	Type of Family	No of cases	Mean	S.D	Critical Ratio	L.S
Youth Problems	Joint	86	48.7093	29.829	0.31	N.S
	Nuclear	216	47.6435	22.170		

INFERENCE

From the table, it is clear that the obtained C.R value (0.31) is lower than the table value (1.96) at 0.05 level. Therefore there is no significant difference between the mean scores of Youth Problem among Higher Secondary Students with respect to Type of Family.

Hence the hypothesis – XI (d) stating that "There is no significant difference between the mean scores of Youth Problem among Higher Secondary students with respect to Type of Family" is accepted.

(e) Influence of BIrth Order on Youth Problem

The scores related to Youth Problem among Higher Secondary Students with respect to Birth Order (first born/ middle born/ last born) have been computed and details are furnished in the following table.

TABLE.9.63: ANOVA Showing the Significant Difference between the mean Scores of Youth Problem with Respect to Birth Order

Variable		df	Sum of Squares	Mean Squares	F Ratio	L.S
Youth Problem	Between Groups	2	2384.2672	1192.1336	1.9914	N.S
	Within Groups	299	178992.8851	598.6384		
	Total	301	181377.1523			

INFERENCE

From the table, it is clear that the obtained 'F' value (1.9914) is lower than the table value (3.03) at 0.05 level. Therefore there is no significant difference between the mean scores of Youth Problem with respect to Birth Order.

Hence the hypothesis – XI (e) stating that "There is no significant difference between the mean scores of Youth Problem among Higher Secondary students with respect to Birth Order" is accepted.

(f) Influence of Parental Monthly Income on Youth Problem

The scores related to Youth Problem among Higher Secondary Students with respect to Parental Monthly Income (below Rs.10,000/ between Rs.10,000 and Rs.25,000 / above Rs.25,000) have been computed and details are furnished in the following table.

TABLE.9.64: ANOVA showing the Significant Difference between the mean Scores of Youth Problem with Respect to Parental Monthly Income

Variable		df	Sum of Squares	Mean Squares	F Ratio	L.S
Youth Problem	Between Groups	2	5251.7836	2625.8918	4.4579	0.05
	Within Groups	299	176125.3687	589.0481		
	Total	301	181377.1523			

INFERENCE

From the table, it is clear that the obtained 'F' value (4.4579) is higher than the table value(3,03) at 0.01 level. Therefore there is significant difference between the mean scores of Youth Problem with respect to Parental Monthly Income.

So, further analysis has been done to find the significant difference between the groups.

TABLE.9.65: Showing the Multiple Comparisons of the mean Scores of Youth Problem with Respect to Parental Monthly Income

Variable	Parental Monthly Income	N	Mean	S.D	Critical Ratio	L.S
Youth Problem	Below Rs.10,000 Vs Between Rs.10,000 and Rs.25,000	142	49.4577	27.695	0.59	N.S
		90	51.3556	21.259		
	Below Rs.10,000 Vs Above Rs.25,000	142	49.4577	27.695	2.68	0.01
		70	40.5000	20.056		
	Between Rs.10,000 and Rs.25,000 Vs above Rs.25,000	90	51.3556	21.259	3.31	0.01
		70	40.5000	20.056		

INFERENCE

In the First case from the table, it is clear that the obtained C.R value (0.59) is lower than the table value (1.96) at 0.05 level. Therefore there is no significant difference between the mean scores of Youth Problem among students whose Parental Monthly Income is Below Rs.10, 000 and whose Parental Monthly Income is Between Rs.10, 000 and Rs.25, 000.

In the Second case from the table, it is clear that the obtained C.R value (2.68) is higher than the table value (2.58) at 0.01 level. Therefore there is significant difference between the mean scores of Youth Problem among students whose Parental Monthly Income is Below Rs.10, 000 and whose Parental Monthly Income is Above Rs.25, 000.

In the Third case from the table, it is clear that the obtained C.R value (3.31) is higher than the table value (2.58) at 0.01 level. Therefore there is significant difference between the mean scores of Youth Problem among students whose Parental Monthly Income is Between Rs.10, 000 and Rs.25,000 and whose Parental Monthly Income is Above Rs.25,000.

Moreover students whose parental monthly income is above Rs. 25,000 have significantly lesser youth problem than the other two groups.

Hence the hypothesis – XI (f) stating that "There is no significant difference between the mean scores of Youth Problem among Higher Secondary students with respect to Parental Monthly Income" is partially verified.

(a) Influence of Gender on Personal Problem and Over Sensitivity-A Dimension of Youth Problem among Higher Secondary Students

The scores related to Personal problem and over sensitivity-a dimension of Youth Problem of Male and Female Higher Secondary Students have been computed and details are furnished in the following table.

TABLE.9.66: Showing the Significant Difference between the mean Scores of Personal Problem and over Sensitivity- a Dimension of Youth Problem among Higher Secondary Student with Respect to Gender

Variable	Gender	No of cases	Mean	S.D	Critical Ratio	L.S
Personal problem and oversensitivity	Males	137	14.1606	10.163	1.02	N.S
	Females	165	15.2727	8.442		

INFERENCE

From the table, it is clear that the obtained C.R value (1.02) is lower than the table value (1.96) at 0.05 level. Therefore there is no significant difference between the mean scores personal problem and over sensitivity- a dimension of Youth Problem among Higher Secondary Students with respect to Gender.

Hence the hypothesis – XII (a) stating that "There is no significant difference between the mean scores of Personal problem and oversensitivity- a dimension of Youth Problem among Higher Secondary students with respect to Gender" is accepted.

(b) Influence of Academic Streams on Personal Problem and Oversensitivity-A Dimension of Youth Problem among Higher Secondary Students

The scores related to Personal Problem and Oversensitivity- a dimension of Youth Problem of Arts and Science streams among Higher Secondary Students have been computed and details are furnished in the following table.

TABLE 9.67: Showing the significant difference between the mean scores of Personal Problem and oversensitivity-a dimension of Youth Problem with respect to Academic Stream

Variable	Academic Stream	No of cases	Mean	S.D	Critical Ratio	L.S
Personal Problem and Oversensitivity	Arts	151	12.5563	8.898	4.26	0.01
	Science	151	16.9801	9.119		

INFERENCE

From the table, it is clear that the obtained C.R value (4.26) is higher than the table value (2.58) at 0.01 level. Therefore there is significant difference between the mean scores of Personal problem and oversensitivity- a dimension of Youth Problem among Higher Secondary Students with respect to Academic Stream.

It is also noted that the Science students have significantly higher Personal problem and oversensitivity than their counterparts.

Hence the hypothesis – XII (b) stating that "There is no significant difference between the mean scores of Personal Problem and Oversensitivity-a dimension of Youth Problem among Higher Secondary students with respect to Academic Stream" is rejected.

(c) Influence of Medium of Instruction on Personal Problem and Oversensitivity-A Dimension of Youth Problem among Higher Secondary Students

The scores related to Personal problem and Oversensitivity -a dimension of Youth Problem of English and Tamil medium Higher Secondary Students have been computed and details are furnished in the following table.

TABLE.9.68: Showing the Significant Difference between the mean Scores of Personal Problem and Oversensitivity- a Dimension of Youth Problem with Respect to Medium of Instruction

Variable	Medium of Instruction	No of cases	Mean	S.D	Critical Ratio	L.S
Personal Problem/ oversensitivity	English	210	14.7524	9.182	0.04	N.S
	Tamil	92	14.8043	9.495		

INFERENCE

From the table, it is clear that the obtained C.R value (0.04) is lower than the table value (1.96) at 0.05 level. Therefore there is no significant difference between the mean scores of Personal Problem and oversensitivity- a dimension of Youth Problem among Higher Secondary Students with respect to Medium of Instruction.

Hence the hypothesis – XII (c) stating that "There is no significant difference between the mean scores of Personal Problem and Oversensitivity- a dimension of Youth Problem among Higher Secondary students with respect to Medium of Instruction" is accepted.

(d) Influence of Type of Family on Personal Problem and Oversensitivity-A Dimension of Youth Problem among Higher Secondary Students

The scores related to Personal Problems and Oversensitivity -a dimension of Youth Problem of students hailing from joint and nuclear families have been computed and details are furnished in the following table.

TABLE.9.69: Showing the Significant Difference between the mean Scores of Personal Problem and Oversensitivity- a Dimension of Youth Problem with Respect to Type of Family

Variable	Type of Family	No of cases	Mean	S.D	Critical Ratio	L.S
Personal Problem/ Oversensitivity	Joint	86	14.8605	11.002	0.10	N.S
	Nuclear	216	14.7315	8.501		

INFERENCE

From the table, it is clear that the obtained C.R value (0.10) is lower than the table value (1.96) at 0.05 level. Therefore there is no significant difference between the mean scores of Personal Problems and Oversensitivity- a dimension of Youth Problem among Higher Secondary Students with respect to Type of Family.

Hence the hypothesis – XII (d) stating that "There is no significant difference between the mean scores of Personal Problem and Oversensitivity - a dimension of Youth Problem among Higher Secondary students with respect to Type of Family" is accepted.

(e) Influence of Birth Order on Personal Problem and Oversensitivity-A Dimension of Youth Problem

The scores related to Personal Problem and Oversensitivity – a dimension of Youth Problem among Higher Secondary Students with respect to Birth Order (first born/ middle born/ last born) have been computed and details are furnished in the following table.

TABLE.9.70: ANOVA Showing the Significant Difference between the mean Scores of Personal Problem and Oversensitivity – a Dimension of Youth Problem with Respect to Birth Order

Variable		df	Sum of Squares	Mean Squares	F Ratio	L.S
Personal Problem and Oversensitivity	Between Groups	2	230.5137	115.2569	1.3464	N.S
	Within Groups	299	25595.2611	85.6029		
	Total	301	25825.7748			

INFERENCE

From the table, it is clear that the obtained 'F' value (1.3464) is lower than the table value (3.03) at 0.05 level. Therefore there is no significant difference between the mean scores of Personal Problem and Oversensitivity – a dimension of Youth Problem with respect to Birth Order.

Hence the hypothesis – XII (e) stating that "There is no significant difference between the mean scores of Personal Problem and Oversensitivity – a dimension of Youth Problem among Higher Secondary students with respect to Birth Order" is accepted.

(f) Influence of Parental Monthly Income on Personal Problem and Oversensitivity-A Dimension of Youth Problem

The scores related to Personal Problems and Oversensitivity- a dimension of Youth Problem among Higher Secondary Students with respect to Parental Monthly Income (below Rs.10,000/ between Rs.10,000 and Rs.25,000 / above Rs.25,000) have been computed and details are furnished in the following table.

TABLE.9.71: ANOVA Showing the Significant Difference between the mean Scores of Personal Problems and Oversensitivity – a Dimension of Youth Problem with Respect to Parental Monthly Income

Variable		**df**	**Sum of Squares**	**Mean Squares**	**F Ratio**	**L.S**
Personal Problems and Oversensitivity	Between Groups	2	60.3690	30.1845	0.3503	**N.S**
	Within Groups	299	25765.4059	86.1719		
	Total	301	25825.7748			

INFERENCE

From the table, it is clear that the obtained 'F' value (0.3503) is lower than the table value (3.03) at 0.05 level. Therefore there is no significant difference between the mean scores of Personal Problems and Oversensitivity – a dimension of Youth Problem with respect to Parental Monthly Income.

Hence the hypothesis – XII (f) stating that "There is no significant difference between the mean scores of Personal Problems and Oversensitivity – a dimension of Youth Problem among higher secondary students with respect to Parental Monthly Income " is accepted.

(a) Influence of Gender on Family Issues-A Dimension of Youth Problem among Higher Secondary Students

The scores related to Family issues-a dimension of Youth Problem of Male and Female Higher Secondary Students have been computed and details are furnished in the following table.

TABLE.9.72: Showing the Significant Difference between the mean Scores of Family Issues- a Dimension of Youth Problem among Higher Secondary Student with Respect to Gender

Variable	**Gender**	**No of cases**	**Mean**	**S.D**	**Critical Ratio**	**L.S**
Family issues	Males	137	19.2336	12.309	0.29	N.S
	Females	165	18.8606	9.685		

INFERENCE

From the table, it is clear that the obtained C.R value (0.29) is lower than the table value (1.96) at 0.05 level. Therefore there is no significant difference between the mean scores of Family issues- a dimension of Youth Problem among Higher Secondary Students with respect to Gender.

Hence the hypothesis – XIII (a) stating that "There is no significant difference between the mean scores of Family Issues- a dimension of Youth Problem among Higher Secondary students with respect to Gender" is accepted.

(b) Influence of Academic Streams on Family Issues-A Dimension of Youth Problem among Higher Secondary Students

The scores related to Family issues-a dimension of Youth Problem of Arts and Science streams among Higher Secondary Students have been computed and details are furnished in the following table.

TABLE.9.73: Showing the Significant Difference between the mean Scores of Family Issues- a Dimension of Youth Problem with respect to Academic Stream

Variable	Academic Stream	No of cases	Mean	S.D	Critical Ratio	L.S
Family issues	Arts	151	19.4570	12.289	0.68	N.S
	Science	151	18.6026	9.413		

INFERENCE

From the table, it is clear that the obtained C.R value (0.68) is lower than the table value (1.96) at 0.05 level. Therefore there is no significant difference between the mean scores of Family issues- a dimension of Youth Problem among Higher Secondary Students with respect to Academic Stream.

Hence the hypothesis – XIII (b) stating that "There is no significant difference between the mean scores of Family Issues- a dimension of Youth Problem among Higher Secondary students with respect to Academic Stream" is accepted.

(c) Influence of Medium of Instruction on Family Issues -A Dimension of Youth Problem among Higher Secondary Students

The scores related to Family issues-a dimension of Youth Problem of English and Tamil medium Higher Secondary Students have been computed and details are furnished in the following table.

TABLE.9.74: Showing the Significant Difference between the mean Scores of Family Issues- a Dimension of Youth Problem with Respect to Medium of Instruction

Variable	Medium of Instruction	No of cases	Mean	S.D	Critical Ratio	L.S
Family issues	English	210	18.2667	10.083	1.69	N.S
	Tamil	92	20.7717	12.558		

INFERENCE

From the table, it is clear that the obtained C.R value (1.69) is lower than the table value (1.96) at 0.05 level. Therefore there is no significant difference between the mean scores of Family issues- a dimension of Youth Problem among Higher Secondary Students with respect to Medium of Instruction.

Hence the hypothesis – XIII (c) stating that "There is no significant difference between the mean scores of Family Issues- a dimension of Youth Problem among Higher Secondary students with respect to Medium of Instruction" is accepted.

(d) Influence of Type of Family on Family issues-A Dimension of Youth Problem among Higher Secondary Students

The scores related to Family issues -a dimension of Youth Problem of students hailing from joint and nuclear families have been computed and details are furnished in the following table.

TABLE.9.75: Showing the Significant Difference between the mean Scores of Family Issues- a Dimension of Youth Problem with respect to Type of Family

Variable	Type of Family	No of cases	Mean	S.D	Critical Ratio	L.S
Family issues	Joint	86	17.7442	13.071	1.15	N.S
	Nuclear	216	19.5417	9.948		

INFERENCE

From the table, it is clear that the obtained C.R value (1.15) is lower than the table value (1.96) at 0.05 level. Therefore there is no significant difference between the mean scores of Family Issues- a dimension of Youth Problem among Higher Secondary Students with respect to Type of Family.

Hence the hypothesis – XIII (d) stating that "There is no significant difference between the mean scores of Family Issues- a dimension of Youth Problem among Higher Secondary students with respect to Type of Family" is accepted.

(e) Influence of Birth Order on Family Issues-A Dimension of Yoth Problem

The scores related to Family issues – a dimension of Youth Problem among Higher Secondary Students with respect to Birth Order (first born/ middle born/ last born) have been computed and details are furnished in the following table.

TABLE.9.76: ANOVA Showing the Significant Difference between the mean Scores of Family Issues – a Dimension of Youth Problem with Respect to Birth Order

Variable		df	Sum of Squares	Mean Squares	F Ratio	L.S
Family Issues	Between Groups	2	300.6284	150.3142	1.2590	N.S
	Within Groups	299	35698.1034	119.3917		
	Total	301	35998.7318			

INFERENCE

From the table, it is clear that the obtained 'F' value (1.2590) is lower than the table value (3.03) at 0.05 level. Therefore there is no significant difference between the mean scores of Family issues – a dimension of Youth Problem with respect to Birth Order.

Hence the hypothesis – XIII (e) stating that "There is no significant difference between the mean scores of Family issues – a dimension of Youth Problem among Higher Secondary students with respect to Birth Order" is accepted.

(f) Influence of Parental Monthly Income on Family Issues-A Dimension of Youth Problem

The scores related to Family issues- a dimension of Youth Problem among Higher Secondary Students with respect to Parental Monthly Income (below Rs.10,000/ between Rs.10,000 and Rs.25,000 / above Rs.25,000) have been computed and details are furnished in the following table.

TABLE.9.77: ANOVA Showing the Significant Difference between the mean Scores of Family Issues- a Dimension of Youth Problem with Respect to Parental Monthly Income

Variable		df	Sum of Squares	Mean Squares	F Ratio	L.S
Family issues	Between Groups	2	2364.9686	1182.4843	10.5121	0.01
	Within Groups	299	33633.7632	112.4875		
	Total	301	35998.7318			

INFERENCE

From the table, it is clear that the obtained 'F' value (10.5121) is higher than the table value (4.68) at 0.01 level. Therefore there is significant difference between the mean scores of Family issues- a dimension of Youth Problem with respect to Parental Monthly Income. So, further analysis has been done to find the significant difference between the groups.

TABLE. 4.78: Showing the Multiple Comparisons of the mean Scores of Family Issues- a Dimension of outh Problem with Respect to Parental Monthly Income

Variable	Parental Monthly Income	N	Mean	S.D	Critical Ratio	L.S
Family Issues	Below Rs.10,000 VsBetween Rs.10,000 and Rs.25,000	F	19.7042	12.068	1.40	N.S
		90	21.7333	9.873		
	Below Rs.10,000 Vs Above Rs.25,000	142	19.7042	12.068	3.96	0.01
		70	14.1857	8.008		
	Between Rs.10,000 and Rs.25,000 Vs above Rs.25,000	90	21.7333	9.873	5.34	0.01
		70	14.1857	8.008		

INFERENCE

In the First case from the table, it is clear that the obtained C.R value (1.40) is lower than the table value (1.98) at 0.05 level. Therefore there is no significant difference between the mean scores of Family issues- a dimension of Youth Problem among students whose Parental Monthly Income is Below Rs.10, 000 and whose Parental Monthly Income is Between Rs.10, 000 and Rs.25, 000.

In the Second case from the table, it is clear that the obtained C.R value (3.96) is higher than the table value (2.58) at 0.01 level. Therefore there is significant difference between the mean scores of Family issues- a dimension of Youth Problem among students whose Parental Monthly Income is Below Rs.10, 000 and whose Parental Monthly Income is Above Rs.25, 000.

In the Third case from the table, it is clear that the obtained C.R value (5.34) is higher than the table value (2.58) at 0.01 level. Therefore there is significant difference between the mean scores of Family issues- a dimension of Youth Problem among students whose Parental Monthly Income is Between Rs.10, 000 and Rs.25,000 and whose Parental Monthly Income is Above Rs.25,000.

Moreover students whose parental monthly income is above Rs.25,000 have significantly exhibited lower family issues than the other two groups.

Hence the hypothesis – XIII (f) stating that "There is no significant difference between the mean scores of Family issues- a dimension of Youth Problem among Higher Secondary students with respect to Parental Monthly Income" is partially verified.

(a) Nfluence of Gender on School Issues-A Dimension of Youth Problem among Higher Secondary Students

The scores related to School issues-a dimension of Youth Problem of Male and Female Higher Secondary Students have been computed and details are furnished in the following table.

TABLE.9.79: Showing the Significant Difference between the mean Scores of School Issues- a Dimension of Youth Problem among Higher Secondary Student with Respect to Gender

Variable	Gender	No of cases	Mean	S.D	Critical Ratio	L.S
School issues	Males	137	12.8905	18.599	2.87	0.01
	Females	165	10.3515	6.363		

INFERENCE

From the table, it is clear that the obtained C.R value (2.87) is higher than the table value (2.58) at 0.01 level. Therefore there is significant difference between the mean scores of School issues- a dimension of Youth Problem among Higher Secondary Students with respect to Gender.

It is also noted that the Male students have significantly higher school issues than their counterparts.

Hence the hypothesis – XIV (a) stating that "There is no significant difference between the mean scores of School Issues- a dimension of Youth Problem among Higher Secondary students with respect to Gender" is rejected.

(b) Influence of Academic Streams on School Issues - A Dimension of Youth Problem among Higher Secondary Students

The scores related to School issues-a dimension of Youth Problem of Arts and Science streams among Higher Secondary Students have been computed and details are furnished in the following table.

TABLE.9.80: Showing the Significant Difference between the mean Scores of School Issues- a Dimension of Youth Problem with Respect to Academic Stream

Variable	Academic Stream	No of cases	Mean	S.D	Critical Ratio	L.S
School issues	Arts	151	11.2119	7.967	0.67	N.S
	Science	151	11.7947	7.132		

FINFERENCE

From the table, it is clear that the obtained C.R value (0.67) is lower than the table value (1.96) at 0.05 level. Therefore there is no significant difference between the mean scores of School issues- a dimension of Youth Problem among Higher Secondary Students with respect to Academic Stream.

Hence the hypothesis – XIV (b) stating that "There is no significant difference between the mean scores of School Issues- a dimension of Youth Problem among Higher Secondary students with respect to Academic Stream" is accepted.

(c) Influence of Medium of Instruction on School Issues - A Dimension of Youth Problem among Higher Secondary Students

The scores related to School issues-a dimension of Youth Problem of English and Tamil medium Higher Secondary Students have been computed and details are furnished in the following table.

TABLE.9.81: Showing the Significant Difference between the mean Scores of School Issues- a Dimension of Youth Problem with Respect to Medium of Instruction

Variable	Medium of Instruction	No of cases	Mean	S.D	Critical Ratio	L.S
School issues	English	210	11.5381	7.440	0.12	N.S
	Tamil	92	11.4239	7.851		

INFERENCE

From the table, it is clear that the obtained C.R value (0.12) is lower than the table value (1.96) at 0.05 level. Therefore there is no significant difference between the mean scores of School issues- a dimension of Youth Problem among Higher Secondary Students with respect to Medium of Instruction.

Hence the hypothesis – XIV (c) stating that "There is no significant difference between the mean scores of School Issues- a dimension of Youth Problem among Higher Secondary students with respect to Medium of Instruction" is accepted.

(d) Influence of Type of Family on School Issues- A Dimension of Youth Problem among Higher Secondary Students

The scores related to School issues -a dimension of Youth Problem of students hailing from joint and nuclear families have been computed and details are furnished in the following table.

TABLE.9.82: Showing the Significant Difference between the mean Scores of School Issues- a Dimension of Youth Problem with Respect to Type of Family

Variable	Type of Family	No of cases	Mean	S.D	Critical Ratio	L.S
School issues	Joint	86	12.8953	8.750	1.84	N.S
	Nuclear	216	10.9491	6.967		

INFERENCE

From the table, it is clear that the obtained C.R value (1.84) is lower than the table value (1.96) at 0.05 level. Therefore there is no significant difference between the mean scores of School Issues- a dimension of Youth Problem among Higher Secondary Students with respect to Type of Family.

Hence the hypothesis – XIV (d) stating that "There is no significant difference between the mean scores of School Issues- a dimension of Youth Problem among Higher Secondary students with respect to Type of Family" is accepted.

(e) Influence of Birth Order on School Issues - A Dimension of Youth Problem

The scores related to School issues – a dimension of Youth Problem among Higher Secondary Students with respect to Birth Order (first born/ middle born/ last born) have been computed and details are furnished in the following table.

TABLE.9.83: ANOVA Showing the Significant Difference between the mean Scores of School Issues – a Dimension of Youth Problem with Respect to Birth Order

Variable		df	Sum of Squares	Mean Squares	F Ratio	L.S
School Issues	Between Groups	2	163.4967	81.7484	1.4366	N.S
	Within Groups	299	17014.0000	56.9030		
	Total	301	17177.4967			

INFERENCE

From the table, it is clear that the obtained 'F' value (1.4366) is lower than the table value (3.03) at 0.05 level. Therefore there is no significant difference between the mean scores of School issues – a dimension of Youth Problem with respect to Birth Order.

Hence the hypothesis – XIV (e) stating that "There is no significant difference between the mean scores of School issues – a dimension of Youth Problem among Higher Secondary students with respect to Birth Order" is accepted.

(f) Influence of Parental Monthly Income on School Issues-A Dimension of Youth Problem

The scores related to School issues- a dimension of Youth Problem among Higher Secondary Students with respect to Parental Monthly Income (below Rs.10,000/ between Rs.10,000 and Rs.25,000 / above Rs.25,000) have been computed and details are furnished in the following table.

TABLE.9.84: ANOVA Showing the Significant Difference between the mean Scores of School Issues – a Dimension of Youth Problem with Respect to Parental Monthly Income

Variable		df	Sum of Squares	Mean Squares	F Ratio	L.S
School Issues	Between Groups	2	185.6391	92.8196	1.6333	N.S
	Within Groups	299	16991.8575	56.8290		
	Total	301	17177.4967			

INFERENCE

From the table, it is clear that the obtained 'F' value (1.6333) is lower than the table value (3.03) at 0.05 level. Therefore there is no significant difference between the mean scores of School issues – a dimension of Youth Problem with respect to Parental Monthly Income.

Hence the hypothesis – XIV (f) stating that "There is no significant difference between the mean scores of School issues – a dimension of Youth Problem among Higher Secondary students with respect to Parental Monthly Income" is accepted.

(a) Influence of Gender on Social Issues - A Dimension of Youth Problem among Higher Secondary Students

The scores related to Social issues-a dimension of Youth Problem of Male and Female Higher Secondary Students have been computed and details are furnished in the following table.

TABLE.9.85: Showing the Significant Difference between the mean Scores of Social Issues- a Dimension of Youth Problem among Higher Secondary Student with Respect to Gender

Variable	Gender	No of cases	Mean	S.D	Critical Ratio	L.S
Social issues	Males	137	3.0438	2.558	3.31	0.01
	Females	165	2.1576	1.991		

INFERENCE

From the table, it is clear that the obtained C.R value (3.31) is higher than the table value (2.58) at 0.01 level. Therefore there is significant difference between the mean scores of Social issues- a dimension of Youth Problem among Higher Secondary Students with respect to Gender.

It is also noted that the Male students have significantly higher social issues than their counterparts.

Hence the hypothesis – XV (a) stating that "There is no significant difference between the mean scores of Social Issues- a dimension of Youth Problem among Higher Secondary students with respect to Gender" is rejected.

(b) Influence of Academic Streams on Social Issues - A Dimension of Youth Problem among Higher Secondary Students

The scores related to Social issues-a dimension of Youth Problem of Arts and Science streams among Higher Secondary Students have been computed and details are furnished in the following table.

TABLE.9.86: Showing the Significant Difference between the mean Scores of Social Issues- a Dimension of Youth Problem with Respect to Academic Stream

Variable	Academic Stream	No of cases	Mean	S.D	Critical Ratio	L.S
Social issues	Arts	151	2.6026	2.458	0.32	N.S
	Science	151	2.5166	2.147		

INFERENCE

From the table, it is clear that the obtained C.R value (0.32) is lower than the table value (1.96) at 0.05 level. Therefore there is no significant difference between the mean scores of Social issues- a dimension of Youth Problem among Higher Secondary Students with respect to Academic Stream.

Hence the hypothesis – XV (b) stating that "There is no significant difference between the mean scores of Social Issues- a dimension of Youth Problem among Higher Secondary students with respect to Academic Stream" is accepted.

(c) Influence of Medium of Instruction on Social Issues - A Dimension of Youth Problem among Higher secondary Students

The scores related to Social issues-a dimension of Youth Problem of English and Tamil medium Higher Secondary Students have been computed and details are furnished in the following table.

TABLE.9.87: Showing the Significant Difference between the mean Scores of Social Issues- a Dimension of Youth Problem with Respect to Medium of Instruction

Variable	Medium of Instruction	No of cases	Mean	S.D	Critical Ratio	L.S
Social issues	English	210	2.4000	2.164	1.71	N.S
	Tamil	92	2.9239	2.573		

INFERENCE

From the table, it is clear that the obtained C.R value (1.71) is lower than the table value (1.96) at 0.05 level. Therefore there is no significant difference between the mean scores of Social issues- a dimension of Youth Problem among Higher Secondary Students with respect to Medium of Instruction.

Hence the hypothesis – XV (c) stating that "There is no significant difference between the mean scores of Social Issues- a dimension of Youth Problem among Higher Secondary students with respect to Medium of Instruction" is accepted.

(d) Influence of Type of Family on Social Issues - A Dimension of Youth Problem among Higher Secondary Students

The scores related to Social issues -a dimension of Youth Problem of students hailing from joint and nuclear families have been computed and details are furnished in the following table.

TABLE.9.88: Showing the Significant Difference between the mean Scores of Social Issues- a Dimension of Youth Problem with Respect to Type of Family

Variable	Type of Family	No of cases	Mean	S.D	Critical Ratio	L.S
Social issues	Joint	86	2.5233	2.678	0.16	N.S
	Nuclear	216	2.5741	2.145		

INFERENCE

From the table, it is clear that the obtained C.R value (0.16) is lower than the table value (1.96) at 0.05 level. Therefore there is no significant difference between the mean scores of Social Issues- a dimension of Youth Problem among Higher Secondary Students with respect to Type of Family.

Hence the hypothesis – XV (d) stating that "There is no significant difference between the mean scores of Social Issues- a dimension of Youth Problem among Higher Secondary students with respect to Type of Family" is accepted.

(e) Influence of Birth Order on Social Issues - A Dimension of Youth Problem

The scores related to Social issues – a dimension of Youth Problem among Higher Secondary Students with respect to Birth Order (first born/ middle born/ last born) have been computed and details are furnished in the following table.

TABLE.9.89: ANOVA Showing the Significant Difference between the mean Scores of Social Issues – a Dimension of Youth Problem with Respect to Birth Order

Variable		df	Sum of Squares	Mean Squares	F Ratio	L.S
Social Issues	Between Groups	2	3.3035	1.6518	.3096	N.S
	Within Groups	299	1595.1236	5.3349		
	Total	301	1598.4272			

INFERENCE

From the table, it is clear that the obtained 'F' value (.3096) is lower than the table value (3.03) at 0.05 level. Therefore there is no significant difference between the mean scores of Social issues – a dimension of Youth Problem with respect to Birth Order.

Hence the hypothesis – XV (e) stating that "There is no significant difference between the mean scores of Social issues – a dimension of Youth Problem among Higher Secondary students with respect to Birth Order" is accepted.

(f) Influence of Parental Monthly Income on Social Issues - A Dimension of Youth Problem

The scores related to Social issues- a dimension of Youth Problem among Higher Secondary Students with respect to Parental Monthly Income (below Rs.10,000/ between Rs.10,000 and Rs.25,000 / above Rs.25,000) have been computed and details are furnished in the following table.

TABLE.9.90: ANOVA Showing the Significant Difference between the mean Scores of Social Issues – a Dimension of Youth Problem with Respect to Parental Monthly Income

Variable		df	Sum of Squares	Mean Squares	F Ratio	L.S
Social Issues	Between Groups	2	34.7247	17.3624	3.3199	0.05
	Within Groups	299	1563.7024	5.2298		
	Total	301	1598.4272			

INFERENCE

From the table, it is clear that the obtained 'F' value (3.3199) is higher than the table value (3.03) at 0.05 level. Therefore there is significant difference between the mean scores of Social issues- a dimension of Youth Problem with respect to Parental Monthly Income. So, further analysis has been done to find the significant difference between the groups.

TABLE.9.91: Showing the Multiple Comparisons of the mean Scores of Social Issues- a Dimension of Youth Problem with Respect to Parental Monthly Income

Variable	Parental Monthly Income	N	Mean	S.D	Critical Ratio	L.S
Social Issues	Below Rs.10,000 Vs Between Rs.10,000 and Rs.25,000	142	2.7324	2.484	0.11	N.S
		90	2.7667	2.234		
	Below Rs.10,000 Vs Above Rs.25,000	142	2.7324	2.484	2.56	0.05
		70	1.9429	1.903		
	Between Rs.10,000 and Rs.25,000 Vs above Rs.25,000	90	2.7667	2.234	2.52	0.05
		70	1.9429	1.903		

INFERENCE

In the First case from the table, it is clear that the obtained C.R value (0.11) is lower than the table value (1.96) at 0.05 level. Therefore there is no significant difference between the mean scores of Social issues- a dimension of Youth Problem among students whose Parental Monthly Income is Below Rs.10, 000 and whose Parental Monthly Income is Between Rs.10, 000 and Rs.25, 000.

In the Second case from the table, it is clear that the obtained C.R value (2.56) is higher than the table value (1.96) at 0.05level. Therefore there is significant difference between the mean scores of Social issues- a dimension of Youth Problem among students whose Parental Monthly Income is Below Rs.10, 000 and whose Parental Monthly Income is Above Rs.25, 000.

In the Third case from the table, it is clear that the obtained C.R value (2.52) is higher than the table value (1.96) at 0.05level. Therefore there is significant difference between the mean scores of Social issues- a dimension of Youth Problem among students whose Parental Monthly Income is Between Rs.10, 000 and Rs.25,000 and whose Parental Monthly Income is Above Rs.25,000.

Moreover, students whose parental monthly income is above Rs. 25,000 have significantly lesser social issues than the other two groups.

Hence the hypothesis – XV (f) stating that "There is no significant difference between the mean scores of Social issues- a dimension of Youth Problem among Higher Secondary students with respect to Parental Monthly Income" is partially verified.

(g) Correlation Between Learning Strategies Along with its Dimensions and youth Problem along with its Dimeansions

The scores related to the correlation between Learning Strategies along with its dimensions and Youth Problem along with its dimensions among Higher Secondary Students are computed and the details of which are tabulated as below.

TABLE.9.92: Showing the Correlation between Learning Strategies along with its Dimensions and Youth Problem Along with its Dimensions.

Youth Problem & its Dimensions / Learning Strategies & its Dimensions	Personal Problem and Oversensitivity	Family Issues	School Issues	Social Issues	Youth Problem in toto
Study Strategy	-.1107*	-.0545	-.1889**	-.0736	-.1296**
Note-Taking/ Listening	-.0387	-.0533	-.1509**	-.1010*	-.0882
Reading/ Comprehension	-.1724**	-.0736	-.2441**	-.1348**	-.1948**
Writing/ Research Skill	-.0701	-.0175	-.1074*	-.0423	-.0592
Test-Taking Strategy	-.0678	-.0274	-.1400**	-.0934*	-.0948*
Organizational Technique	-.0543	-.1278**	-.1422**	-.1209*	-.1313**
Time Management	-.0081	-.1312**	-.1136*	-.0494	-.0926*
Learning Strategy in toto	-.0924*	-.0833	-.2032**	-.1165*	-.1451**

Where * 0.05 level of significance
** 0.01 level of significance

INFERENCE

From the above table, we infer the following,

1. Learning Strategy in toto are significantly and negatively correlated with Youth Problem in toto and its dimensions-personal problem and oversensitivity, family issues, school issues and social issues.
2. Study strategy-a dimension of Learning Strategy is significantly and negatively correlated with Youth problem in toto and its dimensions-personal problem and oversensitivity and school issues.
3. Note-taking/ listening-a dimension of Learning Strategy is significantly and negatively correlated with the dimensions of Youth Problem-school issues and social issues.
4. Reading /Comprehension-a dimension of Learning Strategy is significantly and negatively correlated with Youth problem in toto and its dimension-personal problem and oversensitivity, school issues and social issues.
5. Writing /Research Skill -a dimension of Learning Strategy is significantly and negatively correlated with the dimension of Youth Problem- school issues.
6. Test-taking Strategy -a dimension of Learning Strategy is significantly and negatively correlated with Youth problem in toto and its dimensions-school issues and social issues.
7. Organizational Technique -a dimension of Learning Strategy is significantly and negatively correlated with Youth problem in toto and its dimensions- family issues, school issues and social issues.
8. Time Management-a dimension of Learning Strategy is significantly and negatively correlated with Youth problem in toto and its dimensions-family issues and school issues.

Hence the hypothesis – XVI stating that "There is no significant correlation between Learning Strategies along with its dimensions and Youth Problem along with its dimensions among Higher Secondary Students" is partially verified.

CONCLUSION

This chapter summarizes the analysis of data, testing of the hypotheses description and inferences of the tables. A brief report of the research study together with the major findings and conclusion along with their educational implications has been presented in the succeeding chapter.

10

Summary, Findings and Conclusion

In this chapter, after presenting briefly the statement of the problem and the description of the procedure used in the investigations, the findings and the conclusions are presented. In the light of the findings of the present study, suggestions have been proposed at the end of the chapter for further research in this field.

STATEMENT OF THE PROBLEM

The problem of the research is entitled as, *"A Critical Study on the Learning Strategies in Relation to Certain Personal and Social Issues among Higher Secondary Students"*.

OPERATIONAL DEFINITIONS OF THE TERMs USED

Learning Strategies

A set of steps to accomplish a particular task, such as taking a test, comprehending, text and writing a story to make learning more meaningful. In the present study, it is measured by Learning Strategy Inventory(2000), constructed and validated by Kathy Stroud and Ceil Reyonolds.

Personal Issues and Social Issues

Personal issues are those that individuals deal with themselves and within a small range of their peers and relationships. On the other hand, social issues attribute to values cherished by widespread society.

A social issue is also called a social problem or a social illness refers to an issue that influences and is opposed by a considerable number of individuals within a society. It is often the consequence of factors extending beyond an individual›s control and local geographical environment.

In the present study, it is assessed by Youth Problem Inventory (2004) prepared by Dr. M Varma.

Higher Secondary Students

In the present study, students studying in XI grade are considered as Higher Secondary Students.

OBJECTIVES OF THE STUDY

The following objectives have been set in the present study:

1. To find out the levels of Learning Strategies along with its dimensions among Higher Secondary Students.
2. To find the levels of learning of youth problems in Toto and all its dimensions among Higher Secondary Students.
3. To find whether there are any significant difference in the Learning Strategies along with its dimensions, youth problems in Toto and all its dimensions among Higher Secondary Students with regard to
    - Gender (Male / Female)
    - Academic Stream (Arts / Science)
    - Medium of Instruction (English / Tamil)
    - Type of Family (Joint / Nuclear)
    - Birth Order (First Born / Middle Born / Last Born)
    - Parental Monthly Income (belowRs.10,000/ between Rs10,000 and Rs 25,000/above Rs.25,000)
4. To find whether there is any significant correlation between Learning Strategies along with its dimensions and Youth Problem along with its dimensions among Higher Secondary Students.

HYPOTHESES OF THE STUDY

The following hypotheses have been set in the present study:

1. The levels of Learning Strategies along with its dimensions among Higher Secondary Students are average in nature.

2. The levels of youth problems in toto and all its dimensions among Higher Secondary Students are average in nature.
3. There is no significant difference in Learning Strategy among Higher Secondary Students with regard to
    - Gender (Male / Female)
    - Academic Stream (Arts / Science)
    - Medium of Instruction (English / Tamil)
    - Type of Family (Joint / Nuclear)
    - Birth Order (First Born / Middle Born / Last Born)
    - Parental Monthly Income (belowRs.10,000/between Rs10,000 and Rs25,000/above Rs.25,000)
4. There is no significant difference in Study Strategy – a dimension of Learning Strategy among Higher Secondary Students with regard to
    - Gender (Male / Female)
    - Academic Stream (Arts / Science)
    - Medium of Instruction (English / Tamil)
    - Type of Family (Joint / Nuclear)
    - Birth Order (First Born / Middle Born / Last Born)
    - Parental Monthly Income (below Rs.10, 000/between Rs10,000 and Rs25,000/above Rs.25,000)
5. There is no significant difference in Note-Taking / Listening – a dimension of Learning Strategy among Higher Secondary Students with regard to
    - Gender (Male / Female)
    - Academic Stream (Arts / Science)
    - Medium of Instruction (English / Tamil)
    - Type of Family (Joint / Nuclear)
    - Birth Order (First Born / Middle Born / Last Born)
    - Parental Monthly Income (below Rs.10,000/between Rs10,000 and Rs25,000/above Rs.25,000)
6. There is no significant difference in Reading / Comprehension – a dimension of Learning Strategy among Higher Secondary Students with regard to
    - Gender (Male / Female)
    - Academic Stream (Arts / Science)
    - Medium of Instruction (English / Tamil)
    - Type of Family (Joint / Nuclear)
    - Birth Order (First Born / Middle Born / Last Born)

- Parental Monthly Income (below Rs.10,000/between Rs10,000 and Rs25,000/above Rs.25,000)

7. There is no significant difference in Writing / Research Skills – a dimension of Learning Strategy among Higher Secondary Students with regard to
    - Gender (Male / Female)
    - Academic Stream (Arts / Science)
    - Medium of Instruction (English / Tamil)
    - Type of Family (Joint / Nuclear)
    - Birth Order (First Born / Middle Born / Last Born)
    - Parental Monthly Income (below Rs.10,000/between Rs10,000 and Rs 25,000/above Rs.25,000)
8. There is no significant difference in Test-Taking Strategy – a dimension of Learning Strategy among Higher Secondary Students with regard to
    - Gender (Male / Female)
    - Academic Stream (Arts / Science)
    - Medium of Instruction (English / Tamil)
    - Type of Family (Joint / Nuclear)
    - Birth Order (First Born / Middle Born / Last Born)
    - Parental Monthly Income (below Rs.10, 000/between Rs10, 000 and Rs25,000/above Rs.25,000)
9. There is no significant difference in Organizational techniques – a dimension of Learning Strategy among Higher Secondary Students with regard to
    - Gender (Male / Female)
    - Academic Stream (Arts / Science)
    - Medium of Instruction (English / Tamil)
    - Type of Family (Joint / Nuclear)
    - Birth Order (First Born / Middle Born / Last Born)
    - Parental Monthly Income (below Rs.10,000/between Rs10,000 and Rs25,000/above Rs.25,000)
10. There is no significant difference in Time Management – a dimension of Learning Strategy among Higher Secondary Students with regard to
    - Gender (Male / Female)
    - Academic Stream (Arts / Science)
    - Medium of Instruction (English / Tamil)
    - Type of Family (Joint / Nuclear)
    - Birth Order (First Born / Middle Born / Last Born)

- Parental Monthly Income (below Rs.10,000/between Rs10,000 and Rs25,000/above Rs.25,000)

11. There is no significant difference in Youth Problems among Higher Secondary Students with regard to
    - Gender (Male / Female)
    - Academic Stream (Arts / Science)
    - Medium of Instruction (English / Tamil)
    - Type of Family (Joint / Nuclear)
    - Birth Order (First Born / Middle Born / Last Born)
    - Parental Monthly Income (below Rs.10,000/between Rs10,000 and Rs25,000/above Rs.25,000)
12. There is no significant difference in Personal Problems and Over Sensitivity – a dimension of Youth Problem among Higher Secondary Students with regard to
    - Gender (Male / Female)
    - Academic Stream (Arts / Science)
    - Medium of Instruction (English / Tamil)
    - Type of Family (Joint / Nuclear)
    - Birth Order (First Born / Middle Born / Last Born)
    - Parental Monthly Income (below Rs.10,000/between Rs10,000 and Rs25,000/above Rs.25,000)
13. There is no significant difference in Family issues – a dimension of Youth Problem among Higher Secondary Students with regard to
    - Gender (Male / Female)
    - Academic Stream (Arts / Science)
    - Medium of Instruction (English / Tamil)
    - Type of Family (Joint / Nuclear)
    - Birth Order (First Born / Middle Born / Last Born)
    - Parental Monthly Income (below Rs.10,000/between Rs10,000 and Rs25,000/above Rs.25,000)
14. There is no significant difference in School issues – a dimension of Youth Problem among Higher Secondary Students with regard to
    - Gender (Male / Female)
    - Academic Stream (Arts / Science)
    - Medium of Instruction (English / Tamil)
    - Type of Family (Joint / Nuclear)
    - Birth Order (First Born / Middle Born / Last Born)

- Parental Monthly Income (below Rs.10,000/between Rs10,000 and Rs25,000/above Rs.25,000)

15. There is no significant difference in Social Issues – a dimension of Youth Problem among Higher Secondary Students with regard to
    - Gender (Male / Female)
    - Academic Stream (Arts / Science)
    - Medium of Instruction (English / Tamil)
    - Type of Family (Joint / Nuclear)
    - Birth Order (First Born / Middle Born / Last Born)
    - Parental Monthly Income (below Rs.10,000/between Rs10,000 and Rs25,000/above Rs.25,000)
16. There is no significant correlation between Learning Strategies along with its dimensions and youth problems along with its dimensions.

TOOLS USED IN THE STUDY

To collect the pertinent data for the present investigation, standardized tools have been employed to quantify the variables involved in the study.

The investigator has used the following tools for the data collection.

TABLE.10.1: Showing the Details of the Tools used in the Present Study

S.No	Research Tools	Author
1.	Learning Strategy Inventory(2000)	Kathy Stroud & Cecil Reynolds
2.	Youth Problem Inventory(2004)	Dr. (Mrs.) M. Verma

MAJOR FINDINGS OF THE STUDY

The present investigation had led to the following major findings:

1. The levels of Learning strategies and its dimensions among Higher Secondary Students are moderate in nature.
2. The levels of Youth Problem and its dimensions among Higher Secondary Students are low in nature.
3. There is significant difference between the mean scores of Learning strategy among Higher Secondary Students with respect to Gender. The female students have significantly higher learning strategy then the counterparts.
4. There is no significant difference between the mean scores of learning strategy with respect to Academic Stream among Higher secondary students.
5. There is significant difference between the mean scores of learning strategy with respect to Medium of Instruction. The Tamil medium

students have significantly higher learning strategy then the English medium students.

6. There is no significant difference between the mean scores of learning strategy with respect to the type of family.
7. There is no significant difference between the mean scores of the learning strategy with respect to Birth Order.
8. There is significant difference between the mean scores of Learning strategy with respect to Parental Monthly Income. The students whose parental monthly income below Rs. 10,000 have shown significantly higher learning strategy then the students whose parental monthly between Rs. 10, 000 and Rs. 25, 000 and above Rs. 25, 000.
9. There is significant difference between the mean scores of Study Strategy – a dimension of learning strategy with respect to Gender. The female students have significantly higher study strategy-a dimension of learning strategy then the counterparts.
10. There is no significant difference between the mean scores of study strategy-a dimension of learning strategy with respect to Academic streams.
11. There is significant difference between the mean scores of Study Strategy – a dimension of learning strategy with respect to Medium of Instruction. The Tamil medium students have significantly higher study strategy-a dimension of learning strategy than the English medium students.
12. There is significant difference between the mean scores of Study Strategy – a dimension of learning strategy with respect to Type of family. The students from the Nuclear family have significantly higher study strategy-a dimension of learning strategy than the students from joint family.
13. There is no significant difference between the mean scores of Study Strategy – a dimension of learning strategy with respect to Birth Order.
14. There is significant difference between the mean scores of Study Strategy – a dimension of learning strategy with respect to Parental Monthly Income. It is also noted that students whose parental monthly income is below Rs10,000 have exhibited significantly higher study strategy than the students whose parental monthly income is between Rs.10,000 and Rs.25,000 and above Rs.25,000.
15. There is significant difference between the mean scores of Note-taking/ Listening – a dimension of learning strategy with respect to Gender. The female students have significantly higher Note-taking/ Listening strategy than their counterparts.

16. There is no significant difference between the mean scores of Note-taking/listening – a dimension of learning strategy with respect to Academic Stream.
17. There is significant difference between the mean scores of Note-taking/ Listening – a dimension of learning strategy with respect to Medium of Instruction. Tamil medium students have significantly higher Note-taking/ Listening than their counterparts.
18. There is no significant difference between the mean scores of Note-taking/ listening – a dimension of learning strategy with respect to Type of family.
19. There is no significant difference between the mean scores of Note-taking/Listening – a dimension of learning strategy with respect to Birth Order.
20. There is significant difference between the mean scores of Note-taking/ Listening – a dimension of learning strategy with respect to Parental Monthly Income. The students whose parental monthly income is below Rs.10,000 have higher mean scores of note-taking / listening than the students whose parental monthly income is between Rs.10,000 and Rs.25,000 and above Rs.25,000 which is statistically significant.
21. There is significant difference between the mean scores of Reading/ Comprehension – a dimension of learning strategy with respect to Gender. Female students have significantly higher Reading/ Comprehension strategy than their counterparts.
22. There is no significant difference between the mean scores of Reading/ Comprehension – a dimension of learning strategy with respect to Academic Stream.
23. There is significant difference between the mean scores of Reading/ Comprehension – a dimension of learning strategy with respect to Medium of Instruction, Tamil medium students have significantly higher Reading/Comprehension than their counterparts.
24. There is no significant difference between the mean scores of Reading/ Comprehension – a dimension of learning strategy with respect to Type of family.
25. There is no significant difference between the mean scores of Reading/ Comprehension – a dimension of learning strategy with respect to Birth Order.
26. There is significant difference between the mean scores of Reading/ Comprehension – a dimension of learning strategy with respect to Parental Monthly Income. Students whose parental monthly income is below Rs. 10,000 have significantly higher level of Reading /

Comprehension than the students whose parental monthly income is between Rs.10,000 and 25,000 and above Rs.25,000.

27. There is no significant difference between the mean scores of Writing/ Research Skill – a dimension of learning strategy with respect to Gender.
28. There is no significant difference between the mean scores of Writing/ Research Skill – a dimension of learning strategy with respect to Academic Stream.
29. There is significant difference between the mean scores of Writing/ Research Skill – a dimension of learning strategy with respect to Medium of Instruction, Tamil medium students have significantly higher Writing/Research Skill than their counterparts.
30. There is no significant difference between the mean scores of Writing/ Research Skill – a dimension of learning strategy with respect to Type of family.
31. There is no significant difference between the mean scores of Writing/ Research Skill – a dimension of learning strategy with respect to Birth Order.
32. There is significant difference between the mean scores of Writing / Research Skill – a dimension of learning strategy with respect to Parental Monthly Income. The students whose parental monthly income is below Rs.10,000 have exhibited significantly higher writing/ research skill than the students whose parental monthly income is between Rs.10,000 and 25,000 and above Rs.25,000.
33. There is significant difference between the mean scores of test-Taking Strategy – a dimension of learning strategy with respect to Gender. Female students have significantly higher Test-taking Strategy than their counterparts.
34. There is significant difference between the mean scores of Test-taking Strategy – a dimension of learning strategy with respect to Academic Stream. The Science students have significantly higher Test-taking Strategy than their counterparts.
35. There is significant difference between the mean scores of Test-taking Strategy – a dimension of learning strategy with respect to Medium of Instruction, Tamil medium students have significantly higher Test-taking strategy than their counterparts.
36. There is no significant difference between the mean scores of test-taking strategy – a dimension of learning strategy with respect to Type of family.

37. There is no significant difference between the mean scores of Test-Taking Strategy – a dimension of learning strategy with respect to Birth Order.
38. There is significant difference between the mean scores of Test-taking Strategy – a dimension of learning strategy with respect to Parental Monthly Income.
39. There is significant difference between the mean scores of Organizational Technique – a dimension of learning strategy with respect to Gender. Female students have significantly higher Organizational Technique than their counterparts.
40. There is no significant difference between the mean scores of Organizational Technique – a dimension of learning strategy with respect to Academic Stream.
41. There is significant difference between the mean scores of Organizational technique – a dimension of learning strategy with respect to Medium of Instruction, Tamil medium students have significantly higher Organizational technique than their counterparts.
42. There is no significant difference between the mean scores of Organizational Technique – a dimension of learning strategy with respect to Type of family.
43. There is no significant difference between the mean scores of Organizational Technique – a dimension of learning strategy with respect to Birth Order.
44. There is significant difference between the mean scores of Organizational Technique – a dimension of learning strategy with respect to Parental Monthly Income. Students whose parental monthly income is below Rs.10, 000 have significantly higher organizational technique than the students whose parental monthly income is between Rs. 10,000 and 25,000 and above Rs.25,000.
45. There is significant difference between the mean scores of Time Management – a dimension of learning strategy with respect to Gender. Female students have significantly higher Time Management than their counterparts.
46. There is no significant difference between the mean scores of Time Management – a dimension of learning strategy with respect to Academic Stream.
47. There is no significant difference between the mean scores of Time Management – a dimension of learning strategy with respect to Medium of Instruction.

48. There is no significant difference between the mean scores of Time Management – a dimension of learning strategy with respect to Type of family.
49. There is no significant difference between the mean scores of Time Management – a dimension of learning strategy with respect to Birth Order.
50. There is significant difference between the mean scores of Time Management – a dimension of learning strategy with respect to Parental Monthly Income.
51. There is no significant difference between the mean scores of Youth Problem among Higher Secondary Students with respect to Gender.
52. There is no significant difference between the mean scores of Youth Problem among Higher Secondary Students with respect to Academic Stream.
53. There is no significant difference between the mean scores of Youth Problem among Higher Secondary Students with respect to Medium of Instruction.
54. There is no significant difference between the mean scores of Youth Problem among Higher Secondary Students with respect to Type of Family.
55. There is no significant difference between the mean scores of Youth Problem with respect to Birth Order.
56. There is significant difference between the mean scores of Youth Problem with respect to Parental Monthly Income. Students whose parental monthly income is above Rs. 25,000 have significantly lesser youth problem than the students whose parental monthly income is below Rs.10,000 and between Rs.10,000 and 25,000.
57. There is no significant difference between the mean scores personal problem and over sensitivity- a dimension of Youth Problem among Higher Secondary Students with respect to Gender.
58. There is significant difference between the mean scores of Personal problem and oversensitivity- a dimension of Youth Problem among Higher Secondary Students with respect to Academic Stream. Science students have significantly higher Personal problem and oversensitivity than their counterparts.
59. There is no significant difference between the mean scores of Personal Problem and oversensitivity- a dimension of Youth Problem among Higher Secondary Students with respect to Medium of Instruction.
60. There is no significant difference between the mean scores of Personal Problems and Oversensitivity- a dimension of Youth Problem among Higher Secondary Students with respect to Type of Family.

61. There is no significant difference between the mean scores of Personal Problem and Oversensitivity – a dimension of Youth Problem with respect to Birth Order.
62. There is no significant difference between the mean scores of Personal Problems and Oversensitivity – a dimension of Youth Problem with respect to Parental Monthly Income.
63. There is no significant difference between the mean scores of Family issues- a dimension of Youth Problem among Higher Secondary Students with respect to Gender.
64. There is no significant difference between the mean scores of Family issues- a dimension of Youth Problem among Higher Secondary Students with respect to Academic Stream.
65. There is no significant difference between the mean scores of Family issues- a dimension of Youth Problem among Higher Secondary Students with respect to Medium of Instruction.
66. There is no significant difference between the mean scores of Family Issues- a dimension of Youth Problem among Higher Secondary Students with respect to Type of Family.
67. There is no significant difference between the mean scores of Family issues – a dimension of Youth Problem with respect to Birth Order.
68. There is significant difference between the mean scores of Family issues- a dimension of Youth Problem with respect to Parental Monthly Income. Students whose parental monthly income is above Rs.25,000 have significantly exhibited lower family issues than the students whose parental monthly income is below Rs.10,000 and between Rs.10,000 and Rs. 25,000.
69. There is significant difference between the mean scores of School issues- a dimension of Youth Problem among Higher Secondary Students with respect to Gender. Male students have significantly higher school issues than their counterparts.
70. There is no significant difference between the mean scores of School issues- a dimension of Youth Problem among Higher Secondary Students with respect to Academic Stream.
71. There is no significant difference between the mean scores of School issues- a dimension of Youth Problem among Higher Secondary Students with respect to Medium of Instruction.
72. There is no significant difference between the mean scores of School Issues- a dimension of Youth Problem among Higher Secondary Students with respect to Type of Family.

73. There is no significant difference between the mean scores of School issues – a dimension of Youth Problem with respect to Birth Order.
74. There is no significant difference between the mean scores of School issues – a dimension of Youth Problem with respect to Parental Monthly Income.
75. There is significant difference between the mean scores of Social issues- a dimension of Youth Problem among Higher Secondary Students with respect to Gender. Male students have significantly higher social issues than their counterparts.
76. There is no significant difference between the mean scores of Social issues- a dimension of Youth Problem among Higher Secondary Students with respect to Academic Stream.
77. There is no significant difference between the mean scores of Social issues- a dimension of Youth Problem among Higher Secondary Students with respect to Medium of Instruction.
78. There is no significant difference between the mean scores of Social Issues- a dimension of Youth Problem among Higher Secondary Students with respect to Type of Family.
79. There is no significant difference between the mean scores of Social issues – a dimension of Youth Problem with respect to Birth Order.
80. There is significant difference between the mean scores of Social issues- a dimension of Youth Problem with respect to Parental Monthly Income, students whose parental monthly income is above Rs. 25,000 have significantly lesser social issues than the students whose parental monthly income is below Rs.10,000 and between Rs.10,000 and 25,000.
81.
    - Learning Strategy into to is significantly and negatively correlated with Youth Problem into to and its dimensions- personal problem and oversensitivity, school issues and social issues.
    - Study strategy-a dimension of Learning Strategy is significantly and negatively correlated with Youth problem into to and its dimensions-personal problem and oversensitivity and school issues.
    - Note-taking/ listening-a dimension of Learning Strategy is significantly and negatively correlated with the dimensions of Youth Problem- school issues and social issues.
    - Reading /Comprehension-a dimension of Learning Strategy is significantly and negatively correlated with Youth problem into to and its dimensions-personal problem and oversensitivity, school issues and social issues.

- Writing /Research Skill -a dimension of Learning Strategy is significantly and negatively correlated with the dimension of Youth Problem- school issues.
- Test-taking Strategy -a dimension of Learning Strategy is significantly and negatively correlated with Youth problem into to and its dimensions-school issues and social issues.
- Organizational Technique -a dimension of Learning Strategy is significantly and negatively correlated with Youth problem into to and its dimensions- family issues, school issues and social issues.
- Time Management-a dimension of Learning Strategy is significantly and negatively correlated with Youth problem into to and its dimensions-family issues and school issues.

EDUCATIONAL IMPLICATIONS

Awareness about learning strategies should be created among higher secondary students. Learning strategies are student's general approach to a variety of learning tasks or it is the action taken by the learner to assist in learning more effectively. For learning, students adopt different types of strategies and they are (i) Meta-cognitive strategies, (ii) Cognitive strategies and (iii) Socio-affective strategies. It was proved through early studies that traditional mode of learning is facilitated by learning strategies. So today's student must also be equipped with the knowledge of learning strategies which will enable him to deal with the vast amount of information available through learning. Different subjects or a course of specialization is found to have considerable effect on accessing different kinds of information. Therefore student's interest in different subjects or courses will follow different types of learning strategies.

The primary purpose of the study is to investigate learning and individual learning differences by measuring the complex interplay between the learner and the learning strategies, lower-order learning processes, and the learning experience. Learning strategies provides successful learning support, and helps the learners to improve their learning ability. Explanations about leaning strategies help the educators understand, predict and support learning in different environments, match instructions and presentation, and adapt solutions to a greater success.

The learning strategies help to acquire knowledge and personal enlightenment. The learning strategies provide additional support for an evaluation of the curriculum and instruction at all levels of educational progress

Three strategies to improve learning

- Retrieval Practice- students try to recall what they have learnt.
- Reducing Test Anxiety-students write about their test worries.
- Worked examples-students study worked out examples of problems.
- In order to improve learning strategies among students the following may be adapted:
- The teachers could give quizzes at spaced intervals to reexpose students to key content and to give them practice in retrieving information. This research shows that being quizzed or tested on studied material improves student performance on final tests. Short-answer and fill-in-the-blank quizzes, which require active recall of specific information, are especially useful in helping students remember information longer than they would. This study has shown such quizzes, along with immediate correct-answer feedback, to be more effective than simply reviewing or rereading content.
- Alternate is that between having students look at examples of solved problems and having students solve problems themselves. Research on mathematics and science learning has shown that student learning is enhanced when teachers do this.
- Graphics may be used to illustrate the key points in verbal descriptions, especially when explaining scientific processes when possible.
- Abstract and concrete representations of concepts can be connected and integrated. For example, point out which variables in a mathematical function are related to which aspects of a word problem. This can help students apply a concept, once learned, across various contexts.
- Students can be taught to assess their own degree of learning and to allocate their study time accordingly. For example, students can be trained to summarize the main points of a reading assignment a day after the assignment is given, check to see what points they have missed or forgotten, and plan their study time accordingly.
- In order for the child to remember information, the information needs to be filed away in his brain in an organized way. The information will then be much more easily accessible when it is time to retrieve and use the information in the classroom or on a test. Tests are often used by teachers to evaluate how much students understand and retain after days, weeks, or even months of class work, reading, discussions, homework, and projects. It is important that the child develop organized systems for keeping track of information, or he may become overwhelmed or confused about the many details. Making sure he is doing nightly reading assignments and using a system to record or summarize, such as taking

notes, writing section or chapter summaries on sticky notes, or answering questions at the end of each chapter.

- Student can summarize orally to the teacher what he has read to make sure he derived the main ideas.
- Students in organizing materials, such as cleaning out binders and folders, creating sections with tabs or folders, and making sure all study materials, including study guides or review sheets, are gathered in one place.
- The student will probably remember information better when it is meaningful, familiar, or even silly! The following memory strategies may help the children with those details and facts that just won't stick.
- **Crazy phrases:** If the student has to remember a list of items in order, such as the planets in the solar system, he can come up with a silly sentence using the first letter of each item on the list. The following is an example many teachers use to help students remember the nine planets in order: My Very Eager Mother Just Served Us Nine Pizzas. Otherwise known as: Mercury, Venus, Earth, Mars, Jupiter, Saturn, Uranus, Neptune, and Pluto.
- **Acronyms:** When the order of the information does not matter, the student can take the first letters of each item on the list and try to form them into a word. For example, to help remember the systems of the body, the acronym "RED CRaNES" can be used:
    - Reproductive
    - Excretory
    - Digestive
    - Circulatory
    - Respiratory

      a (no system - place holder)
    - Nervous Endocrine
    - Skeletal
- Cartoons or pictures: If the student is a visual learner, it may help to make cartoons to illustrate concepts (e.g., history, science) or to draw small pictures to trigger his memory for vocabulary words.
- Word associations: the teacher can help the students to make connections to other information he knows by using the sounds or visual representations of words. For example, if he has to remember that the word «distinct» means «different or unmistakable,» the teacher can help him find another word that sounds similar, such as «stink.» If something stinks, it is definitely different and unmistakable!

- For all students, an important part of studying is becoming aware of their most common mistakes, so they can try to avoid making the same errors on the next test. To help the students become more strategic while studying, the teachers can: ask them to look through their graded homework assignments and previous tests to find any patterns of mistakes.
- The students may be helped to make a personalized checklist of test-taking techniques to remember while taking the test, such as remembering to look back to make sure he didn›t miss any questions or remembering to answer all parts of the questions. Checklists can be subject-specific as well.
- Assemble all relevant materials before the student begins, namely, textbooks, class notes, homework, and old quizzes.
- Make strategy cards for important concepts or terms by listing the term on the front of the card. On the back of the card, the student can list the key information and a memory strategy.
- Review class notes, homework, and quizzes, highlighting important information.
- Make a chart of the important events and note their causes and consequences.
- Predict possible essay questions and jot down notes for answering each question.
- Explain the main ideas of the chapter to a parent or friend.
- Have friend or parent quiz him.
- Make a timeline of important events in the chapter.
- Answer questions at the ends of the chapters.
- Review his study plan and set a timer for a certain study period according to the plan.
- In order to reduce youth problem among students, the following may be adapted:
- Communication is key to building rapport. When teachers have open communication with their students, their students will feel more open to talking to them about their problems—including bullying and other issues. Having classroom meetings is one way to build that communication. Classroom meetings provide a way for students to talk about school-related issues beyond academics. These meetings can help teachers and parents stay informed about what's going on at the school and in the child's life. Be sure to listen during these meetings. Empathic Listening is key. Students want to know that they're truly being listened to. They need to feel welcome to talk to their teachers

one-on-one, especially if they feel they've been bullied. Keep in mind that as a target, a student might not want to say something in front of the whole class or if the bully is in the classroom meeting.

- Schools need to have adequate reporting systems as well. They need to encourage teachers and staff to report the incidents that occur. This way the school can provide a way to protect students and prevent these circumstances from occurring again. Reporting also helps track the individual incidents and responses so the teacher can see if there's a trend. By using this system, possible future incidents can be prevented. Make the reporting system easy to use and confidential, and encourage staff to use it.
- Communication is not just verbal. A school can also provide nonverbal cues. These can include interior decorations like signs, it can include teachers and staff, and it can include the exterior of the school. The look of the school sends a strong message to students and parents about whether the school fosters a positive environment. If it does not send a good message, bullying and other problems such as the personal problem, school issues etc., is more likely to occur.
- Many people are involved in children's lives. They all have an impact. When these people work together, the biggest difference can be made in a child's life. Communication with parents about their child's behavior—whether their child is a perpetrator of or on the receiving end of bullying behavior—can be tricky. Thus teachers and staff need to build rapport with the parents of their students.
- Keeping parents informed about their child's grades, friends, behavior, and even attitudes in school is an important tool when addressing behaviors. Working together, parents and teachers can provide a consistent approach to introduce more productive and appropriate replacement behaviors. This makes the message more likely to sink in and stick with the child. It can even help the child recognize the area of interest
- In urban areas, some parents may have had a difficult time with schools in the past and may sense a lack of connection and trust in school staff. Staff should show parents how their school has changed or is changing, and that every student is given an opportunity to succeed. They can convey this message by sending invitations for different events or by having the parents play a specific and active role in their child's life. To help engage hard-to-reach parents, look for meaningful motivators to draw them into the discussion.

DELIMITIATIONS

The study has the following delimitations:

- Geographically, sample area selected was Chennai, Tamil Nadu.
- Six schools were selected at random, of which two were Aided Schools, two were Government Schools and the remaining were Private Schools.
- The present study intended to assess the Learning Strategies; but not to increase the level of Learning Strategies.
- 302 Higher Secondary Student were considered in the present study.

SUGGESSIONS FOR FURTHER RESEARCH

A number of problems were raised in the course of discussion of the findings in the present study. Following are some of the suggestions given by the investigator for undertaking further research.

- The present study is confined to only 302 higher secondary students of Chennai district. A similar study could be conducted on other districts.
- A similar study could be conducted among the college students.
- This study can be extended by adding few psychological variables.
- The same study can also be done to the students of rural areas.

CONCLUSION

This chapter gives the overall picture of the thesis work, which consists of the major findings, summary, suggestions for the further research and educational implications of the study, which is the goal to be reached.

The purpose of the study was to study the learning strategies and the Youth Problem among the higher secondary students. The present study is sure to provide some insight into the field of educational research and the findings of the study can serve a database for further research.

❐

11

Introduction

Teachers have the responsibility of training students to become efficient technicians by enabling them to acquire the necessary knowledge and skill besides assisting them in their personality development. Tight schedules of time table's activities and predetermined pattern of the traditional examinations have been the governing factors in the choice of instructional procedures. Individualization of instruction, which is the most logically accepted pattern in the emerging diversified system, is being given a go by.

Guidance is the assistance given to the individual to deal effectively with two environments or with his adjustment problem. It aims to help in the full growth and development of the individual especially when he is obstructed in his functioning. Hence it intends to develop in a person the ability to help him in varying situations. An infant's life begins with such a help. His motor development seeks assistance. A child seeks guidance in education. An adult may need it in getting suitable placement. In the modern times, the problems of adjustment arise every day. Change affecting the outer environment is not that fast in its effect on the people's life. Hence there is a growing necessity for guidance. Modern education lays great emphasis on guidance and counseling because it aims at total development of the individual to make of them useful members of the society.

Pre-adolescence and are often thought with rapid change and much frustration for the individual. For many it is time for breaking away from child-hood and embarking upon new behavior patterns and roles that call for considerable adoption. The effectiveness of learning to cope with these problems influences subsequent behaviour and many leave an enduring impression on the personality of the individual. A child in the pre-adolescent period is influenced by many factors. His stage of psychological maturity, his previous experiences, his parent's attitude and bodily conditions the pulley and pushes in his immediate environment, his unique personality as it has already developed, his individual growth pattern, and his self concept including his feelings about himself.

Meaning of the Guidance

In its beginnings guidance was centered on problems related to vocations. It was largely concerned with getting jobs for young people. One of the reasons for this was to reduce juvenile delinquency. Teen-age boys and girls, many of them not in school, had nothing to do; they had time on their hands. Such a situation breeds delinquency. Even in its beginning, however, the purpose of guidance was more than just for finding jobs for youth. Much attention was given to a 'wise' choice, that is, one that was suited to the abilities and needs of the individual. Although the vocational aspect has always been stressed, guidance has gone far beyond this; it is now concerned with the entire individual, in all aspects of his life, and with the interrelation between the individual and society. It helps youth to attain a life that is individually satisfying and socially effective.

When we stress the fact that everyone, at one time or another, may be in need of guidance, we must be sure that we understand thoroughly just what it is that he needs and should have made available for his use. Guidance is not giving directions. It is not the imposition of one person's point of view upon another person. It is not making decisions for an individual which he should ask for himself. It is not carrying the burdens of another's life. Rather, guidance is assistance made available by personally qualified and adequately trained men or women to an individual of any age to help him manage his own life activities, develop his own points of view, make his own decisions, and carry his own burdens.

Whenever a person is aided direct or indirect by another person in gaining in knowledge, emotional fitness, mental acuity or stability, social and civic adjustment, or occupational efficiency and job satisfaction, guidance of one kind or another is functioning. It will be noted the guidance, thus conceived, increases the individual's power to think and perform. It should not be considered an activity having for its purpose the lessening of an individual's ability to act independently or to follow his own initiative. Guidance is operating whenever a child, adolescent, or adult is helped in any way by another person or persons to come to a decision, improve his behaviour, or change his attitude.

Concerning people adults are constantly guiding the life of a young person, either by precept or by example. This is accomplished many times without specific purpose or even awareness on the part of the person who is responsible for the guidance. The young person who has benefited from his association with a fine adult, who has imitated his behaviour, or who has been influenced by his words may be equally unaware of the eventual effect upon him of what he has observed or heard.

Definition of Guidance

Guidance is the help given by one person to another in making choices and adjustments and in solving problems. Guidance aims at aiding the recipient to grow in his independence and ability to be responsible for him. It is a service that is universal-not confined to the school or the family. It is found in all phases of life-in the home, in business and industry, in government, in social life, in hospitals, and in prisons; indeed it is present wherever there are people who need help and wherever there are people who can help.

1. "Fundamental of all the guidance is the help or assistance given by one competent person to another individual so that the latter may direct his life by developing his point of view, make his own decisions and carry out those decisions" **- Crow and Crow.**
2. "Effective education is guidance, and realistic guidance is self-guidance" **- Carmicheal.**
3. "Guidance is inherent in education and as such should be done largely by classroom teacher. He should try to help pupils set up dynamic, reasonable and worthwhile objectives for themselves" **- Cox**.
4. "Guidance involves personal help to promote the growth of an individual in self-direction. The help may be given to the individual along or in a group; it is the individual who is the focus of attention and not the group. Also this attention is to be paid to the individual and not to the problem" **-Jones**.
5. "Assistance given to an individual in solving problems related to occupational choice and progress with due regard for the individual's characteristics and their relation to occupational opportunity"
-The General Conference, ILO, 1949
6. "All guidance is education, but some aspects of education are to guidance, the objectives of both education and guidance may be the

same viz., the development of individual,. But the methods used are different" - **B.B. Taneja.**

7. "Guidance is a process of helping individuals through their own efforts to discover and develop their potentialities both for personal happiness and social usefulness" - **Labh Singh.**
8. "Guidance is the process of helping individuals to understand themselves and their world" - **Shertzer and Stone.**

Importance of the Guidance

The basic question which may be asked here is – what is the need for guidance? Why should it be given to an individual? Man when born is not capable of independent working. He is born with certain biological inheritance which does not render him capable of adjustment in his physical environment. The human child main dependent for the longest period is on his parents who are responsible for his development in early childhood. Guidance is an integral part of Education. Guidance is necessary for the following reasons.

1. Guidance services if properly organized help to eliminate wastage and stagnation by developing the curriculum according to the needs and abilities of student.
2. Students are helped to select courses according to their abilities, interests and aptitudes.
3. Guidance service decreases the number of misfits by helping such cases to see things realistically and adjust themselves.
4. Students are prepared for professional leadership in the changed socio-economic and industrial conditions in which different occupations have emerged which require specialized training.
5. The child's healthy growth is encouraged.
6. Problems of discipline and delinquency are solved.
7. It helps to supply the right personnel for various jobs in private and public sectors.
8. The population in our country is increasing at a tremendous rate and if it is not checked it will create chaotic conditions in the country. The individuals require guidance to plan their family.
9. Individuals differ in Physical, mental, Social and emotional characteristics. To provide for the maximum development of individuality, guidance is essentially needed, particularly for exceptional children.
10. Problems of women are merging as a new area where guidance is needed for proper adjustment in the family. The cases of divorce, separation and desertion are very rapidly increasing in our society which is posing a new threat to our traditional social system.

11. There are other problems which are unique to our society as for instance problems of scheduled castes, problems of social conflicts problems of retired persons and problems of industrial relations where guidance in needed.
12. To help the adolescent pupils to know and develop their abilities and interests: Adolescence is that period of time, in which the child experiences a number of changes. The period roughly runs below 12 to early 20's. He moves from childhood to adulthood, mentally, emotionally, socially and physically. In this age, an individual is capable of begetting off springs. At this stage he is in dire need of guidance.
13. To help pupils to understand their strengths and limitations and to do scholastic work at the level of their abilities: Generally, the adolescents either over estimate or under estimate their abilities. Guidance is to clarify their concepts and to bring them to the level of their actual position. So that they become aware of the real situation of his personality and other allied areas such as interest, aptitudes etc.
14. To help pupils to make realistic educational and vocational choices: The pupils should be guided to select the subjects and activities according to their abilities, interests, achievements etc. In India generally the students do not think in terms of their abilities,. Capacities and capabilities, but are guided to select the subject the subject of studies either by the peer group or by their parents. The parents, so often, project their own frustrations upon their children and guide them to go in for a profession what they themselves had liked, but could not enter in that. This leads to the failure, frustration, dropout or stagnation. If proper guidance facilities are made available this type of wastage can be considerably avoided.
15. To provide information of educational opportunities: The pupils should be informed about the desirability and possibility of further schooling. They should be informed about the schools or colleges, training, vocational and professional courses so that they can, with the help of guidance workers, be able to go in for the courses of study which are most appropriate for them.
16. To help the pupils in personal and social adjustment: Guidance is not making some decisions for some body, it to enable him to make appropriate. To help the school to understand their student: For organizing suitable educational programmes in the college, the headmasters and the teachers must understand their pupils individually. The teachers can understand it in a perfect way if they are involved in the process of guidance activity. In that case they can find out way and

means to study their students in a more appropriate way. This improves upon the class room teaching. College discipline, college environments and college atmosphere.

Scope of Guidance

In the light of modernization and industrialization the scope of guidance is ever increasing. In the words of Crow and Crow,"As now interpreted, guidance touches every aspect of an individual's personality-physical, mental, emotional and social. It is concerned with all aspects of an individual's attitudes and behavior patterns. It seeks to help the individual to integrate all of his activities in terms of his basic potentialities and environmental opportunities."

The following factors are responsible for the expansion of the scope of guidance.

Complex Nature of Personality

Industrialization brings with it a number of tensions such as adjustment with the job, with the place of work, with the physical and social environment, and also with the advancement of technology and modernization. One is to cope with all such problems, tensions and anxiety in an effective way, for which guidance is needed not only on one occasion but throughout the life. So its scope in the field of adjustment with almost all spheres of life is increased. The discussion about the types of guidance services will make it amply clear that it is needed in almost all spheres of life and throughout the life span.

Complexity of Occupation

In the process of industrialization, automation and cybernetics, many new occupations are coming up and a few old occupations are dying. In U.S.A., an average man changes, seven occupations thought his life. The trend is bound to effect as the process of development will need very complex, sophisticated and complicated occupations for which higher educational background and intensive training will be necessary. All this process of the complexity of occupation is bound to increase the scope of guidance not only in one way, but in so many ways.

Complexity of Training

For the new jobs, new type of training, new courses of studies, use of new types of the machines and above all to prepare himself for employment in the changing world, are some of the problems which will have to be tackled in an effective way, with the help of guidance. When numbers of training facilities with different levels of specializations are being conceptualized, guidance will have to be introduced to avoid the chances of going of the right man in the wrong job.

Increasing Areas

The passing of time and complexity of circumstance, scholars like Brewer have prepared about 10 areas of guidance i.e, educational, vocational, religious, home relationship, citizenship, leisure time and recreation, personal well being, freight doing, co-operation and cultural action. The areas do embrace almost all the spheres of life into its grip and as such its scope is further increasing. The fact remains that; the more complex the society more will be the need for guidance.

The expansion of Education

The days are gone when only a few privileged were to be educated. Now, in the name of democracy, all needs to be educated to become good citizens. When all are to be educated to their capacities, capabilities, and potentialities, it becomes essential that the proper man is directed to go in for the proper channel i.e, subjects of study. It can be possible only when facilities for educational guidance are available in schools, colleges and employment exchanges.

Types of Guidance

Broadly speaking, there are a dozen types of guidance in accordance with various fields and situations where guidance is needed. The various fields or Types are 1. Personal social guidance 2. Education guidance 3. Vocational guidance, 4. Physical guidance, 5. Hygiene guidance, 6. Marital guidance, 7. Home guidance, 8. Collage guidance 9. Leadership guidance. 10. Religious guidance, 11. Leisure guidance 12. Old age guidance. Out of these types the first three are the major ones, and the test are either minor ore already included in any of the first three. For instance fourth to tenth types re some now included in personal social guidance. The eleventh can form a part of educational guidance the twelfth is not related to college pupils, and hence it may be left out. Briefly speaking the three main types are as follows.

1. Personal Social Guidance

This assists the child to adjust well with physical and social environment and solves all the emotional and Psychological problems. It makes the child socially well adjusted and emotionally balanced and helps his all round development of personality.

Higher Secondary Stage

At this stage the pupil makes a transition from adolescence to adult hood. The specifics Psychological problems that arise are adjustment with the college environment and persistence of the old problems from the adolescent life. The function of the guidance services is to helps the college student solve old problems, adjustment to new environment, build a philosophy of life imbibe healthy ideas and goals, acquaint themselves will the social surroundings and participate in social activities.

2. Educational Guidance

It pertain the choice of the various educational courses available to the child in accordance with his innate capacities interests, personality traits and aspirations. If seeks to recognize the individual differences in pupils and adjust these with diversified courses.

Higher Secondary Stage

This is the higher stage when the pupil is in the age group 16-20 and he develops into a youth full nature personality. He becomes conscious of his self his responsibilities towards the parents the family members and towards the society. But many of them are not clear about their goals. They are blind about their purposes. The guidance programmed at this stage is to help the college student in realizing there aims. Not all are fit of college education. They deserve to be directed to other channels such as short term causes after matriculation apprenticeship in a vocation are a direct employment.

3. Vocational Guidance

It is an extension of the educational guidance pertaining to the judicious choice of the profession or employment after the completion of the studies in accordance with the ability aptitude and trait of the pupil.

Higher Secondary Stage

The objective of guidance at this stage is to assist the college student in acquiring knowledge about memories vacation after the university education making him conscious of his responsibility and redirecting him from service jobs of technical and professional nature so as make him a better contributor to the society a better producer in the economic sense, and a happy citizen. This type of guidance is to be provided through a well know organization at the directed level or at the university or at the college itself. The specific tasks of organization will be to impart knowledge of various vocations, knowledge of higher avenues in terms of study or jobs and knowledge of financial assistance available from the Government in terms of scholarship, fellowships, travel grants and apprenticeship allowance.

Guidance Needs Categories

Different authors classified guidance needs different ways. Grewal, J.C. classified guidance needs into five categories.

- Physical Needs
- Social Needs
- Psychological Needs
- Educational Needs
- Vocational Needs

Delimitations of the study

It is difficult to concentrate all the things in a single study. The investigator has delimited her study. They are;

- This study is limited to Higher Secondary Schools of Shillong only.
- This study is limited to the academic year 2014-15.
- This study is limited to few socio-demographic variables only.

❐

12

Review of Related Literature

A Review of Related Literature is the process of collecting, selecting and reading books, journals, reports, abstracts and other references. A literature review is a systematic explicit and reproductive method for identifying, evaluating and interpreting the existing body of recorded work produced by research scholars and practitioners. It is an essential aspect of any research work that gives insight to the investigator about the issues or problems under study. According to Best J.W (1986) "A brief summary of previous research and writing of recognized experts provides evidences that the researcher is familiar with what is already known and with what is still unknown and untested". Good (1959) "A survey of related literature is necessary for proper planning, execution and right concept of the problems and solutions".

The objectives of review of related literature are to identify the gap in area and avoid duplication of research. To prevent researcher from repeating previous errors or redoing the work that has already been done. To get information about methodology and techniques for selected research problem. To search for suitable research problem. To think on process of formation of hypothesis for a research problem. To get information about tools and conclusions comparatively. To study reference material and contribute in knowledge.

Thus a systematic review of related literature will help to get sources of significant ideas, theories and hypothesis and valuable information regarding problems and evaluation of current practices and empirical researcher.

Guidance

Guidance is the process of helping an individual to help himself ever individual requires it whether he is infancy or an adult, a genius or a dullard, average or a person above or below average. For in the course of growing and developing he is faced with a number of alternative ways of behaviours and depending upon his choice, he can make or mark his life opportunities. "Guidance" has become one of the most essential terms of the modern educational philosophy and has been drawing the special attention of various educational and psychological experts during the recent years. Guidance is comparatively new field with in larger and more inclusive field of education and many of its terms are not adequately defined and stabilized.

Guidance is a concept that teacher varied aspects of an individual; physical emotional social occupation etc. it is therefore concerned with all the attitudes and behaviour patterns of individuals in therefore concerned with all the attitudes and behaviour patterns of individuals in different sphere. The attitudes and behavioral patterns of individuals are not found in a day, rather they shape gradually under the influence of changing environmental conditions. The entire way of an individual's life is conditioned to a high by his choice of an occupation which includes appropriate preparation, actual entry and degree of success or failure in it.

This means that information pertaining to educational back ground. Scholarship foreign studies, training apprenticeship, employment etc. so that an individual may plan his future career in accordance with his potentialities, available educational facilities and occupational opportunities. In general however, guidance has been accepted as the personalization of education both in theory and in practice.

According to Mathewson (1955) "Guidance should be constructed to mean as a continuous and pervasive process as a favorable directional influence upon appropriate social behaviour personal effectiveness in every day affairs, academic competence and progress and assimilation of right values and attitude".

Knapp (1953) stressed that "guidance is learning about the individual student helping him to understand himself effecting changes in had in his environment which help him to grow develop as much a possible."

Hoyt (1962) expressed guidance as "that part of pupils personal service aimed at maximal development of individual potentialities through devoting school wide assistance to youth in the personal problems, choices and decisions each must face, as he moves toward maturity.

Grant (1965) defined "Guidance has assisting students in adjusting, solving problems and maturing and added that guidance includes a constitution of services as informal, planning and placement, counseling and student appraisal".

According to palane (1966) "Guidance is the assistance which the college gives the pupil to aid him in fulfilling his potential, negotiating the facts of development and solving his special problems". Thirtha (1973) says "guidance has to mean helping the individual to become increasingly self directive and capable of creative and purposeful living".

Brief History of Guidance

It is very difficult to trace back the history of the origin of the guidance movement as it exists today because it has been the result of continuous efforts of individuals and institutions who from time to time have contributed to the growth of the guidance movement. Here, it is not possible to mention the names of all individuals and institution which have contributed in the development of guidance. Only those important individuals and institutions will be referred to whose contribution has been most relevant to the movement in the present form.

As a part of the educational system in ancient India, seats of learning flourished in different regions of the country. Taxila and Nalanda Universities were supposed to be the highest seats of learning where scholars came not only from India but also other countries i.e. China, Japan, Cambodia, Ceylon etc. to receive education at the hands of distinguished scholars. The admission to these universities was processed through a very strict admission text conducted by Dwarpandita who worked as a counselor for the new entrants to the campus. This process of admission worked, in more or less the same way as our present-day educational guidance.

In ancient India, the whole of the society was divided into four "Varnas"- Kshatriya, Brahmin, Vaishya and Sudras. Sudras were not entitled to education. The three high castes were educated in accordance with their assigned duties. Education, in a strict sense, was only confined to Brahmins. Therefore was hardly any question of providing guidance.

In the Muslim period, education was given in mosques and temples and was mostly of a religious nature. The mass of people remained without educational facilities. Hardly any kind of guidance was provided to the students as regards the selection of courses for study.

Maharashtra and Gujarat, formerly part of the state of Bombay, started a guidance bureau in 1950 to cater to the needs of school-going children. The bureau emphasized the importance of collecting and disseminating occupational information and to train the guidance personnel to effectively manage the guidance services in college and the community. The bureau has been making consistent efforts to create awareness about the utility of guidance among principals, teachers and parents in the state.

The Secondary Education Commission was appointed in the year 1952 to study the conditions of secondary education and to make recommendations for its improvement. The Commission emphasized the importance of guidance in colleges. The Government of India established a Central Bureau of Educational and Vocational Guidance in 1954. The main objective of the central bureau was to coordinate the activities of state bureaus which were afterwards opened in almost all the states and to provide leadership in the field of guidance.

Keeping into consideration the importance of guidance, the all India Educational and Vocational Association was formed in 1956 to coordinate the work being done in different states. The guidance movement is gaining ground in our country. Needless to mention, there is great wastage and stagnation in our educational system right from primary to university level. The guidance services will certainly reduce the amount of wastage and stagnation.

Adjustment

The term 'adjustment's ordinarily taken as a smoothly functioning adaptation to some aspect or aspects of an individual's environment. Poor adjustment implies inadequate adaptation, and frequently implies also a degree of association fiction, tension or emotional disturbances.

The word 'adjustment' came into popular use during the 1930's and was given strong endorsement by Shaffer (1936), in his classical work psychology of adjustment. He emphasized the biological adaptation of the organism to it is environment as the central meaning of the term. The mechanistic approach to human behaviour shows the imprint of behaviorists who dominated the scene since 1920. Gestalt psychologists and psycho analysts criticized this definition of adjustment as given by Shaffer. They criticized the definition to have given emphasis to mechanical adaptation of human being to the demands of the environments. They pointed that man not only adopts himself to the environment but through the use of his intelligence and his imagination changes his environment to meet his need s more effectively.

According to Boring (1948) "Adjustment is a process by which a living organism maintains balance between its needs and circumstances that influence the satisfaction of these needs". Adjustment is therefore, a state of harmony between the needs, activities and resources of a person and the conditions of his milieu. Accordingly personality-adjustment indicates how well a particular individual has been able to cope with himself and with the environment in and around him. A person is considered to be well adjusted, if he accepts himself and the way of life he has to follow without getting into trouble.

Mathews (1960) defines a successful person as "one who lives and grows in such a way that he is actively aware,. Relatively satisfied and feels largely successful with his internal adjustment and as a result of exhibits behaviours that is generally approved by him and relatively acceptable to the outside world". Huston (1971) found that measures of psychological adjustment seem to be better predictors of future than current academic performance.

This is the definition adopted by Bell (1962) in the developing of his adjustment inventory. This viewing operationally one who has the least number of problems in adjusting with his environment may be considered as well adjusted.

STUDIES DONE ON GUIDANCE NEEDS

Studies on Guidance Needs

As problems of life are getting more and more complicated day by day, man needs help to understand and solve them. In every field of life man has to face great hardships. These tremendous changes are not only seen in any one dimension of human life but the whole scheduling of human affairs is affected by it. In such condition we have to accept the need of proper assistance for the sake of adjustment in this complicated and developing society. Change in society and social norms and values have brought revolutionary changes in every aspect of human life. This structure needs proper and organized mode of help or assistance; recognized as guidance. Guidance is a process which helps every individual to help himself by the recognition and utilization of the innate potentialities. It provides clear vision about setting life goals, future plans and problems of religious and civic affairs. The concept of guidance in human race is not new; it is as old as human himself. It can trace back in Greek societies as informal resource by the philosophies of Plato and Aristotle or by the follow ship of traditional educational ways.

Many psychologists have emphasized that fact that if problems of children are not identified early and remedial measures taken; they will lead to serious complications in their later scholastic achievement and other areas of adjustment. Many investigators have compared counseled and non-counseled groups of student s and found that the counseled were superior to the counseled were superior to the non-counseled in many respects.

Williamson and Boarding (1930) compared a group of counseled and a matched group of non-counseled students. They found that the counseled group got better grades and were better adjusted academically. These students were followed up after 32 years in 1962, by Campbell (1965). He found that the counseled groups were more successful as adults on several criteria. In another follow up study of counseled students, Rotheny (1958) also reported similar findings.

Gribbons (1960) found that the guidance programmed aided pupils to make accurate appraisal of their abilities, values and interests and provided information about educational and vocation opportunities and helped the pupils to integrate their self appraisal and the information.

Students seek counsel from some source on other at crucial periods. If a qualified persona is not available, they have no choice; expect to get guidance from those with who they are in close contact. Krishna (1957) and Prasad (1957) reported that most students get counsel from the members of their families Krishna (1957) reported that as many as 31 percent of the parents of the students he studied were illiterates. This shows the extent of pseudo guidance that the students will be receiving and speaks for importance of guidance services in institutions.

The issue of self-confidence is a critical one in education and more especially in elementary education. The non-confident child is a source is a source of worry to both, his parents and teachers. This is especially true if he is also deemed academically capable. It has been found by Rajagopal (1968) that backward children have feelings of insecurity, emotional imbalance and anxiety.

However, it is not only the backward children that need help but also the gifted children who do good work in school and yet sit quietly seldom interacting within the academic environment. At higher levels of education this form of shyness can adversely affect the individual chances of success (Flowes and Maston, (1972).

From the results of a 10 years follow up study of 70 men who graduated from a western University, highly selective in its admissions, Decent (1957) argues that the student of high environment deserves more counseling attention than ordinarily receives, not only the good student be much better, but he might become more productive graduate if counseling services were more accessible to him. Wedemezer (1953) Gowan (1960) and many others also advocated that the gifted also must be given guidance.

In a follow up study of high ability achieving and non-achieving college freshman, Smith (1971) found that many of the non-achievers would have achieved better had they received counseling.

An elaborate research was done in the university of Illinois were two groups of gifted under achievers were given counseling. It was found that the counseled group improved in personal adjustment, but immediate classroom performance was not improved. However, achievement measured after four months showed some improvement (Paterson, 1962).

The voluminous literature, while somewhat contradictory does engender a fairly coherent picture of the dropout. The dropout is more is more likely to be a male. He comes from a home of lower socio-economic status (Hollingstead, 1949) likely to have but difficulty in school as reflected in low reading achievement scores (Perty, 1956) is marked by absenteeism and is non participant in extracurricular actives (Paniel and Dillon, 1956) and low previous grade averages (Panel, 1960). The National Education Research Division observes that he withdraw from school at age 16 while he was in the 10th class. His IQ was likely to be below 100 (Blough and Telfore) and he was less likely to have resided in a home with both natural parents present (Vanlyke and Hoyt, 1958).

Thus many investigators have emphasized the fact that had guidance been given many of the maladjusted would have been better adjusted. Many of those who are classified as underachievers would have not have been in that group. The school dropout would have become a much more productive graduate had been given counseling.

Mc Daniel, H.B. & John E. Lalls (1961) stated that;"Freud's contribution to guidance practice is extensive for the psychoanalytic methods of psychotherapy have had strong impact upon most of the current theories of counseling for example, catharsis, the process of lessening psychological tensions by talking through one's problems. Galton in England laid the foundations of many of the current statistical procedures which underlie testing. It remained for Binet and Simon in France to construct the first successful intelligence test. Many of the new measurement devices of intelligence, achievement, aptitude, interest and personality have proved to have value from both the curriculum and guidance functions of the schools."

It means that the entrance in 20th century guidance movement took a new turn and several tests were made for the better investigation of individual's interest and for the exact measurement of his capabilities. That test concept was followed by Terman after few years of Binet& Simon. The purpose was to provide better and right direction to the individual. These raw efforts got the shape of proper guidance movement in the year1908 by Frank Parson in America.

Milton L. Blum (1961) quoted that; "*With the end of the World War II, in America guidance again assumed great importance in the shifting of people* *back to their civilian occupations and in designating civilian occupation for those who went directly in to the armed forces from schools."*

It proves that movement took little bit different shape here but the main purpose of guidance was to solve the adjustment problems of the students that if they are not anymore interested to continue armed life so they had the opportunity to change their life pattern in common civilian life.

1. *"In 1951 Rogers introduced the concept of client centered counseling which was highly appreciated by people. In 1970s there was an emphasis on accountability of services provided by school counselors and the benefits that could be obtained with structured evaluations. The educational and counseling needs of students with disabilities we readdressed with the passage of the Education for All Handicapped Children Act in 1975 in America. In 1990s proper school counseling program was scheduled and ASCA set standards for school counseling and showed the roles and responsibilities of counselors at different levels. Like at middle and higher level Counselors deal with a vast array of student problems–personal, academic, social, and career issues."*
2. *"Guidance has been conceptualized as a programme of activities which has provided us with the gateway out of the existing numerous problems in our present age of complex scientific and technological development"* **-(Okobiah and Okorodudu 2004).**

Robert L. Gibson (1986) stated that;"In the early civilizations, the philosophers, priests, or other representatives of the Godsand religion assumed the function of advising and offering counsel of these early Greekcounsellors, Plato more than any other person is generally recognized as one of the first to organize psychological insights into a systematic theory."

In every era we can study the concept of guidance in different shades. In America with the start of 20th century it was observed that the complexities of life were growing increasingly due to which psychological investigation was done by different psychologists, resulted in the start of guidance movement.

In the words of Gibson (1986); *"In America during the 1930s, possible directions for guidance in the elementary school were put forth by the child study movement, which took the position that it was the teacher's role to provide guidance for each pupil in the self contained class room."*

After that need of guidance got crucially increased, and many new guidance efforts indifferent countries broke out.

The UNESCO module on guidance and counseling (2000) also posited that Guidance is a programme of services to individuals based on their needs and the influence of environmental factors. Guidance and counseling is a professional field which has a broad range of activities, programmes and services geared towards assisting individuals to understand themselves, their problems, their school environment and their world and also to develop adequate capacity for making wise choices and decisions.

Shrivastava, K.K. (2003) discussed the contribution of Frank Parson; *"In 1908, Frank Parson working in Boston settlement house, proposed and developed an occupational counseling program for young people seeking a job. Within a year his vocational bureau began to work in cooperation with the Boston schools to guide children and adolescents into suitable schools and curricula."*

It means Frank parson is considered as father of guidance movement in world due to his contribution in solving complexities of young generation. His book and his bureau set an example for many upcoming guides and counselors within their county America.

On the other hand, generally speaking, *"placement is ensuring that people are in the right place at the right time. It has to do with helping people find a place that will contribute to their physical, mental, emotional, and spiritual health and well* -being (Villar, 2007, p. 150).

Guidance and counseling is usually referred to as *"a process of helping individuals to understand themselves by discovering their own needs, interests and capabilities in order to formulate their own goals and make plans for realizing those goals"* -(Egbochuku, 2008, p. 44).

Various studies have been conducted on guidance and its varied needs by many Indian and Western educationists. It is evident from these researches that most of the research works done on guidance and its varied needs have been done in western countries. In India, comparatively less work has been done. From the studies, it is evident that, guidance and counseling leaves a positive effect on the academic achievement of under achievers. Career guidance develops higher career maturity. Guidance needs are influenced by the intelligence level of the students. There is a difference in the vocational interests of the socio-economically advantaged and non- advantaged students. Nicholas (2002) revealed lectures and professional help outside the university as the preferred sources of guidance for first year university students. Wright (2005) identified social class, gender, ethnicity and academic attainment as key factors involved in the complex process of choices that young pupils make during their 14-19 transition. Pius et. al. (2007) highlighted the importance of using assessment instruments to identify students' counseling needs. Giovazolias (2010) revealed that those students who face psychological difficulties had negative attitude towards counseling. Eyo et. al. (2010) revealed that students' attitude at secondary school stage towards guidance and counseling was significantly positive and that the gender and school location significantly influenced students' attitude towards guidance services. Guidance is the bedrock for achieving self-actualization. It is a process of helping individuals to understand themselves by discovering their own needs, interests and capabilities in order to formulate their own goals and make plans for realizing those goals. An analysis of guidance needs of secondary school students is of paramount importance; hence this study.

Specifically, *"the aims of guidance and counseling programs in schools are to assist individuals to develop the ability to understand themselves, to solve their own problems, and to make appropriate adjustments to their environment*"(Lunenberg, 2010, p. 8). Assessments, placements, and counseling are some of the major services of a guidance and counseling program.

Assessment services are designed *"to collect, analyze, and use a variety of objective and subjective personal, psychological, and social data"*(Lunenburg, 2010, p. 4). These collected data can be used to better understand students and better guide them in decision-making especially in providing admissions, placements, and counseling services. The use of both grades and examination to identify students with a high potential for future success are an example of multi-dimensional screening (Armstrong and Rochet, 1999).

"Outcomes based solely on one predictor (e.g., test score or grades) have consistently been proven to be inferior to prediction models that employ multiple predictors" **(Camara, Wiley & Wyatt, 2010, p. 6).**

Specifically, placement services are designed to include *"assessment, informational services, and counseling assistance appropriate to the pupil's choices of school subjects, co-curricular activities, and employment"* **(Lunenburg, 2010, p. 4).**

"The counseling service is designed to facilitate self-understanding and development through dyadic or small group relationships. The aim of such relationships tends to be on personal development and decision making that is based on self-understanding and knowledge of the environment" **(Lunenburg, 2010, p. 4).**

"Counseling is the heart of the guidance program. It is the counseling that integrates all the data gathered about the individual and his environment, in order for them to make sense" **(Villar, 2007, p. 86).**

Stephen (2002) in his item "Helping children with attention problems" stated as follows. 'As student with attention problems are a heterogeneous group, there is no one intervention (or set of interventions) that will improve the class room functioning of all of these students. Thus, it is suggested that classroom modifications be tailored to the unique needs of each student. In developing these modifications it is perhaps best to begin by examining how the classroom environment might be changes to set up the student with attention problems for success.

The next step is to consider the implementation of a contingency management system designed to provide external incentives for appropriate class room behaviours. In doing so it is important to remember that behaviour management programmes must be consistently applied. Further it is essential to avoid excessive use to negative consequences.

Students must experiences success. In other words, it is essential that students be frequently reinforced for what we want them to do, rather than simply punished for what we do not want them to do.

Davis (1996) in Ridge Spring Monetta Schools Guidance and counseling constructed Twelve Grades. In each grade he followed three strands. They are

1. Knowledge of self and others.
2. Career planning and Exploration
3. Educational and vocational development

By using these strand in different grades Davis had given guidance in his school to provide them the necessary follow up after school age.

Studies on Adjustment and Achievement

Greenland (1959) found that socially accepted children show better adjustment to school life than isolated ones. People however; differ in their strategies of coping with the environment. This difference in adjustment may be ascribed to various factors such as sex, social and cultural settings attitudes towards life, etc.,

Mittel (1962 and 1965) Anderson et.al (1963), Chowla (1964), Watlay (1965) and Davis (1967) found that when ability was controlled better adjustment resulted in better attainment. Hoyt et.al (1954) reported on insignificant relation between adjustment and achievement. Brown (Jr) (1959) found that most of the inter correlations between anxiety scores; measures of intelligence academic achievement and extravertism are negative, low and statistically insignificant.

Studies on Adjustment and other Variables

Locality

Time and again Psychologists in the past have studied the differences between rural, semi-urban and urban populations not only in their ways, attitudes and behaviour but nearly in all traits. For example, mc Nemon (1942) studied these differences in school subjects. Moisr and kuder (1949) studied the differences between the two groups in their professional characteristics; Mc Arthur (1955) and Knapp et.al. (1959) studied, the differences in social values; Lehman (1959) and other studied the difference in I.Q and Sharma and Labn Singh (1968) studies the differences in interest. The differences are observable in many of traits; particularly because of the cultural idiosyncrasies and cultural constancies of these two sub-cultures though they do not exist much apart in space.

In a study of personality differences among urban, sub-urban and rural students, Munsow (1959) reported that the best adjusted were sub-urban, urban and rural children in that order. Sinha and Pandey (1966) also found a significant difference between the number of problems of rural and urban children.

Venkata Rami Reddy (1972) administered a problem check-list to 510 students in VIII, IX and X grades in urban, semi-urban and rural areas to determine whether any significant difference between the levels of adjustment of pupils was hailing from these three localities. The mean adjustment scores for the three groups were 55046 for urban, 50.29 for semi-urban and 60.34 for rural. So pupils from urban localities had less number of problems than those from rural localities. But the differences were not significant at 0.05 level. Mathew and Assaiah (1973) found that the mean attitude scores of the pupils towards school were 88.1 and 85.2 for urban and rural localities respectively. However, Suhasini (1974) T.Venkataiah (1980) found significant differences between urban and rural pupils in their adjustment in some areas.

Sex

Sex is considered to be an important variable in various studies conducted in social sciences with reference to various problem areas like home, health, school society etc.

The incidence of a sex differences in learning of school children has been documented sincc 1932 (Swamy Temple. John, (1932). According to reports from learning Clinics Lindquist (1942) and Marlow (1967) surveyed elementary school Population and found girls in the lower grades are superior to boys in ability to read but observed that these differences tended to diminish as age increases. Similarly surveys of reading clinics by Wyatt (1966) have reported that the percentage of problem readers (Boys) ranged from 75 to 90. His study was restricted to boys only.

Ram Deopathak (1970) aimed at comparing boys and girls in their levels of adjustment. He found that girls had more problems in each area of adjustment. But, the critical ratios for scholastic and home adjustment are insignificant. In the rest of the areas the critical ratios were found to be significant at 0.001 level. He concluded that boys are better adjusted than girls. His sample was 400 boys and girls in the age range 14-16.

Venkata Rami Reddy (1972) did not find any significant difference between adjustment scores of boys and girls on many of the problem areas except on the area finance and living conditions in which boys were significantly less adjusted than girls.

Some psychologists found that girls had more favorable school related attitudes while boys tended to have a better academic self image, socially better adjusted and less anxious in the classroom situation. Modesen (1967) found that very young children both boys and girls (0-9) years respond to cues for co-operation and competition in a similar fashion.

Parents, Home and Health

The younger the child, the more flexible is his growth process. During infancy, the child needs help in many aspects especially because he must relinquish the secure dependence on parents and develop a degree of independence appropriate to his age. The emotional problems of youth can be classified as home centered school centered, and community centered problems. Bell adjustment inventory (Palsane, 1970) reveals that health adjustment is positively correlated with home adjustment (r = 0.43), social adjustment (r = 0.24) and emotional adjustment (r = 0.53). The healthy students were significantly superior in over all adjustment compared to those with poor health.

The study of caplow (1954) revealed that father specific interest may lead to both direct and indirect encouragement of similar interest in his son. The study of parental education as a variable in the overall adjustment has approved inconclusive with boys, the results have been significant meaning that those with good background of parental education tend to be better adjusted on the whole than those with poor parental education. In the case of girls, though the difference has been in favor of those with good parental education, it is not statistically significant, may be on account of few cases studied and a large standard error of difference the results of the study of Charles and Donivan (1972) indicated that sons and daughters excel in the particular skills used in their father's occupation.

Venkata Rami Reddy (1972) found that occupation status of fathers had a significant influence on the level of adjustment of VIII, IX and X graders. He found that sons of clerks are better adjusted than children of agriculturists. Suhasini (1974) in her investigation on IV and V graders reported, however, no relationship between parental occupations and level of adjustment. She reported that children of working mothers were better adjusted than children of non-working mothers, contributing Venkata Rami Reeddy's (1972) fin dings that of children of working and non-working mothers did not differ in their level of adjustment.

Mohan Mathew and Asssaiha (1973) using Likert type of attitude towards family and this was more so I the case of female pupils. Children of parents belonging to high professions had more favourable attitude towards family. The mean attitude score of pupils from families with one or two children was 88.7 and that of pupil from larger families was 84.3 ties with more favourable attitude towards the family scored higher marks in the examinations.

Kesavulu (1975) in his investigation into guidance needs of the academically talented pupils studying VIII and IXclasse4s in some selected secondary schools reported that there is significant difference between the intellectually superior and below average groups. He also reported that there was significant guidance needs of boys than girls-within 'above average' groups.

Gopal Chetty (1975) reported that there was a significant difference between the subjects hailing from different localities with regard to their adjustment. He found that the urban students were better adjustment than the semi-urban students in all the areas. He reported that the female subjects were found to better adjusted than the male subjects. He also reported that economic status of the parents, father's educational level and occupational level and mother's education had influenced a lot in the level of adjustment of the students.

Venkata Subbaiah (1989) in his investigation into the guidance needs of the students studying in the second year degree courses of Cuddapah district in A.P. reported that the occupation and education of the parents had a great influence on the guidance needs.

Attitudes

Attitudes are defined as "The degree of positive or negative associated with some psychological object" (Edward, 1957). Thus attitude is related to so many aspects like attitude towards home, college, sex, locality, parental income, parent's profession etc.

Shri Ram Murthy (1973) studied the attitude of present VI graders and X graders towards school - students of VI graders had more favourable attitude towards school than those of the X class.

❒

13

Methodology

This chapter is related with the methodology and procedure followed in conducting the present investigation. The characteristic of any good research is good methodology and procedure which directs and leads the investigation to the target where he/she desire to reach. This chapter present the details of the processes followed in collecting data to achieve the objectives of the present investigation. it also describes the population and sample, tools used, title of the study, objectives of the study, procedure for data collection and delimitation of the study.

Population

A population refers to any collection of specific group of human beings or of non-human entities such as objects, educational institution, time units and geographical areas, prices or salaries drawn by the individual. The population of the present study includes of the Higher Secondary Schools of Shillong in East Khasi Hills District. The total number of Higher Secondary Schools in Shillong is 27. Gender wise enrolment of students for the academic year 2014-15 is as follows:

TABLE.13.1: Population of the Study

<table>
<tr><th>Type of School</th><th>No of Schools</th><th>No of Male Students</th><th>No of Female Students</th><th>Grand Total</th></tr>
<tr><td>Government</td><td>3</td><td rowspan="3">1466</td><td rowspan="3">2154</td><td rowspan="4">3620</td></tr>
<tr><td>Govt. Aided</td><td>16</td></tr>
<tr><td>Private Unadided</td><td>8</td></tr>
<tr><td>Total</td><td>27</td><td>1466</td><td>2154</td></tr>
</table>

Sample

A sample is a portion of people from larger population. A sample is typically and relatively small portion of that large area which is chosen for statistical study. It helps to reduce greater precision and accuracy. Sampling procedure provide generalization on the basis of a relatively small portion of the population is called sample. Random sampling technique is used to select the sample. The sample of the study consists of 6 higher secondary schools among them 2 Government; 2 Government Aided and 2 Private management schools.

Sampling Method

Random sampling method was adopted and the schools were randomly selected.

TABLE.13.2: Sample Distribution

Category	Sample
Boys	41
Girls	124
Total	165

Variables

Dependent Variable: Scores of Guidance Needs (Whole and Five areas)

Independent Variables: Sex, Age, Class, Management, Native Place and Type of Family

Title of the Study

The title of the present study is stated as *"A Study on Guidance Need of Higher Secondary School Students in Shillong"*.

Objective of the Study

The study is designed with the following specific objectives:

1. To find out the Guidance need by area wise of Higher Secondary School Students in Shillong.

Research Questions

- How many students really require Guidance Need as a whole?
- How many students require Guidance Need by area wise?

Tool

The instrument which are using for gathering new facts for exploring new fields are called tools. In order to obtain information or data several tools may be uses according to the requirement of the study. The investigator was adopted the following tool for the present study:

1. Guidance Needs Inventory developed by Grewal, J.S., Retired Professor of Education, RIE, Bhopal.

   About the tool: There are 65 items in the tool. All are positive items.

TABLE.13.3: Areas Guidance Need

S.No.	Area	Questions
1	Physical Need	1-10
2	Social Need	11-25
3	Psychological Need	26-38
4	Educational Need	39-57
5	Vocational Need	58-65

Scoring Pattern: Highly True (HT) has weightage of '0'; Mostly True (MT) has weightage of '1'; Quite True (QT) has weightage of '2'; Least True has weightage of '3'and Not True (NT) has weightage of '4'.

For more information about inventory please refer Appendix-A and Appendix-B.

Data Collection

After selection the process data collection procedure was performed in a well sequenced manner. In the present study, the investigator personally visited the schools and met the Headmaster/Principal explained the purpose of her visit. After obtaining permission, the tool was distributed among the students. The investigator then collected back the tool sheets from the students.

Data Analysis and Discussion

The collected data was entered in the excel sheet. After thorough checking the analysis was done with the help of SPSS (Statistical Package for Social Science). Interpretation of analysis was done in the separate chapter entitled Analysis and Discussion.

❐

14

Analysis and Discussion

This Chapter deals with analysis and discussion of data. The data was presented in the form of:

1. Frequency distribution tables

Distributions Characteristics of Guidance Need Scores of Higher Secondary School Students.

TABLE.14.1: Frequency Distribution of (Whole Group) Higher Secondary School Students towards Guidance Need Scores

Class Interval (CI)	Frequency (f)	Percent (%)	Valid Percent	Cumulative Percent (cpf)
10-29	10	6.1	6.1	6.1
30-49	25	15.2	15.2	21.3
50-69	33	20.0	20.0	41.2
70-89	47	28.5	28.5	69.7
90-109	30	18.2	18.2	87.9
110-129	13	7.9	7.9	95.8
130-149	5	3.0	3.0	98.8
150-169	1	.6	.6	99.4
170-199	1	.6	.6	100.0
Total	**16.5**	**100.0**	**100.0**	

TABLE. 14.2: Frequency Distribution of Higher Secondary School Students towards Guildance Need (AllScores)

GN Score	Frequency (f)	Percent (%)	Valid Percent	Cumulative Percent
10	1	.6	.6	.6
11	1	.6	.6	.1.2
15	1	.6	.6	.1.8
16	1	.6	.6	2.4
19	1	.6	.6	3.0
20	1	.6	.6	.3.6
21	1	.6	.6	4.2
24	1	.6	.6	4.8
27	1	.6	.6	5.5
28	1	.6	.6	6.1
30	1	.6	.6	6.7
32	1	.6	.6	7.3
35	2	1.2	1.2	8.5
36	4	2.4	2.4	10.9
37	1	.6	.6	11.5
38	2	1.2	1.2	12.7
39	1	.6	.6	13.3
40	1	.6	.6	13.9
42	1	.6	.6	14.5
44	2	1.2	1.2	15.8
45	1	.6	.6	16.4
46	2	1.2	1.2	17.6
47	2	1.2	1.2	18.8
48	1	.6	.6	19.4
49	3	1.8	1.8	21.2
51	2	1.2	1.2	22.4
52	1	.6	.6	.23.0
53	2	1.2	1.2	24.2
54	1	.6	.6	24.8
55	2	1.2	1.2	26.1
56	1	.6	.6	26.7

57	2	1.2	1.2	27.9
60	3	1.8	1.8	29.7
61	2	1.2	1.2	30.9
62	2	1.2	1.2	32.1
63	3	1.8	1.8	33.9
64	3	1.8	1.8	35.8
65	2	1.2	1.2	37.0
66	2	1.2	1.2	38.2
67	2	1.2	1.2	39.4
68	1	.6	.6	40.0
69	2	1.2	1.2	41.2
70	2	1.2	1.2	42.4
71	1	.6	.6	43.0
72	3	1.8	1.8	44.8
73	1	.6	.6	43.5
74	2	1.2	1.2	46.7
75	2	1.2	1.2	47.9
76	2	1.2	1.2	49.1
77	1	.6	.6	49.7
78	3	1.8	1.8	51.5
79	2	1.2	1.2	52.7
80	3	1.8	1.8	54.5
81	2	1.2	1.2	55.8
82	4	2.4	2.4	58.2
83	3	1.8	1.8	60.0
84	4	2.4	2.4	62.4
85	1	.6	.6	63.0
86	4	2.4	2.4	65.5
87	3	1.8	1.8	67.3
88	1	.6	.6	67.9
89	3	1.8	1.8	69.7
90	1	.6	.6	70.3
91	3	1.8	1.8	72.1
92	4	2.4	2.4	74.5

93	4	2.4	2.4	77.0
95	1	.6	.6	78.2
98	5	3.0	3.0	81.2
99	1	.6	.6	81.8
100	3	1.8	1.8	83.6
101	1	.6	.6	84.2
102	2	1.2	1.2	85.5
105	1	.6	.6	86.1
106	1	.6	.6	86.7
107	1	.6	.6	87.3
109	1	.6	.6	87.9
111	1	.6	.6	88.5
112	1	.6	.6	89.2
113	1	.6	.6	89.7
115	2	1.2	1.2	90.9
116	1	.6	.6	91.5
118	1	.6	.6	92.1
120	3	1.8	1.8	93.9
124	1	.6	.6	94.5
126	1	.6	.6	95.2
127	1	.6	.6	95.8
132	2	1.2	1.2	97.0
133	1	.6	.6	97.6
143	1	.6	.6	98.2
148	1	.6	.6	98.8
155	1	.6	.6	99.4
172	1	.6	.6	100.
Tpta;	165	100.0	100.0	

High scores are an indication of less need and low scores on the inventory are an indication of more need. The minimum score in the inventory is 0 and maximum score is 260.

From the Table-4.1 & 4.2 it is found that 95.8% of students scored below 130 score (50% score of total score). It shows that, nearly 96% of students want guidance need.

TABLE.14.3: Frequency Distribution of Higher Secondary School Students towards Guidance Need under the area Physical Need

Physical Need				
Score	**Frequency**	**Percent**	**Valid Percent**	**Cumulative Percent**
0	2	1.2	1.2	1.2
1	1	.6	.6	1.8
2	4	2.4	2.4	4.2
3	3	1.8	1.8	6.1
4	9	5.5	5.5	11.5
5	5	3.0	3.0	14.5
6	4	2.4	2.4	17.0
7	8	4.8	4.8	21.8
8	11	6.7	6.7	28.5
9	11	6.7	6.7	35.2
10	14	8.5	8.5	43.6
11	11	6.7	6.7	50.3
12	12	7.3	7.3	57.6
13	7	4.2	4.2	61.8
14	5	3.0	3.0	64.8
15	12	7.3	7.3	72.1
16	5	3.0	3.0	75.2
17	5	3.0	3.0	78.2
18	8	4.8	4.8	83.0
19	8	4.8	4.8	87.9
20	2	1.2	1.2	89.1
22	3	1.8	1.8	90.9
23	4	2.4	2.4	93.3
24	1	.6	.6	93.9
25	1	.6	.6	94.5
27	2	1.2	1.2	95.8
28	2	1.2	1.2	97.0
29	1	.6	.6	97.6
30	1	.6	.6	98.2
32	3	1.8	1.8	100.0
Total	**165**	**100.0**	**100.0**	

There are 10 items in Physical Need area of Guidance Need. The maximum Score in this area is 40 and minimum is zero. 87.9% of students scored below 20 (50 per cent of total scores). It shows that nearly 88% of students want physical need. 2 students need 100 per cent Guidance of Physical Need.

TABLE14.4: Frequency Distribution of Higher Secondary School Students towards Guidance Need under the area Social Need

Social Need				
Score	**Frequency**	**Percent**	**Valid Percent**	**Cumulative Percent**
2	1	.6	.6	.6
3	1	.6	.6	1.2
4	3	1.8	1.8	3.0
5	1	.6	.6	3.6
6	2	1.2	1.2	4.8
7	2	1.2	1.2	6.1
8	4	2.4	2.4	8.5
9	6	3.6	3.6	12.1
10	5	3.0	3.0	15.2
11	8	4.8	4.8	20.0
12	6	3.6	3.6	23.6
13	7	4.2	4.2	27.9
14	8	4.8	4.8	32.7
15	9	5.5	5.5	38.2
16	4	2.4	2.4	40.6
17	5	3.0	3.0	43.6
18	6	3.6	3.6	47.3
19	10	6.1	6.1	53.3
20	15	9.1	9.1	62.4
21	11	6.7	6.7	69.1
22	5	3.0	3.0	72.1
23	12	7.3	7.3	79.4
24	3	1.8	1.8	81.2
25	2	1.2	1.2	82.4
26	3	1.8	1.8	84.2
27	5	3.0	3.0	87.3
28	5	3.0	3.0	90.3
29	1	.6	.6	90.9
30	3	1.8	1.8	92.7
31	3	1.8	1.8	94.5
32	1	.6	.6	95.2
33	1	.6	.6	95.8
34	2	1.2	1.2	97.0
36	1	.6	.6	97.6
37	1	.6	.6	98.2
39	1	.6	.6	98.8
45	1	.6	.6	99.4
50	1	.6	.6	100.0
Total	**165**	**100.0**	**100.0**	

There are 15 items in Social Need area of Guidance Need. The maximum score in this area is 60 and minimum is zero. 90.9 % of students scored below 30 score (50% of total score). It shows that 91% of students want Social Need.

TABLE. 14.5: Frequency Distribution of Higher Secondary School Students towards Guidance Need under the area Psychological Need

Psychological Need				
Score	**Frequency**	**Percent**	**Valid Percent**	**Cumulative Percent**
0	1	.6	.6	.6
2	3	1.8	1.8	2.4
3	4	2.4	2.4	4.8
4	1	.6	.6	5.5
6	4	2.4	2.4	7.9
7	2	1.2	1.2	9.1
8	8	4.8	4.8	13.9
9	5	3.0	3.0	17.0
10	7	4.2	4.2	21.2
11	3	1.8	1.8	23.0
12	4	2.4	2.4	25.5
13	4	2.4	2.4	27.9
14	4	2.4	2.4	30.3
15	4	2.4	2.4	32.7
16	5	3.0	3.0	35.8
17	4	2.4	2.4	38.2
18	1	.6	.6	38.8
19	5	3.0	3.0	41.8
20	12	7.3	7.3	49.1
21	9	5.5	5.5	54.5
22	2	1.2	1.2	55.8
23	12	7.3	7.3	63.0
24	8	4.8	4.8	67.9
25	7	4.2	4.2	72.1
26	6	3.6	3.6	75.8
27	9	5.5	5.5	81.2
28	9	5.5	5.5	86.7
29	4	2.4	2.4	89.1
30	6	3.6	3.6	92.7
31	4	2.4	2.4	95.2
32	1	.6	.6	95.8
34	1	.6	.6	96.4
35	3	1.8	1.8	98.2
40	1	.6	.6	98.8
43	1	.6	.6	99.4
47	1	.6	.6	100.0
Total	**165**	**100.0**	**100.0**	

There are 13 items in Psychological Need area of Guidance Need. The maximum score in this area is 52 and minimum is zero. 72.1 % of students scored below 26 score (50% of total score). It shows that 72% of students want Guidance of Psychological Need. Only one student needs 100 per cent of Guidance of Psychological Need.

TABLE.14.6: Frequency Distribution of Higher Secondary School Students towards Guidance Need under the area Education Need

Educational Need				
Score	**Frequency**	**Percent**	**Valid Percent**	**Cumulative Percent**
0	3	1.8	1.8	1.8
2	2	1.2	1.2	3.0
3	4	2.4	2.4	5.5
4	9	5.5	5.5	10.9
5	7	4.2	4.2	15.2
6	3	1.8	1.8	17.0
7	2	1.2	1.2	18.2
8	5	3.0	3.0	21.2
9	8	4.8	4.8	26.1
10	9	5.5	5.5	31.5
11	4	2.4	2.4	33.9
12	3	1.8	1.8	35.8
13	5	3.0	3.0	38.8
14	10	6.1	6.1	44.8
15	4	2.4	2.4	47.3
16	8	4.8	4.8	52.1
17	5	3.0	3.0	55.2
18	4	2.4	2.4	57.6
19	5	3.0	3.0	60.6
20	7	4.2	4.2	64.8
21	7	4.2	4.2	69.1
22	6	3.6	3.6	72.7
23	4	2.4	2.4	75.2
24	3	1.8	1.8	77.0
25	4	2.4	2.4	79.4
26	3	1.8	1.8	81.2
27	3	1.8	1.8	83.0
28	2	1.2	1.2	84.2
29	5	3.0	3.0	87.3
30	1	.6	.6	87.9
31	4	2.4	2.4	90.3
33	4	2.4	2.4	92.7
34	1	.6	.6	93.3
36	2	1.2	1.2	94.5
37	1	.6	.6	95.2
38	1	.6	.6	95.8
40	1	.6	.6	96.4
41	1	.6	.6	97.0
42	2	1.2	1.2	98.2
48	1	.6	.6	98.8
50	2	1.2	1.2	100.0
Total	**165**	**100.0**	**100.0**	

There are 19 items in Educational Need area of Guidance Need. The maximum score in this area is 76 and minimum is zero. 90.3 % of students scored below 36 score (50% of total score). It shows that 90 % of students want Guidance of Educational Need. Only three students need 100 per cent of Guidance of Educational Need.

TABLE.14.7: Frequency Distribution of Higher Secondary School Students towards Guidance Need under the area Vocational Need

Vocational Need				
Score	**Frequency**	**Percent**	**Valid Percent**	**Cumulative Percent**
0	7	4.2	4.2	4.2
1	7	4.2	4.2	8.5
2	10	6.1	6.1	14.5
3	11	6.7	6.7	21.2
4	11	6.7	6.7	27.9
5	11	6.7	6.7	34.5
6	18	10.9	10.9	45.5
7	16	9.7	9.7	55.2
8	18	10.9	10.9	66.1
9	7	4.2	4.2	70.3
10	4	2.4	2.4	72.7
11	12	7.3	7.3	80.0
12	11	6.7	6.7	86.7
13	5	3.0	3.0	89.7
14	6	3.6	3.6	93.3
15	3	1.8	1.8	95.2
16	4	2.4	2.4	97.6
17	2	1.2	1.2	98.8
18	1	.6	.6	99.4
20	1	.6	.6	100.0
Total	**165**	**100.0**	**100.0**	

There are 8 items in Vocational Need area of Guidance Need. The maximum score in this area is 32 and minimum is zero. 90.3 % of students scored below 16 score (50% of total score). It shows that 95.2 % of students want Guidance of Vocational Need. Only seven students need 100 per cent of Guidance of Vocational Need.

❐

15

Summary and Conclusion

This chapter deals with the Summary, Major Findings, Conclusions, Recommendations and Suggestions for further research.

Guidance

Guidance is the assistance given to the individual to deal effectively with to environment or with his adjustment problem. It aims to help in the full growth and development of the individual especially when he is obstructed in his functioning. Hence it intends to develop in a person the ability to help him in varying situations. An infant's life begins with such a help. His motor development seeks assistance. A child seeks guidance in education. An adult may need it in getting suitable placement. In the modern times, the problems of adjustment arise every day. Change affecting the outer environment is not that fast in its effect on the people's life. Hence there is a growing necessity for guidance. Modern education lays great emphasis on guidance and counseling because it aims at total development of the individual to make of them useful members of the society.

Definition of Guidance

Guidance is the help given by one person to another in making choices and adjustments and in solving problems. Guidance aims at aiding the recipient to grow in his independence and ability to be responsible for him. It is a service that is universal-not confined to the school or the family. It is found in all phases of life-in the home, in business and industry, in government, in social life, in hospitals, and in prisons; indeed it is present wherever there are people who need help and wherever there are people who can help.

1. "Fundamental of all the guidance is the help or assistance given by one competent person to another individual so that the latter may direct his life by developing his point of view, make his own decisions and carry out those decisions" **–Crow and crow**
2. "Effective education is guidance, and realistic guidance is self-guidance" **– Carmicheal**
3. "Guidance is inherent in education and as such should be done largely by classroom teacher. He should try to help pupils set up dynamic, reasonable and worthwhile objectives for themselves"**–Cox.**
4. "Guidance involves personal help to promote the growth of an individual in self-direction. The help may be given to the individual along or in a group; it is the individual who is the focus of attention and not the group. Also this attention is to be paid to the individual and not to the problem" **–Jones.**
5. "Assistance given to an individual in solving problems related to occupational choice and progress with due regard for the individual's characteristics and their relation to occupational opportunity"
–The General Conference, ILO, 1949.
6. "All guidance is education, but some aspects of education are to guidance, the objectives of both education and guidance may be the same viz., the development of individual,. But the methods used are different."

Guidance Needs Categories

Different authors classified guidance needs different ways. Grewal, J.C. classified guidance needs into five categories.

1. Physical Needs
2. Social Needs
3. Psychological Needs
4. Educational Needs
5. Vocational Needs

Population

A population refers to any collection of specific group of human beings or of non-human entities such as objects, educational institution, time units and geographical areas, prices or salaries drawn by the individual. The population of the present study includes of the Higher Secondary Schools of Shillong in East Khasi Hills District. The total number of Higher Secondary Schools in Shillong is 27. Gender wise enrolment of students for the academic year 2014-15 is as follows:

TABLE.15.1: Population of the Study

<table>
<tr><th>Type of School</th><th>No of Schools</th><th>No of Male Students</th><th>No of Female Students</th><th>Grand Total</th></tr>
<tr><td>Government</td><td>3</td><td rowspan="3">1466</td><td rowspan="3">2154</td><td rowspan="4">3620</td></tr>
<tr><td>Govt. Aided</td><td>16</td></tr>
<tr><td>Private Unadided</td><td>8</td></tr>
<tr><td>Total</td><td>27</td><td>1466</td><td>2154</td></tr>
</table>

Sample

A sample is a portion of people from larger population. A sample is typically and relatively small portion of that large area which is chosen for statistical study. It helps to reduce greater precision and accuracy. Sampling procedure provide generalization on the basis of a relatively small portion of the population is called sample. Random sampling technique is used to select the sample. The sample of the study consists of 6 higher secondary schools among them 2 Government; 2 Government Aided and 2 Private management schools.

Sampling Method

Random sampling method was adopted and the schools were randomly selected.

TABLE15.2: Sample distribution

Category	Sample
Boys	41
Girls	124
Total	**165**

Variables

1. Dependent Variable: Scores of Guidance Needs (Whole and Five areas)
2. Independent Variables: Sex, Age, Class, Management, Native Place and Type of Family.

Title of the Study

The title of the present study is stated as ***"A Study on Guidance Need of Higher Secondary School Students in Shillong".***

Objective of the Study

The study is designed with the following specific objectives:

1. To find out the Guidance need by area wise of Higher Secondary School Students in Shillong.

Research Questions

1. How many students really require Guidance Need as a whole?
2. How many students require Guidance Need by area wise?

Tool

The instrument which are using for gathering new facts for exploring new fields are called tools. In order to obtain information or data several tools may be uses according to the requirement of the study. The investigator was adopted the following tool for the present study:

1. Guidance Needs Inventory developed by Grewal, J.S., Retired Professor of Education, RIE, Bhopal.

   About the tool: There are 65 items in the tool. All are positive items.

TABLE.15.3: Areas Guidance Need

S.No.	Area	Questions
1	Physical Need	1-10
2	Social Need	11-25
3	Psychological Need	26-38
4	Educational Need	39-57
5	Vocational Need	58-65

Scoring Pattern

Highly True (HT) has weightage of '0'; Mostly True (MT) has weightage of '1'; Quite True (QT) has weightage of '2'; Least True has weightage of '3'and Not True (NT) has weightage of '4'.

For more information about inventory please refer Appendix-A and Appendix-B.

Data Collection

After selection the process data collection procedure was performed in a well sequenced manner. In the present study, the investigator personally visited the schools and met the Headmaster/Principal explained the purpose of her visit. After obtaining permission, the tool was distributed among the students. The investigator then collected back the tool sheets from the students.

Data Analysis and Discussion

The collected data was entered in the excel sheet. After thorough checking the analysis was done with the help of SPSS (Statistical Package for Social Science). Interpretation of analysis was done in the separate chapter entitled Analysis and Discussion.

Delimitations of the study

It is difficult to concentrate all the things in a single study. The investigator has delimited her study. They are;

1. This study is limited to Higher Secondary Schools of Shillong only.
2. This study is limited to the academic year 2014-15.
3. This study is limited to few socio-demographic variables only.

Major Findings

1. High scores are an indication of less need and low scores on the inventory are an indication of more need. The minimum score in the inventory is 0 and maximum score is 260. It is found that 95.8% of students scored below 130 score (50% score of total score). It shows that, nearly 96% of students want guidance need.
2. There are 10 items in Physical Need area of Guidance Need. The maximum Score in this area is 40 and minimum is zero. 87.9% of students scored below 20 (50 per cent of total scores). It shows that nearly 88% of students want physical need. 2 students need 100 per cent Guidance of Physical Need.
3. There are 15 items in Social Need area of Guidance Need. The maximum score in this area is 60 and minimum is zero. 90.9 % of students scored below 30 score (50% of total score). It shows that 91% of students want Social Need.
4. There are 13 items in Psychological Need area of Guidance Need. The maximum score in this area is 52 and minimum is zero. 72.1 % of students scored below 26 score (50% of total score). It shows that 72% of students want Guidance of Psychological Need. Only one student needs 100 per cent of Guidance of Psychological Need.
5. There are 19 items in Educational Need area of Guidance Need. The maximum score in this area is 76 and minimum is zero. 90.3 % of students scored below 36 score (50% of total score). It shows that 90 % of students want Guidance of Educational Need. Only three students need 100 per cent of Guidance of Educational Need.

6. There are 8 items in Vocational Need area of Guidance Need. The maximum score in this area is 32 and minimum is zero. 90.3 % of students scored below 16 score (50% of total score). It shows that 95.2 % of students want Guidance of Vocational Need. Only seven students need 100 per cent of Guidance of Vocational Need.

Recommendations

Based on the above findings, the investigator likes to give few important and urgent recommendations for all round development of students.

1. Overall, all students need all types of guidance need.
2. Few students need 100 per cent guidance need. It is the foremost duty of government to recruit counselors in the schools.
3. It is better to organize workshops on guidance need in schools and colleges.

CONCLUSION

The study revealed that, there is an urgent need to take care about guidance needs of students studying in higher secondary schools. All students (more than 90% of students) need all types of (physical need, social need, psychological need, educational need and vocational need). The government should think towards recruitment of counselor in the schools for all round development of students for sustainable development.

❐

Bibliography

1. Agnes Sujatha (2003) Study of Mental health and Teacher Effectiveness of Graduate Teacher, University of Madras
2. Basumalik T and Bhattacharya, K.P. Views on Mental Health a primary study on Psychometric research and service unit ISI Calcutta 1084 "Second Survey of Research in Education" Vol. 1, P.449.
3. Black, Deb (1994) this booklet " creative class room problem solving"
4. Christensen, Kp W Martin, Loren (1992). Teaching Creative Problem Solving. Technology Teacher, v52 n3 p.9-11
5. Ciarrochi, Joseph sad Terr, Deame, Frank . P . (2005), When simplifying life is not be bad. The link between rigidity, stressful life events and mental health in an undergraduate population British Journal of Guidance and Counselling, V33. N.2 p. 185 -197.
6. Communitye College Journal of Research and Practice Volume 26/5, 2002, Pp.383 - 399
7. Clode Linda, (1992). A Futuristic Stimulation Using Creative problem Solving Gifted Child Today
8. Danielson, Mary Ann and Mitchell, Nancy (1995). "the relationship between problem solving and group decision- making"
9. Devaraj &.Srnivasan (2003) Educational Psychology, Ram publishers, Chennai Pp.256-257.
10. Dillon , Rchard, (1995). Using a Robotics contest to Enhance Students Creativity and Problem Solving Skill. Technology Teacher, vol.55/1, pp.11-14

11. Eenjamin C Amick (III) The Health institute, New England Medical Center, Boston, MA: Deggy Mc donough, York Univeristy, York, Canada and Carl Pieper, Duke University, Chapel Hill. N.
12. Ethaney Sandra. MC (1993) Children's mental health and their ability to learn, Journal of National health and education Consortium
13. Felix, Robert H (1957), " Evolution of community mental health concepts," Medical Journal of Psychiatry, P. 673 -679
14. Flak, V.F & Sheldon, K.M (2003) Student Psychological Need satisfactions and college teacher – Course Evaluations. Educational Psychology Vol 23, N.3 pp. 235 -247.
15. Frank, Lawrence K (1953), the promotion of mental health, " American academy of political and social science, P. 167 -174
16. Gupta, A (1980) Personality and Mental health Consistency of Research in Education volume 1 p.630
17. Hoy, W.K. (1987) Educational Administration: Theory, Research and Practice. New York; Random House.
18. Jahada (1963) " Mental health – book" Vol 3 P.1067 – 1079
19. Jarhead, Magic (1963)," Mental Health" Encyclopedia of Mental Health,Vol.3,Pp.1067-1079
20. Journal of Amercan college of health (2005)," The mental health needs of today's college students, challenges and recommendations" Helder publications. Helen Dwight raid education foundation, Vol.3/4, P. 157
21. Kabr Singh Sidhu (2002) Methodoly of Research in Education Sterling Publishers Ltd. Jalundar.
22. Kalpan Diane (1996) mental health implication of not graduating from high school Journal of Experimental Education Vol.62, Pp.105-23
23. Klein, Donald (1960), Some concepts concerning the mental health of the individual, " Journal of Consulting Psychology.
24. L.N. Dubey, (1980). Problem Solving Ability Test, Agra: National Psychological Corporation.
25. Mark. J. (1996). " the relationship between mental imagery and problem solving ability"
26. Maslow, A.H. (1970). Motivation and personality 2nd edition, New York Harper and Row
27. Muralidharan Rajalakshmi, Kaur Paramjeet (1995) A mental health programme for primary school children; International Journal of early years educaton; Vol.3/2, Pp.19-28
28. Mulia, R.D.,(1993) Journal of Educaton and Psychology, Vol.48, p.145
29. Nagarajan K (1996) Handbook of Statistics, Ram publishers, Chennai, Pp.258-259

30. Norma Catts. F and Moslay. (1991) Practical School Discipline and Mental Hygiene, Hoghnton Publishers, Boston, Vol.2, Pp.172-192
31. Rao. V.N and Parthasarathy. R. (1988), Mental Health in the class room: what is to be done."? New frontiers in education, vol.4, Pp.440-445
32. Sharma, Indra, (2007). Problem Solving Ability and Scientific attitude as determinant of academic achievement. Journal of Social Science, Pp.68-69 March & June 2007
33. Santhanam. S (1992), " Importance of mental health of Teacher Pp.141-149
34. Shorndrick, Denise. D et. Al., (1992) "Test Of Interpersonal problem solving"
35. Thinklin T, Ridell.S. Wilson. A. (2005). Support for students certain mental health difficulties in higher education. The student's prospective. British Journal of Guidance and Counselling Vol.33/4, pp. 495-512.
36. V.N. Rao and R. Parthasarathy (1998) "Mental Health n the Classroom: What is to be done? New Frontiers in Education, Vol.4, Pp. 440-445
37. Watson Anmy, C. Corrgon, Patrick W. Angell, beth, (2005) What motivates public support for legally mandated mental health treatment? " Social Work Research" Vol.29/2, P.87, Jan 2005.
38. Watson, Amy et al (2005) Public support for legally mandated mental health treatment social work research Vol. 29/2.
39. Yang, B., & Clum, G.A., (1994, summer) Life stress, social support, and problem-solving skills predictive of depressive symptoms, hopelessness, and sauced ideation in an Asian student population: A test of a model Suicide & Life-Threatening Behaviour, Vol.24/2,pp. 127 -139.
40. Adesoji, F.A (1997). *Average students and effectiveness of problem-solving instructional Strategies,* e-Journal of Educational studies,4(1), 16-19.
41. Adesoji, F.A (2002).Modern strategies in the teaching of integrated science. In S.O *Ayodele(Ed.), Teaching strategies for Nigeria secondary school.*Idandan: Power House Press Publishers p.205-212.
42. Akinbobola, A.O. (2004). Effects of Corporative and competitive learning strategies on the performance of students. *Journal of Research in Education.* 1(1) 71-75.
43. Anderman, E.M., &Yooung, A.J (1994).Motivation and strategy used by the students: Individual differences and classroom effects. *Journal of Research in Science Teaching.* 21, 811-831.

44. Ann Kovalchick & Kara Dawson (2006) Encyclopedia of Education & Technology (Volume 1 & 2) Neelkamal publication PVT. LTD.
45. Armbruster, B.B. (2000). Taking notes from lectures. In R.F. Flippo& D.C. Caverly (Eds.), *Handbook of college reading and study strategy research* (pp. 175-199).
46. Bhatia, K.K&Damral, B.D (2005) *"Education in Emerging Indian Society"* Kalyani publishers.
47. Bostrom R.P., Olfaman L., Sein M.K. (1990). The importance of learning style in end-user training. MIS Quarterly, 101-119.
48. Chamot, A.U., Barnhardt, S., El-Dinary, P.B., & Robbins, J.(1999). *The learning strategies handbook.* White Plains, NY: Addison Wesley Longman.
49. Davidson G.V., Savenye W.C., Orr K.B (1992). How do learning style relate to performance in a computer application course? *Journal of Research in Computing in Education.*24 (3), 349-358.
50. Derry, S.J (1990). Learning Strategies for acquiring useful knowledge. InB.F. Jones & I. Idoil. (Eds). Dimensions of thinking cognitive instruction. NJ. Erlbaum.
51. Dunn R. (1986). Learning Style: State of the science.*Theory and practice,* 24 (1), 10-19.
52. Graham, S., Harris, KR., Mac Arthur, C.A.,&Schwartz, S. (1991). Writing and writing instruction for students with learning disabilities: review of a research program. Learning Disability Quarterly, 14(2), 89-114.
53. Hamman, D. (1998). Preservice teachers' value for learning strategies instruction. *Journal of Experimental Education,* 66, pp.209-222.
54. Hughes, C.A.,&Schumaker, J.B (1991). Test-taking strategy instruction for adolescents with learning disabilities. Exceptionality, 2, pp.205-221.
55. Joyce, B & Weil, Masha (1980) Models of teaching Engleword cliffs N.J USA; Prentice Hall international, Inc.
56. Klinger, J., Vaughn, S., Hughes, M., Schumm, J., &Elbaum, B. (1988). Outcomes for students with and without learning disabilities in inclusive classrooms. Learning Disabilities Research & Practice, 13(3), pp.153-161.
57. Kothari, C.R (1990) *"Research Methodology Methods and Techniques"* wiely Easter Ltd New Delhi.
58. LokeshKoul (1984) *"Methodology of Educational Research"* Vani Educational Book Vikas Publishing house Pvt. Ltd.

59. Nagarajan & Srinivasan. R (1994) *"Research Methodology in Education"* Ram Publishers, Gandhi Nagar, Madras.
60. Abzug, Bella., and Davis, Susan. 1998. "India." Mapping Progress: Assessing Implementation of the Beijing Platform.
61. Basu, S. (2008). Gender stereotypes in Corporate India: A glimpse. New Delhi: Response Books.
62. Budhwar, P. S., Saini, D. S., & Bhatnagar, J. (2005, June). Women in management in the new economic environment: The case of India. Asia Pacific Business Review, 11(2), 179-193.
63. Bunch, Charlotte. "The Intolerable Status Quo: Violence Against Women and Girls." The Progress of Nations 1997 New York: UNICEF
64. Burns, John F. "Though Illegal, Child Marriage is Popular in Part of India." The New York Times. May 11, 1998.
65. Carr, Marilyn., and Chen, Martha., and Jhabvala, Renana. 1996. Speaking Out: Women's Economic Empowerment in South Asia. Southampton Row, London: Intermediate Technology Publications LTD.
66. Catalyst. (2009, March). Women CEOs of the Fortune 1000. Retrieved April 2, 2009, from http://www.catalyst.org/
67. Desai, Sonalde. 1994. Gender Inequalities and Demographic Behavior: India. New York: The Population Council, Inc.
68. Differentials by Sex: Evidence from India," Artha Vijnana, Vol. 38, No. 4, pp. 372-386.
69. Dube, Leela and Rajni Palriwala, eds., 1990, Structures and Strategies: Women, Work, and Family, New Delhi.
70. Dwyer, Daisy and Judith Bruce, eds., 1988, A Home Divided: Women and Income in the Third World, Stanford, CA.
71. Gupta, A., Koshal, M., & Koshal R. K. (2006). Women managers in India: Challenges and opportunities. In H. J. Davis, S. R. Chatterjee & M. Heuer (Eds.), Management in India (pp. 285-312). New Delhi: Response Books.
72. Handy, F., Ranade, B., & Kasam, M. (2007, Summer). To profit or not to profit: Women entrepreneurs in India. Nonprofit Management & Leadership, 17(4), 383-401.
73. Heitzman, James and Robert L. Worden, eds., 1996, Area Handbook Series, India–A Country Study, Washington, DC. International Labour Office, 1997, Yearbook of Labour Statistics 1997, Geneva.
74. Khandelwal, P. (2002, April-June). Gender stereotypes at work: Implications for organizations. Indian Journal of Training and Development. XXXII (2), 72-83.

75. Kishwar, Madhu and Ruth Vanita, eds., 1985, In Search of Answers: Indian Women's Voices From Manushi, London.
76. Liddle, Joanna and Rama Joshi, 1986, Daughters of Independence: Gender, Caste and Class in India, New Brunswick,
77. National Commission for Women India, 1993, Proceedings of the National Workshop on "Employment, Equality and Impact of Economic Reform on Women," New Delhi.7
78. National Sample Survey Organization, 1994, Sarvekshana, Vol. 17, No. 3, January-March.
79. Neft, Naomi., and Levine, Ann D. 1997. Where Women Stand: An International Report on the Status of Women in 140 Countries. New York: Random House.
80. NJ. Madheswaran, S. and T. Lakshmanasamy, 1996, "Occupational Segregation and Earnings.
81. Omvedt, Gail. 1990. "Violence against Women: New Movements and New Theories in India." Kali Primaries.
82. President of India. (2009, August 21). Speech by Her Excellency, the President of India, Shrimati Pratibha Devisingh Patil, at the meeting with the Ladies' Circle International. Retrieved August 24, 2009, from http://presidentofindia.nic.in/sp210809.html
83. Purushothaman, Sangeetha. 1998. The Empowerment of Women in India: Grassroots Women's Networks and the State. New Delhi: Sage Publications.
84. Ramalingaswami, Vulimiri., and Jonsson, Urban., and Rohde, Jon. "The Asian Enigma." The Progress of Nations. 1996 New York: UNICEF
85. Rajan. "Will India's Ban on Prenatal Sex Determination Slow Abortion of Girls?" Internet.
86. Registrar General and Census Commissioner, 1993, Census of India 1991, Final Population Totals: Brief Analysis of Primary Census Abstract, Series 1, New Delhi.
87. Sen, A. (2005). The argumentative Indian: Writings on Indian history, culture and identity. New York: Farrar, Straus and Giroux.
88. United States Department of Labor/Women's Bureau. (2008). Quick stats on women workers, 2008. Retrieved August 25, 2009, from www.dol.gov/wb/stats/main.htm
89. Women workers in India in the 21st century-Unemployment and underemployment. (2004, February). Retrieved April 30, 2009.

❑❑❑